GUARDIANS OF THE GOAL

GUARDIANS OF THE GOAL

A Comprehensive Guide to New York Rangers Goaltenders, from Hal Winkler to Ed Giacomin, Henrik Lundqvist, and All Those in Between

GEORGE GRIMM

FOREWORD BY STAN FISCHLER

SPORTS PUBLISHING

Sports Publishing books may be purchased in bulk at special discounts for sales promotion, corporate gifts, fund-raising, or educational purposes. Special editions can also be created to specifications. For details, contact the Special Sales Department, Sports Publishing, 307 West 36th Street, 11th Floor, New York, NY 10018 or sportspubbooks@skyhorsepublishing.com.

Sports Publishing® is a registered trademark of Skyhorse Publishing, Inc.®, a Delaware corporation.

Visit our website at www.sportspubbooks.com.

10 9 8 7 6 5 4 3 2 1

Library of Congress Cataloging-in-Publication Data is available on file.

Jacket design by Tom Lau
Jacket photographs: Getty Images

Print ISBN: 978-1-68358-327-1
Ebook ISBN: 978-1-68358-328-8

Printed in the United States of America

This book is dedicated to all the past, present, and future goaltenders of the New York Rangers, and to all of us who wished we could have joined their ranks even for just the pregame warmup.

Contents

FOREWORD BY STAN FISCHLER

About Goalies and Me

Goalies have captured my attention since I was a little guy.

The year was 1939. I was nine years old and had seen my first hockey game at the old Madison Square Garden, no relation to the current "World's Most Famous Arena."

In those days, The Garden was situated on Manhattan's Eighth Avenue between 49th and 50th Street. You could get all the hockey you ever wanted from that MSG.

We had two National Hockey League teams then—the Rangers and New York Americans—as well as the New York Rovers and four Metropolitan League teams.

On a typical winter Sunday, you could catch the Met League game at 1:30, followed by the Rovers playing in the Eastern Amateur Hockey League at 3:30.

If that wasn't enough puck-watching, there was the Ranger—or Amerks—game at 8:30; which meant you had enough time to down spaghetti and meatballs for half a buck at Buitoni's down Eighth Avenue.

My love of goaltending first paid off handsomely the day after my first game at the Garden. I was attending P.S. 54 in Williamsburg, Brooklyn, and was asked by my third-grade teacher, Mrs. Gould, to pick a subject for the traditional "Show and Tell" exercise.

Since I remembered how much the goaltenders had fascinated me the day before, I got before the class and demonstrated a kick save, a catch with the big goalie mitt, and a few other action episodes in the crease.

For my efforts, Mrs. Gould gave me an "A" and that endeared me to her—and hockey—for life.

Not surprisingly, goalies became a fascinating subject for me through the years—especially those who played for the Rangers.

At the start, there was Davey Kerr who helped the Blueshirts to their third Stanley Cup and Earl Robertson followed by Charlie Rayner guarding the Amerks' twines.

Wartime hockey was tough on every NHL team but especially the Rangers, who lost Sugar Jim Henry to the armed forces after he paced the Blueshirts to first place in the 1941–42 campaign.

During the war years, we were treated to the likes of Steve Buzinski, Ken "Tubby" McAuley, Doug Stevenson, and others who tasted a cup of coffee and then disappeared into the Goalie Netherland.

After the war—and the beloved Amerks had disappeared—"Bonnie Prince Charlie" Rayner took over and he became one of the most beloved Blueshirts of all time. Chuck couldn't bring the Rangers a Cup in 1950, but came within a save of doing so.

I knew and loved Charlie and was able to get close to him since I then had become vice-president of the Rangers Fan Club. In his last season, Rayner mentored young Lorne Worsley who would win the Calder Trophy and then have the distinction of being demoted to the minors.

Don't ask me why; I still don't know.

Johnny "China Wall" Bower followed and posted a 2.60 goals-against average; that the Rangers just missed a playoff berth was not his fault. Trouble was, he, too, got the hook when Worsley returned.

That was in 1954–55, the season I went to work for the Rangers in publicity en route to a lifetime watching hockey without having to purchase a ticket.

We had Worsley—now known all over the hockey world as "Gump" because he resembled comic book character Andy Gump (from *The Gumps*)—and what a character he turned out to be.

Gump's problem was his coach, Phil Watson—a very dislikable character behind the bench or not—since they never could stand each other's presence.

Watson eventually brought up fellow French-Canadian Marcel Paille who impressed me two ways:

1. Despite his many moves in the crease, not one hair on his head ever moved;

2. The ultimate standup goalie, Paille considered it sinful to ever drop to the ice to make a save.

I saw them all—Mike Richter, a personal favorite since he visited my ailing son, Simon, in the hospital while he was awaiting a new heart via transplant—but loved one more than any other.

Before joining the Rangers Fan Club, I had been a Maple Leafs fan and when they won the Stanley Cup in 1951, Al Rollins shared the champagne—and the Vezina Trophy—with Turk Broda.

I was nuts about Rollins. I remembered him as a Rangers farmhand with the Rovers when everyone called him "Allie," and I was tickled when he was signed by the Blueshirts during the 1959–60 season when he was thirty-three.

A friend of mine and I took Rollins to dinner and we just had a whale of a time talking hockey left and right. Al had looked good even at that advanced age.

Then something strange happened. Uncle Sam won a gold medal at Squaw Valley with Jack McCartan in goal. Next thing I knew the Rangers signed him to a contract and that was the end of my buddy Rollins's career in New York.

As you must have figured by now, I could go on and on about Rangers netminders right up to the King himself, Henrik Lundqvist.

But if that had happened, I'd be writing this book and not my buddy George.

I'd better stop now and point you in the direction of the chap who put his heart, soul, mind, and computer into this most worthy contribution to hockey—and Rangers and goaltending—history.

P.S. I thought I'd let you know in passing that I liked them better without a mask!

—Stan Fischler, 2018, Kibbutz El Rom, Israel

Preface

Rangers fans have always loved their goaltenders and, throughout their history, the club has been blessed with some of the very best in the game. Through the first nine-plus decades of their existence, eighty-eight men from Canada, the United States, and six European countries have toiled between the pipes for the Blueshirts. They all shared the same responsibility, yet each brought their own style, personality, character, and idiosyncrasies to the position and provided unique memories for those of us watching them.

This book profiles each one of these brave "Guardians of the Goal" in chronological order, as well as providing an overview of their era and the general managers and coaches they played for. This link between the goalies and team management is important because both need the other to succeed. A coach and GM cannot win without a competent goaltender, and the poor guy in net will not have a chance if he is the last line of defense behind a non-competitive, disorganized team. It also helps to explain why many of these netminders achieved fame and glory before or after they passed through the Rangers' crease during what might have been a rough patch in franchise history.

Guardians of the Goal highlights the careers of eight "franchise goaltenders": Davey Kerr, Chuck Rayner, Gump Worsley, Ed Giacomin, John Davidson, John Vanbiesbrouck, Mike Richter, and Henrik Lundqvist, who were each uniquely identified with the Rangers and set the standard for those that followed.

The book also looks at the practice and emergency goaltenders who bravely and often anonymously served the team during the early decades, as well as the many rule changes that have affected goalies. We also look at the young netminders who are in the Rangers' pipeline and evaluate their chances of moving up to the big stage of Madison Square Garden.

Regardless of whether they were a franchise goalie, a flash in the pan, or an emergency fill-in, each of these "Lone Rangers," or as Steve Baker once called them, "The few, the proud, and the very busy," have one thing in common: They all tried their best to keep that little one-inch by three-inch piece of frozen, vulcanized rubber out of the gaping twenty-four-square-foot chasm behind them. Some were more successful than others but, as you will see, although they may occasionally "steal" a game, in most cases a goaltender is only as good as the team in front of him.

Introduction

"Goalies should have hard skulls, quick hands and the skin of a rhinoceros. The hard skulls and quick hands will take care of the flying pucks while the thick skin will defy the slings and arrows of critical coaches and customers."

—Lorne "Gump" Worsley

Goaltending is a thankless profession. The men in the nets rarely get credit for a win but are very often blamed for a loss. It's also a very stressful and dangerous position. Hall of Famer Glenn Hall, who was known to become physically ill before every game, once said, "Our first priority was staying alive. Our second was stopping the puck."

Over the years, many very good goaltenders have had to either retire or take a season off in the prime of their careers due to what was once called "nervous exhaustion." Part of that stress was because they were sitting ducks in a shooting gallery. With shots coming at them at speeds of more than 100 miles per hour and early equipment providing minimal protection, severe injuries were quite common. But today, with better protection, goaltenders might not dread injury as much as their predecessors. However, there is still the fear of allowing a goal that changes the outcome of a game, letting down their teammates, or hearing about it from the crowd. As Jacques Plante once complained, "How would you like it in your job if every time you made a small mistake, a red light went on over your desk and 15,000 people stood up and yelled at you?"

Rangers goaltenders have historically faced a lot of pressure, as well as a lot of shots (due to the fact that for many years the Blueshirts just weren't a very competitive team). The franchise got off to a great start, winning a Stanley Cup in only their second season and adding two more in the next twelve years. But then came World War II, when Lester Patrick's poor decisions put the franchise in a hole which took years to dig out of. Those years included a long stretch in which it seemed that team management was not truly committed to winning or to acquiring the kind of players that could take the team to the next level; that of being competitive every season instead of just once or twice every decade. In fact, during a twenty-five-year span, from 1942 to 1967, when there were only six teams in the league and four of them made the playoffs, the Rangers still only managed to reach the post-season seven times. Even after going all the way to the Stanley Cup Finals in 1950, they regressed and missed the playoffs for the next five seasons. That all changed in the mid-1960s when Emile Francis restored pride and respectability to the franchise and presided over one of the most successful eras in team history. They didn't win a Cup, but they qualified for the playoffs in nine consecutive seasons.

Since then the Rangers have burned through seven general managers and twenty-two coaches, producing mostly competitive squads culminating in a Stanley Cup victory in 1994. In the quarter-century since that most recent highlight, there have been dry spells for sure, but none of which could or should have been blamed on their goaltender. From top management to the players, each one of those failures was a team effort.

A Look Back

When goalie Hal Winkler skated onto the ice at Madison Square Garden for the Rangers' first game on November 16, 1926, hockey was very different from the sport we know today. Yes, the object of the game may have been the same—shooting a round rubber disk into a goal using a stick—but the rules were different, the players were smaller, and the game was played at a much slower pace.

Compared to what goaltenders wear today, Winkler's equipment was primitive. It was heavy and provided only minimal protection. Depending on their preference, goaltenders wore either felt-backed canvas pads on their upper body or used chest protectors that were similar to those worn by a catcher in baseball. Elbow pads were worn on the outside of the sweater and they used standard player's gloves with a small webbing sewn between the thumb and forefinger of their catching hand. Those gloves would remain basically unchanged until the mid-1940s, when Emile "The Cat" Francis created early versions of the trapper and blocker gloves that netminders wear today. Goaltenders also originally used the same sticks as skaters but by the 1926 season could use a stick with a wider blade and paddle to help them stop shots.

Goaltenders originally used cricket pads to protect their legs. But one day, Emile "Pop" Kenesky, a harness maker from Hamilton, Ontario, was watching a local game and noticed how often pucks were glancing off the curved edges of the pads and into the net. Kenesky modified the pads, redesigned the strapping, and added an extra roll on the outer edge that stabilized the pad and made it stand out from the leg rather than wrap around it as the cricket pads had done. This helped the goaltender control rebounds. Kenesky's pads were handcrafted and made of horsehide stuffed with deer hair. Although they were limited by the league to a narrow 12 inches in width they often weighed in at as much as 40 pounds a pair when they became waterlogged. Kenesky's pads became an instant hit and he soon began taking orders from goaltenders around the league.

Goaltenders of the day often wore a small cap, but they all braved the barrage of shots barefaced. Goalie Clint Benedict of the Montreal Maroons briefly wore a crude leather mask in 1929 to protect a broken nose, but it took another three decades until Jacques Plante came along with his own mask in 1959 for facial protection to gain acceptance.

Many of the NHL's early rules affected the way goaltenders played their position. For example, when the league began play in December 1917, goaltenders were not allowed to drop to the ice to make a save. The rule resulted in a slew of high-scoring games and was quickly changed in January 1918. Despite the rule change, most goaltenders played what is known as a "stand-up style" throughout most of the twentieth century. Some stood straight up while others crouched. They dropped to the ice when necessary, but spent most of the time on their skates. "Stand up as much as you can," advised Hall of Famer Johnny Bower, citing the prevailing wisdom. "If you fall down, you'll be in trouble." Standing up gave the goaltender more mobility, but it was also a means of self-preservation. "You protect your head," said Ken Dryden, another Hall of Fame netminder. "Keep it out of the way, above the bar. It didn't have anything to do with effectiveness. Even after the mask, standup was still the style."

Goalies were also not allowed to hold the puck and were penalized with a faceoff at their doorstep, 10 feet directly in front of their net if they did. The crease, which is the goalie's safe haven, measured only three feet by seven feet, leaving netminders little room to maneuver unimpeded. They were also forced to serve their own penalties, thus requiring a skater to take his place in the net. The substitute was not even allowed to borrow the goalie's stick and gloves until the 1939–40 season. Forward passing was not allowed in the attacking zone until 1929–30 and defensemen usually remained behind their own blue line even when the puck went up ice.

The playing conditions were also very different in those early days. Except for chicken wire behind each of the goals, there was nothing above the boards to protect spectators from errant pucks, sticks, and skates, or to guard players from fans. Eventually the chicken wire was extended around the entire rink, but that caused some unforeseen problems. "When I started in 1939–40," said Hall of Fame referee Bill "The Big Whistle" Chadwick, "if I sat on the boards to let a player go by, fans would stick me with a hatpin." It wasn't until the 1946–47 season that Plexiglass (then called Herculite) was first installed in Toronto's Maple Leaf Gardens and became the league standard.

The league did not begin flooding the ice between periods until 1940, merely scraping away the snow with shovels. As a result, by the third period the playing surface was usually deeply rutted and difficult to skate and pass on. Coupled with the fact that teams were only allowed to dress twelve skaters plus a goaltender, fatigue had to be a factor, which most likely accounted for the lower scores and greater number of shutouts of the day. The ice looked very different as well. NHL teams didn't begin to add white coloring to the ice until the 1949–50 season, so the cement flooring was visible through the clear ice giving it a dull grey color, making it difficult for the fans and players to see the puck.

By the mid-1940s, the NHL put even more pressure on their goaltenders by adding the center ice red line which changed hockey from a passing game to a quicker, more frenzied game with more screens and rebounds, as well as increased scoring for American fans. Then, in the 1960s, the position became even more dangerous with the introduction of the curved stick, which added at least 20 mph to slapshots but took away a certain degree of accuracy.

Since those early days the game has continued to evolve—as has the art of goaltending, the styles they play, and the equipment they wear.

Today's goaltenders are bigger and better-conditioned than their predecessors. They now have their own coaches and specialized training. Their equipment is also larger and much lighter than the pads worn by goaltenders even as recently as twenty years ago. Most of today's netminders have eschewed the strict stand-up style of the past in favor of the "butterfly" or "hybrid butterfly" techniques, both of which have them dropping to their knees more often and spreading their pads out in a "V" to cover the lower half of the net, while using their glove and upper body to protect the top.

What hasn't changed, however, is the pressure on these valiant men in the nets, the skills and mental and physical toughness needed to play the position, and their overall importance to the game.

A Note About Statistics: The statistics in the book were provided by Hockey-Reference.com. However, the hockey research community is constantly working on updating these stats as new information is found. Therefore, the stats printed in this book sometimes may not match those found online.

CHAPTER ONE

The Early Years

The New York Rangers joined the NHL in 1926 along with the Chicago Black Hawks and Detroit Cougars—as the league expanded from seven to ten teams.

However, their path to fruition actually began two years earlier in 1924, when the New York Life Insurance Company decided to foreclose on the second Madison Square Garden building at 24th Street, tearing it down and constructing an office building in its place.

After the closing of the Garden, boxing promoter George "Tex" Rickard, a wealthy westerner who had made a name for himself in New York, needed an arena in which to hold his bouts. Rickard was a cigar-smoking hustler who had run gambling saloons in Alaska and Nevada. He formed a syndicate of "600 millionaires" and created the Madison Square Garden Corporation, naming himself president at an annual salary of $30,000. He then announced plans to build a new Garden at a site on Eighth Avenue and 50th Street, which was then being used as a car barn.

The new Garden was built in a remarkable 249 days at a cost of $5.6 million. It opened on November 28, 1925, with a six-day bicycle race.

Realizing that it would take more than boxing and bicycles to keep the Garden afloat, Rickard began looking at other events to fill out the schedule. His partner, Col. John S. Hammond, had seen a hockey game while visiting Montreal and thought the game would sell in New York. Rickard, however, was cool to the idea of owning a hockey team, but wouldn't mind having one as a tenant.

About the same time in 1925, the Hamilton Tigers of the NHL folded and the franchise was purchased by bootlegger "Big Bill" Dwyer for $75,000. Dwyer wanted to move the team to New York, but needed a guarantee from Rickard that he would have the only hockey team in town. Tex, who still had no interest in the game, gave his word and "Big

Bill" moved his team into the Garden and called them the New York Americans.

But as hockey caught on in the city and the Americans became a success at the box office, if not on the ice, Tex began to reconsider the sport as an investment. When the NHL announced that it would be adding three teams for the 1926–27 season, Rickard reneged on his agreement with Dwyer as he and Hammond took steps to acquire a team of their own. The expansion was made necessary when the Pacific Coast Hockey League (PCHL) and the Western Hockey League (WHL) folded, leaving many hockey players out of work. So, in 1926, "Tex's" Rangers, the Chicago Black Hawks, and the Detroit Cougars joined the now 10-team NHL.

Once the Garden was granted a franchise, Col. Hammond hired Conn Smythe to build the Rangers. Smythe had been recommended to Hammond by Charles Adams, owner of the Boston Bruins, who had seen Smythe coach the University of Toronto hockey team against Ivy League squads in the Boston Garden.

Smythe accepted Hammond's offer of $10,000 to build the Rangers and assembled an impressive squad around a nucleus that included Bill and Bun Cook, Frank Boucher, Lorne Chabot, Taffy Abel, Ching Johnson, and Murry Murdoch. But Hammond didn't think the Rangers were good enough and wanted Smythe to acquire winger Cecil "Babe" Dye, one of the league's top goal scorers. Smythe didn't think the Rangers needed Dye and the two men argued, leading to Smythe's dismissal after less than a month as a Garden employee.

Hammond then talked Lester Patrick out of retirement to run the organization. "The Silver Fox" had a long history as a hockey player, coach, and owner. He and his brother Frank had organized the Pacific Coast Hockey League years earlier and had just sold the contracts of every player in the league to the NHL for $250,000. Lester was looking forward to relaxing in sunny California, but agreed to come east and ran the Rangers for the next two decades.

Smythe was invited to the team's opening night game by Rickard, but at first declined the offer. Only after his wife insisted did Conn change his mind and attend. He took the opportunity to remind Rickard that he had only been paid $7,500 of the $10,000 he had been promised.

Rickard paid Smythe the $2,500 owed to him and Conn turned around and bet it all on a football game between the University of Toronto and McGill University, winning the bet and doubling his money. He then bet all his winnings on the Rangers to beat the Toronto St. Pats in the latter's home opener at the Arena Gardens on November 20. Once again, he won and doubled his money, turning the original $2,500 into $10,000 in a few short days. He eventually formed a syndicate of investors to buy the St. Pats and renamed them the Maple Leafs. He then oversaw the building of Maple Leaf Gardens and turned the Leafs into a Canadian institution.

The Rangers were an instant hit on and off the ice. They played their first game at Madison Square Garden on November 16, 1926, beating the Montreal Maroons, 1–0, and became the toast of the town, finishing in first place in their inaugural season and winning the Stanley Cup the following year. They won two more Cups—in 1933 and 1940—and easily surpassed the Americans in popularity. In 1935, Dwyer, who was earlier convicted of bootlegging charges and sent to prison, sold the team to defenseman Mervyn "Red" Dutton, whose father was a millionaire. In an effort to attract a local following, Red changed the team's name to the "Brooklyn" Americans and served as player, coach, and general manager until 1942, when a combination of World War II and their increasing debts forced the Americans to fold.

Dutton went on to become NHL president from 1943 until 1946, when he resigned with the intention of resurrecting the Americans. The NHL, however, encouraged by Garden management, reneged on their promise to allow the Americans to return. A bitter Dutton then declared that the Rangers would never win the Stanley Cup again for as long as he lived, which became known as the "Curse of Red Dutton." Red died in 1988, and the Rangers didn't win another Stanley Cup until 1994.

Rickard died in 1929, and his body was shipped by train from Florida to lie in state in the Garden. Hammond and William J. Carey then took control of the Rangers. In 1934, Col. Hammond became Chairman of the Board of the Garden and Lester Patrick took full charge of the club.

Patrick coached the Rangers from their inaugural campaign until the 1939–40 season when he handed the coaching reins over to Frank Boucher but continued to hold the post of general manager.

Rule Changes:

1927–28: To encourage offense, forward passing was allowed in the defending and neutral zones and goalie pads were reduced in width from 12 to 10 inches.

1929–30: Forward passing was now permitted inside all three zones but not permitted across either blue line.

1931–32: Although there is no record of a team attempting to play with two goaltenders on the ice, a rule was instituted which stated that each team was allowed only one goaltender on the ice at one time.

1934–35: A penalty shot was awarded when a player is tripped and thus prevented from having a clear shot on goal, having no player to pass to other than the offending player. The penalty shot was taken from inside a 10-foot circle located 38 feet from the goal. The goaltender was not allowed to advance more than one foot from his goal line when the shot was taken. In 1938 the rule was modified to allow the puck carrier to skate in towards the goal before shooting.

1940–41: Flooding the ice surface between periods was made mandatory. Prior to that, the ice only had to be scraped. This left the ice surface deeply rutted, making it difficult to skate and pass on.

Hal Winkler
Born: March 20, 1892 in Gretna, Manitoba
Died: May 29, 1956
5-8, 150lb
Caught: Right
Rangers Debut: November 16, 1926 vs. Montreal Maroons
Uniform #1
Seasons with Rangers: 1, 1926–27

Hal Winkler was the first of fifteen goaltenders the Rangers used during Lester Patrick's 20-year tenure as general manager. At thirty-four years of age, Winkler was the oldest player in the Rangers' opening night lineup. He began his hockey career in 1913, playing for Winnipeg of the Manitoba Hockey League. Thirteen years later, after playing for various senior teams in Manitoba, Saskatoon, and Alberta, he was acquired from the Calgary Tigers of the WCHL by then-Rangers GM Conn Smythe for cash in October 1926.

Winkler and Lorne Chabot competed for the number one goaltender position in training camp at Ravina Gardens in Toronto, with

Hal getting the opening night nod. In the opening game, he would shut out the defending Stanley Cup champion Montreal Maroons 1–0. With the blanking, Winkler became the first goaltender in league history to post a shutout in his NHL debut.

But in January 1927, after compiling a 3–4–1 record with two shutouts and a 1.65 GAA (goals-against average), Winkler was sent to the Boston Bruins for $5,000. It seems that at the time Boston GM Art Ross wasn't happy with his goaltender, Charles "Doc" Stewart, a licensed dentist, and Lester Patrick was more than happy to sell Winkler to him—especially since he had the younger and bigger Lorne Chabot waiting in the wings.

Once settled in Boston, Winkler led the Bruins to the playoffs, beating the Rangers in the semifinals but losing to the Ottawa Senators in the Finals, two games to none. The next season, Winkler played in all 44 regular-season games, leading the league in games and minutes played as well as shutouts (15) as the Bruins finished in first place in their division but lost to the Rangers in the first round of the playoffs.

Winkler then returned to the minor leagues, playing for the Minnesota Millers (AHA) and Seattle Eskimos (PCHL) before finishing his career with the Boston Tigers/Cubs (CAHL) in 1930–31.

Regular Season

Season	Team	GP	W	L	T	GA	GAA	SO	MIN	G	A	PTS	PIM
1926–27	NYR	8	3	4	1	13	1.65	2	473	0	0	0	0
1926–27	BOS	23	12	9	2	40	1.66	4	1445	0	0	0	0
1927–28	BOS	44	20	13	11	70	1.51	15	2780	0	0	0	0
NYR Totals	-	8	3	4	1	13	1.65	2	473	0	0	0	0
Career	-	75	35	26	14	123	1.57	21	4698	0	0	0	0

Playoffs

Season	Team	GP	W	L	T*	GA	GAA	SO	MIN	G	A	PTS	PIM
1926–27	BOS	8	2	2	4	13	1.50	2	520	0	0	0	0
1927–28	BOS	2	0	1	1	5	2.50	0	120	0	0	0	0
Career	BOS	10	2	3	5	18	1.69	2	640	0	0	0	0

**Note: Prior to the 1935–36 season, some playoff series were "total-goals" series where games were allowed to end in a tie.*

Fast Fact: Hal Winkler was not only the Rangers' first goaltender, but also the first of only eleven of eighty-eight Blueshirt netminders who caught the puck with their right hand. The others were Davey Kerr, Ken McAuley, Bob DeCourcy, Lorne Anderson, Julian Klymkiw, Marcel Pelletier, Gilles Villemure, Don Simmons, Glen Hanlon, and Terry Kleisinger.

Lorne Chabot
Born: October 5, 1900 in Montreal, Quebec
Died: October 10, 1946
6-1, 185lb
Caught: Left
Rangers Debut: November 20, 1926 at Toronto St. Pats
Uniform #1
Seasons with Rangers: 2, 1926–27 to 1927–28
Stanley Cups: 2, Rangers (1927–28), Toronto (1931–32)
Vezina Trophy: 1934–35 (with Chicago)

Lorne Chabot was a veteran of the First World War and had been a Canadian Mountie even before he made his NHL debut with the Rangers in 1926. He had been an outstanding amateur netminder in Canada, having led the Port Arthur Bearcats to the Allen Cup in 1925 and 1926, playing one of those series with his goalie stick taped to his broken hand.

He was signed by Conn Smythe in 1926, and took over for the Blueshirts' original goaltender Hal Winkler eight games into the 1926–27 season. Chabot posted a 22–9–5 record in his rookie season with 10 shutouts and a 1.51 GAA, leading the first-year Rangers to a first-place finish in the NHL's American Division.

During his rookie season, Rangers publicists Johnny Bruno and Dick Blythe thought they could increase interest in the team by giving Chabot, a French Canadian from Montreal, a more ethnic sounding surname by adding an 's-k-y.' But when Lester Patrick and Chabot saw "Leopold Chabotsky" on press releases and scoresheets, they weren't pleased and the practice was quickly ended. The publicists had also changed the name of forward Oliver Reinikka to Ollie Rocco in an effort to attract Italian fans.

Chabot had an outstanding playoff series that first season, allowing only three goals in a two-game total-goal loss to former teammate Hal Winkler and the Boston Bruins. The next year, Chabot—who was called "Sad Eyes" due to his dour countenance—played in all 44 games, posting a 19–16–9 record with 11 shutouts and a 1.74 GAA for the second-place Blueshirts.

At 6-foot-1 and 185 pounds, Chabot was the biggest netminder in the league at the time, measuring an inch taller and 20 pounds heavier than Maroons goaltender Clint Benedict. But Lorne was quick and agile for a man his size. In February 1928, Chabot recorded four consecutive shutouts, going 297 minutes and 42 seconds without allowing a goal. He also had an interesting quirk. Attesting to the perils of his position, Chabot insisted on shaving right before games because he "stitched better when his skin was smooth."

During the 1927–28 season, Chabot was offered a bribe to throw a game against the Maroons, but immediately alerted Lester Patrick of the offer and was known as "an honest player who couldn't be tempted."

That spring, Chabot led the Rangers through the first two rounds of the playoffs, first beating the Boston Bruins and then the Pittsburgh Pirates in two total-goal series. But in the second game of the Finals, Nels Stewart of the Maroons unleashed a shot that caught Chabot squarely in the left eye. Chabot was taken to Montreal's Royal Victoria Hospital where it was first thought he would lose his eye.

Stuck without a spare or even practice goaltender, Lester Patrick asked Montreal GM Eddie Gerard for permission to use Ottawa's Alex Connell or minor leaguer Hugh McCormick to replace Chabot. When Gerard refused, Patrick himself donned the pads as the Rangers beat the Maroons in overtime, 2–1, and thus a legend was born.

Joe Miller played the rest of the series in goal as the Blueshirts won the Stanley Cup while Chabot watched from the stands with a black patch covering his eye.

Chabot would make a full recovery, but Patrick had lost confidence in his big goaltender, fearing that he would become "puck shy." So, a few weeks before the beginning of the following season, Chabot was sent to Toronto along with winger Alex Gray and $10,000 for goaltender John Ross Roach and winger Butch Keeling.

Chabot regained his form in Toronto and remained one of the league's top netminders for the next seven years, winning another Cup with the Leafs in 1931–32 and a Vezina Trophy with the Black Hawks in 1934–35. Lorne also saw action with the Montreal Canadiens, Montreal Maroons, and New York Americans before retiring at the end of the 1936–37 season.

Regular Season

Season	Team	GP	W	L	T	GA	GAA	SO	MIN	G	A	PTS	PIM
1926–27	NYR	36	22	9	5	59	1.51	10	2347	0	0	0	0
1927–28	NYR	44	19	16	9	79	1.74	11	2730	0	0	0	0
1928–29	TOR	43	20	16	5	64	1.52	10	2534	0	0	0	2
1929–30	TOR	42	16	20	6	110	2.54	6	2600	0	0	0	0
1930–31	TOR	37	21	8	8	80	2.09	6	2300	0	0	0	0
1931–32	TOR	44	21	16	6	106	2.36	4	2698	0	0	0	2
1932–33	TOR	48	24	18	6	111	2.26	5	2946	0	0	0	4
1933–34	MTL	47	21	20	6	101	2.07	8	2928	0	0	0	2
1934–35	CBH	48	26	17	5	88	1.80	8	2940	0	0	0	0
1935–36	MTM	16	8	3	5	35	2.08	2	1010	0	0	0	0
1936–37	NYA	6	2	3	1	25	4.05	1	370	0	0	0	0
NYR Totals	-	81	41	25	14	138	1.63	21	5077	0	0	0	0
Career	-	412	200	146	62	858	2.03	71	25,403	0	0	0	10

Playoffs

Season	Team	GP	W	L	T	GA	GAA	SO	MIN	G	A	PTS	PIM
1926–27	NYR	2	0	1	1	3	1.50	1	120	0	0	0	0
1927–28	NYR	6	2	2	1	8	1.31	1	367	0	0	0	0
1928–29	TOR	4	2	2	0	5	1.24	0	242	0	0	0	0
1930–31	TOR	2	0	1	1	4	1.72	0	139	0	0	0	0
1931–32	TOR	7	5	1	1	15	2.05	0	438	0	0	0	0
1932–33	TOR	9	4	5	0	18	1.57	2	686	0	0	0	0
1933–34	MTL	2	0	1	1	4	1.83	0	131	0	0	0	0
1934–35	CBH	2	0	1	1	1	0.48	1	125	0	0	0	0
1935–36	MTM	3	0	3	0	6	1.21	0	297	0	0	0	0
NYR Totals	-	8	2	3	2	11	1.36	2	487	0	0	0	0
Career	-	37	13	17	6	64	1.51	5	2545	0	0	0	0

Lester Patrick
Born: December 30, 1883 in Drummondville, Quebec
Died: June 1, 1960
6-1, 180lb
Caught: Left
Rangers Debut: March 20, 1927 vs. New York Americans
Uniform #16
Seasons with Rangers: As Player: 2, 1926–27 to 1927–28 As Coach: 13, 1926–27 to 1938–39 As GM: 19, 1926–27 to 1945–46
Stanley Cups as Coach and GM: 3, Rangers, 1927–28, 1932–33, 1939–40
Hockey Hall of Fame: 1947

Public Domain

Rangers patriarch Lester Patrick cemented his place in Blueshirts lore on the evening of April 7, 1928. The Rangers had eliminated the Pittsburgh Pirates and Boston Bruins and were playing the second game of the Stanley Cup Finals against the Montreal Maroons, who had won the opener, 2–0, behind the steady goaltending of Clint Benedict.

Early in the second period, Rangers goaltender Lorne Chabot was struck in the left eye by a Nels Stewart shot, forcing him to leave the game. Patrick now found himself without a goaltender since, either due to poor planning or in an effort to save a little money, he had decided not to bring along a spare netminder, even though all of the games would be played in Montreal due to the circus taking over Madison Square Garden.

Patrick asked Montreal coach and GM Eddie Gerard for permission to use Alex Connell of the Ottawa Senators, who was a spectator at the game, as a replacement. Connell was one of the better goaltenders in the league at the time so Gerard refused. Patrick then asked permission to use minor-league goalie Hugh McCormick, but that request was also denied. He was then given 10 minutes to produce a goaltender or the Rangers would have to forfeit the match.

"The place became bedlam," author Eric Whitehead wrote of the Rangers locker room in his book *The Patricks: Hockey's Royal Family*.

"Well-meaning outsiders burst in with suggestions for ways out of the dilemma."

Rangers defenseman Leo Bourgeault volunteered to take Chabot's place in goal, but Frank Boucher and Bill Cook, the team's captain, told Lester that having Bourgeault in goal would leave the team short a valuable player. Instead, they suggested that Patrick himself strap on the pads, promising that the team would block as many shots as possible and keep the Maroons' skaters away from the net.

Patrick thought about it for a few moments and finally called out to trainer Harry Westerby, "Harry I'm going in goal." He then told Westerby to gather Chabot's equipment and get him a clean set of underwear and socks. During the commotion, Pittsburgh Pirates coach Odie Cleghorn wandered into the Rangers dressing room and Lester asked him to run the bench for him while he was in the net. Cleghorn agreed. Yes, the NHL was a very different place back then.

Patrick was forty-four years old at the time, thirteen years older than his captain Bill Cook and nine years the senior of Montreal goaltender Clint Benedict. This would not be Patrick's first experience between the pipes. Years earlier as a defenseman in the Pacific Coast Hockey Association, he had occasionally gone into the net when his team's goaltender was penalized. On one occasion, he had blocked a shot and proceeded to skate the length of the ice to score.

Patrick was welcomed onto the ice with curiosity and what could be called bemused applause.

Montreal Star sports editor Baz O'Meara described the bizarre scene thusly: "There was 'Laughing Lester,' who has done everything in hockey sauntering out with a little black cap askew over his whitening thatch, his lanky legs upholstered by brown pads that seemed to fit him like his father's old trousers."

Patrick made a great show of the situation, pointing at the Maroons and yelling, "Let them shoot!" But wiser heads prevailed. Before the faceoff, Cleghorn gathered the skaters around him and cautioned, "Stay back to protect Lester. Don't let 'em get close. Wait for a break. If you can protect Lester, one goal might win it."

When the game resumed the Rangers checked frantically in front of their coach. The Maroons managed to get a few shots off, but they were blocked by Patrick and the period ended with the game still scoreless.

Bill Cook scored 30 seconds into the third period to give the Rangers the lead, which they held on to until Nels Stewart scored to tie the score with 5:40 left in the period.

The game went into sudden-death overtime and the Maroons were sure that the old man in net would fold. But Patrick held on, stopping an early surge by the Maroons. The momentum of the play changed quickly, and soon Frank Boucher grabbed a loose puck and stickhandled past a Montreal defenseman and beat Benedict with a hard, low shot for the game-winner.

Lester Patrick was the hero. The Rangers jumped over the boards and hoisted their white-haired, GM/coach/goaltender on their shoulders and carried him off the ice. As Eric Whitehead concluded: "An ageless and unquenchable love of the fray and the courage of an old bull seal returned to protect his herd, yes. It was vintage Patrick family stuff!"

Patrick was lucky. He turned out to be a hero when it could have very easily gone the other way. But knowing that he couldn't pull off another miracle, the next day he asked for and received permission to use Joe Miller of the New York Americans. Miller turned in an outstanding performance in the remaining three games of the series, and the Rangers won their first Stanley Cup on April 14.

In honor of Patrick's remarkable performance, James Burchard, who covered hockey for the *New York World-Telegram*, composed the following poem about Lester's adventure:

'Twas in the spring of twenty-eight
A golden Ranger page,
That Lester got a summons
To guard the Blueshirt cage.
Chabot had stopped a fast one,
A bad break for our lads,
The Cup at stake and no one
To don the Ranger pads.
"We're cooked," lamented Patrick,
"This crisis I had feared."
He leaned upon his newest crutch.
And wept inside his beard.

Then suddenly he came to life,
No longer halt or lame.
"Give me the pads," he bellowed,
"I used to play this game."
Then how the Rangers shouted.
How Patrick was acclaimed.
Maroons stood sneering, gloating,
They should have been ashamed.
The final score was two to one.
Old Lester met the test.
The Rangers finally won the Cup,"
But Les has since confessed.
"I just spoke up to cheer the boys,
"I must have been delirious.
"But now, in reminiscence,
"I'm glad they took me serious."

Ironically, six years earlier, Lester's brother Frank was faced with a similar situation that also involved Eddie Gerard.

In the Stanley Cup Finals of 1922, the Vancouver Millionaires, champions of the PCHL, had traveled to Toronto to face the NHL champion St. Pats. In the second game of the series, Toronto defenseman Harry Cameron injured his shoulder and was unable to continue playing. Toronto asked for permission to use Eddie Gerard, a player borrowed from the Ottawa Senators, as an emergency replacement. In a show of good sportsmanship, Frank Patrick agreed. Although he played only one game, Gerard won his third consecutive Stanley Cup when the St. Pats defeated Vancouver. As captain of the Senators, he had led Ottawa to the Stanley Cup in 1920 and 1921 and would do so again in 1923.

Playoffs

Season	Team	GP	W	L	T	GA	GAA	SO	MIN	G	A	PTS	PIM
1927–28	NYR	1	1	0	0	1	1.71	0	35	0	0	0	0
Career	NYR	1	1	0	0	1	1.71	0	35	0	0	0	0

Fast Fact: At forty-four years of age, Lester Patrick was the oldest man ever to tend goal for the Rangers. Seventeen-year-old Harry Lumley was the youngest (1943).

Joe Miller
Born: October 6, 1900 in Morrisburg, Ontario
Died: August 12, 1963
5-9, 170lb
Caught: Left
Rangers Debut: April 10, 1928 at Montreal Maroons
Uniform #1
Seasons with Rangers: 1, 1927–28 (playoffs)
Stanley Cup: Rangers, 1927–28

Joe Miller went from hockey's outhouse to its penthouse in just a matter of weeks.

On March 22, 1928, Miller and the last-place New York Americans finished their season with their fifth consecutive loss, this time a 5–0 blanking in Ottawa. His season seemingly over, Miller returned to his Morrisburg, Ontario, home to relax and keep tabs on the Amerks' co-tenants at the Garden, the Rangers, who had finished in second place and were in the Stanley Cup playoffs.

The Rangers got through the first two rounds of the playoffs fairly easily but ran into a serious problem in the finals against the Montreal Maroons. Goaltender Lorne Chabot had been struck in the eye by a shot from Nels Stewart in the second game of the series and could not continue. The injured goaltender had been famously replaced by forty-four-year-old Rangers GM and coach Lester Patrick for the remainder of that game but the Blueshirts now needed to find a netminder for the rest of the series.

Patrick asked the Maroons for permission to use either George Hainsworth or Charlie Gardiner. Both were top goalies in the league at the time, so Montreal boss Eddie Gerard refused to allow Patrick to use either one of them.

Working on the premise that any goalie is better than no goalie—and out of desperation—Patrick submitted Miller's name. Joe had finished the season with an 8–16–4 record, allowing 77 goals in 28 games for the last-place Amerks and had picked up the nickname "Red Light Miller" for all the goals that he had allowed. Gerard agreed to allow the Rangers to use him, most likely while rubbing his hands together, assuming that his Maroons now had the Stanley Cup in the bag.

Joe played well in the third game of the series, but the Rangers were shut out, 2–0, by Clint Benedict, giving the Maroons a two-games-to-one lead in the five-game series. In the fourth game, Miller protected a one-goal lead and shut out Montreal, 1–0. Miller's shining moment came in the fifth game on April 14 as he too suffered an eye injury when struck by a shot—this time from the stick of Hooley Smith. The game was delayed for 10 minutes as Miller was helped into the dressing room for repairs. When he returned his right eye was nearly swollen shut, but the little goalie held his ground as the Blueshirts beat the Maroons, 2–1, to win the franchise's first Stanley Cup.

The next season, the Americans sent Miller and $20,000 to the Pittsburgh Pirates for goaltender Roy "Shrimp" Worters. Miller played two seasons with the Pirates and then moved with the franchise to Philadelphia, where they became the Quakers. He then retired in 1932 after a season in the IHL.

Miller is a prime example of a goalie being only as good as the team in front of him. He spent four seasons in the NHL playing for some bad teams. But when the pressure was on, and with a better team in front of him, Joe proved to be a quality netminder.

Regular Season

Season	Team	GP	W	L	T	GA	GAA	SO	MIN	G	A	PTS	PIM
1927–28	NYA	28	8	16	4	77	2.68	5	1721	0	0	0	0
1928–29	PTP	44	9	27	8	80	1.73	11	2780	0	0	0	0
1929–30	PTP	43	5	35	3	179	4.08	0	2630	0	0	0	0
1930–31	PHQ	15	2	11	1	47	3.43	0	821	0	0	0	0
Career	-	130	24	89	16	383	2.89	16	7952	0	0	0	0

Playoffs

Season	Team	GP	W	L	T	GA	GAA	SO	MIN	G	A	PTS	PIM
1927–28	NYR	3	2	1	0	3	1.00	1	180	0	0	0	0
Career	NYR	3	2	1	0	3	1.00	1	180	0	0	0	0

John Ross Roach
Born: June 23, 1900 in Port Perry, Ontario
Died: July 9, 1973
5-5, 130lb
Caught: Left
Rangers Debut: November 15, 1928 at Detroit Cougars
Uniform #1
Seasons with Rangers: 4, 1928–29 to 1931–32
Stanley Cup: Toronto St. Pats, 1921–22

Public Domain

John Ross Roach played junior hockey for the Toronto Aura Lee team in 1919–20 before moving up to the seniors the following year with the Toronto Granites. He turned pro in 1921–22 and led the Toronto St. Pats to a Stanley Cup victory in his rookie season. He stayed in Toronto for a total of seven seasons as the St. Pats evolved into the Maple Leafs.

But in October 1928, the twenty-seven-year-old netminder was traded—along with winger Butch Keeling—to the Rangers for Lorne Chabot, Alex Gray, and $10,000. Roach was reportedly looking for more money from the Leafs so Conn Smythe was more than happy to trade him, even to Lester Patrick's Rangers. The acquisition of Roach also set up a rivalry between he and Roy "Shrimp" Worters of the New York Americans, who were considered the two best goaltenders in the league at the time.

At a mere 5-foot-5 and 130 pounds, "Little Napoleon" was the smallest goaltender to play for the Rangers. But despite his small stature, he proved to be a durable performer, starting every game for the Rangers over the next four seasons. He was very fidgety in goal and in constant motion. He could also be feisty and somewhat moody off the ice.

John made his Rangers debut on November 15, 1928, shutting out the Detroit Cougars, 2–0. He went on to post a 21–13–10 record with a 1.41 GAA and a total of 13 shutouts while helping the Blueshirts reach the Stanley Cup Finals.

During his four seasons with the Rangers, Roach set many team records—some of which still stand today—including most shutouts in one season (13 in 1928–29), lowest goals-against average in one season (1.48 in 1928–29), and most consecutive playoff shutouts (three in 1929).

He also led the NHL in games played four times (1928–29, 1929–30, 1930–31, 1931–32), minutes played (2,760 in 1930–31), shutouts (nine in 1931–32), playoff games played by a goaltender (six in 1929, and seven in 1932), playoff minutes played by a goaltender (1929 and 1932), lowest playoff goals-against average (1.00 in 1931), and most playoff shutouts (three in 1929 and one in 1932).

The Rangers made it to the postseason three more times with Roach in net, including one more trip to the Finals in 1931–32. But it was during that final series against Toronto that Roach lost the confidence of Lester Patrick when he surrendered six goals in each of his three appearances as the Leafs easily took the series, 3–0, to win the Stanley Cup. Roach was then sold to the Detroit Red Wings before the start of the next season for $10,000 as Patrick turned to young Andy Aitkenhead to be his goaltender.

Roach played the next season with the Red Wings, barely being edged out for the Vezina Trophy by the man he was traded for, Lorne Chabot, who was now with Chicago. He then spent the next two seasons bouncing between the Wings and their minor-league clubs, and retired at the end of the 1934–35 season at the age of thirty-four.

Regular Season

Season	Team	GP	W	L	T	GA	GAA	SO	MIN	G	A	PTS	PIM
1921–22	TRS	22	11	10	1	91	4.07	0	1340	0	0	0	0
1922–23	TRS	24	13	10	1	88	3.59	1	1469	0	0	0	0
1923–24	TRS	23	10	13	0	80	3.48	1	1380	0	0	0	0
1924–25	TRS	30	19	11	0	84	2.80	1	1800	0	0	0	0
1925–26	TRS	36	12	21	3	114	3.07	2	2230	0	0	0	0
1926–27	TOR	44	15	24	5	94	2.04	4	2764	0	0	0	0
1927–28	TOR	43	18	18	7	88	1.96	4	2690	0	0	0	0
1928–29	NYR	44	21	13	10	65	1.41	13	2760	0	0	0	0
1929–30	NYR	44	17	17	10	143	3.10	1	2770	0	0	0	0
1930–31	NYR	44	19	16	9	87	1.89	7	2760	0	0	0	0
1931–32	NYR	48	23	17	8	112	2.23	9	3010	0	0	0	0
1932–33	DET	48	25	15	8	93	1.88	10	2970	0	0	0	0

Season	Team	GP	W	L	T	GA	GAA	SO	MIN	G	A	PTS	PIM
1933–34	DET	18	9	8	1	45	2.62	1	1030	0	0	0	0
1934–35	DET	23	7	11	5	62	2.55	4	1460	0	0	0	0
NYR Totals	-	180	80	63	37	407	2.16	30	11,300	0	0	0	0
Career	-	492	219	204	68	1246	2.46	58	30,433	0	0	0	0

Playoffs

Season	Team	GP	W	L	T	GA	GAA	SO	MIN	G	A	PTS	PIM
1921–22	TRS	2	1	0	1	4	0.56	1	425	0	0	0	0
1924–25	TRS	2	0	2	0	5	2.50	0	120	0	0	0	0
1928–29	NYR	6	3	2	0	5	0.77	3	392	0	0	0	0
1929–30	NYR	4	1	2	1	7	1.36	0	308	0	0	0	0
1930–31	NYR	4	2	2	0	4	1.00	1	240	0	0	0	0
1931–32	NYR	7	3	4	0	27	3.38	1	480	0	0	0	0
1932–33	DET	4	2	2	0	8	2.00	1	240	0	0	0	0
NYR Totals	-	21	9	10	1	43	1.82	5	1420	0	0	0	0
Career	-	29	12	14	2	60	1.63	7	2205	0	0	0	0

Fast Fact: At 5-foot-5 and 130 pounds, John Ross Roach was the shortest and lightest Ranger goaltender. Steve Valiquette and Magnus Hellberg at 6-foot-6 were the tallest and Jason LaBarbera the heaviest at 232 pounds.

Andy Aitkenhead
Born: March 6, 1904 in Glasgow, Scotland
Died: October 21, 1968
5-9, 145lb
Caught: Left
Rangers Debut: November 10, 1932 at Montreal Maroons
Uniform #1
Seasons with Rangers: 3, 1932–33 to 1934–35
Stanley Cup: Rangers, 1932–33

Andy Aitkenhead was born on March 6, 1904, in Glasgow, Scotland, but was raised in Saskatoon, Saskatchewan, and began his hockey career at the age of seventeen with the Yorkton Terriers of the N-SSHL. The

"Glasgow Gobbler" then played for a number of teams and leagues in British Columbia, leading many of them in wins, goals-against average, and shutouts. He caught the eye of Rangers scouts and signed with the Blueshirts in 1931, where he was assigned to the Bronx Tigers of the Can-Am League for the 1931–32 season.

The next season, Rangers GM Lester Patrick sold his starting netminder for the previous four seasons, John Ross Roach, to the Detroit Red Wings for $10,000 and gave the job to the twenty-eight-year-old rookie.

The bushy haired, blue eyed Aitkenhead won his first start, 4–2, over the Montreal Maroons and went on to post a 23–17–8 record with three shutouts and a 2.17 GAA for the Rangers, who finished in third place in the NHL's American Division. Aitkenhead, who was known to wear a tweed cap in goal, played in all eight playoff games, winning six and recording two shutouts as the Blueshirts went on to beat the Maple Leafs for the Stanley Cup.

The acrobatic Aitkenhead also had a pretty good sophomore year as well, going 21–19–8 with seven shutouts and a 2.27 GAA. But the stress of playing goal in the NHL began to take its toll, and in March he suffered what was called a "nervous breakdown." Lester Patrick tried to borrow Alex Connell from Ottawa to use in the playoffs, but Aitkenhead regained his composure and played the rest of the season and the playoffs. Andy performed well in the postseason, giving up only two goals in the two-game, total goals series. But the Blueshirts could only put one shot past future Ranger Davey Kerr of the Montreal Maroons and were eliminated.

By then, Aitkenhead's nerves were shot. It was reported that he would lock himself in his room after a game and replay each shot over and over. After losing seven of his first ten starts in 1934–35, Patrick acquired goaltender Percy Jackson from Boston for defenseman Jean Pusie. But Jackson surrendered eight goals in his only start as a Ranger and was sent back to Boston for cash. Patrick then purchased the contract of Davey Kerr from the Maroons for $10,000 and Aitkenhead returned to the PCHL, where he played mostly with the Portland Buckaroos before retiring in 1941.

Regular Season

Season	Team	GP	W	L	T	GA	GAA	SO	MIN	G	A	PTS	PIM
1932–33	NYR	48	23	17	8	107	2.16	3	2970	0	0	0	0
1933–34	NYR	48	21	19	8	113	2.27	7	2990	0	0	0	0
1934–35	NYR	10	3	7	0	37	3.64	1	610	0	0	0	0
Career	NYR	106	47	43	16	257	2.35	11	6570	0	0	0	0

Playoffs

Season	Team	GP	W	L	T	GA	GAA	SO	MIN	G	A	PTS	PIM
1932–33	NYR	8	6	1	1	13	1.60	2	488	0	0	0	0
1933–34	NYR	2	0	1	1	2	1.00	1	120	0	0	0	0
Career	NYR	10	6	2	2	15	1.48	3	608	0	0	0	0

Fast Fact: Scotsman Andy Aitkenhead was the Rangers' first European-born goaltender. Overall, Sweden leads the Blueshirts' import list with four goaltenders, followed by Czechoslovakia and Finland with two each and Bulgaria, Scotland, and the USSR, one.

Percy Jackson
Born: September 21, 1907 in Canmore, Alberta
Died: September 16, 1972
5-9, 165lb
Caught: Left
Rangers Debut: November 15, 1934 at Detroit Red Wings
Uniform #1
Seasons with Rangers: 1, 1934–35

Percy Jackson began his hockey career with the Trail Smoke Eaters in 1927–28, and then played the next three seasons with the Vancouver Lions, where he led the PCHL in wins twice as well as shutouts and goals-against average.

Jackson made his NHL debut with the Boston Bruins in 1931–32, going 1–1–1. Two years later, on March 18, 1934, the Bruins loaned him to the New York Americans to replace the injured Roy Worters in the final game of the season. Jackson surrendered nine goals to the Bruins that night as the Americans lost, 9–5.

He was traded to the Rangers for defenseman Jean Pusie before the start of the 1934–35 season and played his first and only game for the Blueshirts on November 15, 1934, an 8–2 loss to Detroit. His rights were sold back to the Bruins three days later. He made one more appearance with Boston and spent the rest of his career in the minor leagues.

Regular Season

Season	Team	GP	W	L	T	GA	GAA	SO	MIN	G	A	PTS	PIM
1931–32	BOS	4	1	1	1	8	2.09	0	230	0	0	0	0
1933–34	NYA	1	0	1	0	9	9.00	0	60	0	0	0	0
1934–35	NYR	1	0	1	0	8	8.00	0	60	0	0	0	0
1935–36	BOS	1	0	0	0	1	1.50	0	40	0	0	0	0
NYR Totals	-	1	0	1	0	8	8.00	0	60	0	0	0	0
Career	-	7	1	3	1	26	3.98	0	392	0	0	0	0

Davey Kerr—Franchise Goaltender
Born: January 11, 1910 in Toronto, Ontario
Died: May 11, 1978
5-10, 160lb
Caught: Right
Rangers Debut: December 13, 1934 vs. Boston Bruins
Uniform #1
Seasons with Rangers: 7, 1934–35 to 1940–41
Stanley Cup: Rangers, 1939–40
Vezina Trophy: 1939–40
All-Star selections: 1937–38 (Second Team), 1939–40 (First Team)

Before there was a Chuck Rayner, a Gump Worsley, an Ed Giacomin, John Davidson, John Vanbiesbrouck, Mike Richter, or Henrik Lundqvist, there was Davey Kerr.

Kerr was the Rangers' original franchise goaltender, the guy who set the standard for what all future Blueshirts netminders would aspire to accomplish.

David Alexander Kerr began his amateur career with the Toronto Canoe Club of the OHA in 1924. He moved on to the Montreal AAA of the MCHL in 1929, and led the club to the Allen Cup championship in

1930. He was then signed by the Montreal Maroons in 1930 and played 102 games for them over three seasons (46–37–18 with 11 shutouts and a 2.36 GAA). But in 1934, the Maroons needed cash and Rangers GM/coach Lester Patrick, whose Blueshirts had started the season 3–8, needed a goaltender. Kerr was purchased by the Rangers for $10,000, the going price for a netminder at the time. It proved to be money well spent.

In the first eight years of the Rangers' existence, goaltending was a mostly unsettled position, with seven different players taking turns between the pipes—including Lester Patrick himself. However, once Kerr was acquired the goaltending situation was in good hands for the next seven seasons.

Kerr made his Rangers debut on December 16, 1934, in a 2–1 victory over Boston. A durable netminder, he would miss only one game for the rest of his seven-year Blueshirts career. He backstopped the team into the playoffs six of those seven years and led them to the finals twice, first in 1937 when he set a franchise record with four shutouts in a playoff year (since tied by Mike Richter) in a losing effort against Detroit, and then again in 1940 when they won the Stanley Cup.

Kerr enjoyed his best season in 1939–40 when the Rangers set a franchise record with a 19-game unbeaten streak (14–0–5). Davey posted a 1.54 GAA and recorded eight shutouts to lead the league in both categories, won the Vezina Trophy, and was named a First Team All-Star.

Perhaps his defining moment as a Ranger came during the 1940 playoffs, in the semifinals against Boston. The Rangers had won the series opener but dropped the next two games and were in obvious trouble. Kerr shut the Bruins out, 1–0, in both of the next two games, and then held them to a single goal in the Rangers' 4–1 victory, sending them to the Finals. He then led them to a four-games-to-two series victory over the Toronto Maple Leafs, the last two games going into sudden-death overtime. If not for Kerr's heroics in those two series, the Blueshirts' 54-year Cup drought would have been a lot longer.

Kerr was a fan favorite and, in March 1938, became the first active hockey player to appear on the cover of *Time* magazine in a portrait by artist S. J. Wolff. It was an amazing tribute considering that two of the sport's biggest stars at the time, Eddie Shore and Howie Morenz, had never appeared on *Time*'s cover; and it wasn't until the 1950s that Montreal's Maurice Richard was afforded the same honor.

The Toronto native always kept himself in great shape. At 5-foot-10 and 160-pounds, he was solidly built with strong legs and arms while still being very agile. He had an excellent glove hand and would challenge teammates in practice by laying his stick flat on the ice in front of him. He would then prop his feet against the left and right posts, leaving himself spread-eagled with a large space between his legs—but had both of his hands free to stop the puck while the stick deflected shots along the ice.

Kerr was also very well respected by his teammates, being able to shout commands to his defensemen without offense. In addition, he never blamed a teammate for a goal scored against him, always taking full responsibility. Kerr also found a clever way to circumvent the NHL's rule forbidding goaltenders from holding the puck to stop play. He had his leg pads customized to rise up a little higher over the knee to give him a place to drop the puck to halt play when needed.

Off the ice, Kerr was deliberate and methodical. He smoked a pipe and wore sunglasses while traveling with the team by train to protect his eyes from the glare of the sun off the snow. He attended McGill University and was a stockbroker in Toronto. He played tennis and handball in the offseason to stay in shape and keep his reflexes sharp. He also preferred to be called a *goaltender* rather than a *goalkeeper*, feeling that the latter was more a soccer term. After his retirement, he confessed that he would occasionally sip a little wine with his pregame meal. This was done in the privacy of his home, since it would certainly have been frowned upon by Lester Patrick.

Kerr retired at the age of thirty-one following the 1940–41 season to accept an offer of year-round employment with a Toronto-based beverage company. It was believed that Kerr's decision to retire was influenced by many years of butting heads with Patrick over his contract and Lester's desire to trade him—along with five other members of the 1940–41 Rangers following their first-round playoff ouster.

At the time of his retirement, Kerr held every franchise goaltending record including regular season games (324), wins (157), and shutouts

(40), as well as playoff games (32), wins (17), shutouts (seven), and most shutouts in a single playoff year (four). Kerr also led the league in games played five times and shutouts twice. He also led all playoff goaltenders in 1937 and 1940 in games played, minutes, wins, shutouts, and goals-against average.

Regular Season

Season	Team	GP	W	L	T	GA	GAA	SO	MIN	G	A	PTS	PIM
1930–31	MTM	31	14	12	4	71	2.33	1	1830	0	0	0	0
1931–32	NYA	1	0	1	0	6	6.00	0	60	0	0	0	0
1932–33	MTM	26	14	8	4	58	2.15	4	1620	0	0	0	0
1933–34	MTM	48	19	18	11	122	2.39	6	3060	0	0	0	0
1934–35	NYR	37	19	12	6	94	2.47	4	2287	0	0	0	0
1935–36	NYR	47	18	17	12	95	1.91	8	2980	0	0	0	0
1936–37	NYR	48	19	20	9	106	2.10	4	3030	0	0	0	0
1937–38	NYR	48	27	15	6	96	1.95	8	2960	0	0	0	0
1938–39	NYR	48	26	16	6	104	2.10	6	2970	0	0	0	0
1939–40	NYR	48	27	11	10	77	1.54	8	3000	0	0	0	0
1940–41	NYR	48	21	19	8	125	2.49	2	3010	0	0	0	0
NYR Totals	-	324	157	110	57	697	2.07	40	20,237	0	0	0	0
Career	-	430	204	149	76	954	2.14	51	26,807	0	0	0	0

Playoffs

Season	Team	GP	W	L	T	GA	GAA	SO	MIN	G	A	PTS	PIM
1930–31	MTM	2	0	2	0	8	4.00	0	120	0	0	0	0
1932–33	MTM	2	0	2	0	5	2.50	0	120	0	0	0	0
1933–34	MTM	4	1	2	1	7	1.75	1	240	0	0	0	0
1934–35	NYR	4	1	1	2	10	2.50	0	240	0	0	0	0
1936–37	NYR	9	6	3	0	10	1.08	4	553	0	0	0	0
1937–38	NYR	3	1	2	0	8	1.83	0	262	0	0	0	0
1938–39	NYR	1	0	1	0	2	1.01	0	119	0	0	0	0
1939–40	NYR	12	8	4	0	20	1.56	3	769	0	0	0	0
1940–41	NYR	3	1	2	0	6	1.88	0	192	0	0	0	0
NYR Totals	-	32	17	13	2	56	1.57	7	2135	0	0	0	0
Career	-	40	18	19	3	76	1.74	8	2615	0	0	0	0

Bert Gardiner
Born: March 25, 1913 in Saskatoon, Saskatchewan
Died: August 28, 2001
5-11, 160lb
Caught: Right
Rangers Debut: March 22, 1936 vs. Boston Bruins
Uniform #1
Seasons with Rangers: 2, 1935–36 and 1939 (playoffs)

Bert Gardiner came close to becoming part of Rangers folklore but unfortunately wound up as a footnote to an opponent's remarkable performance.

Gardiner was signed as a free agent by Lester Patrick in 1934 following an impressive junior career in Western Canada. The Rangers assigned Gardiner to their EAHL affiliate, the Brooklyn Crescents, where he led the league in wins, shutouts, goals-against average, playoff wins, playoff shutouts, and playoff GAA.

He made his Rangers debut in a 3–1 win in Boston in the final game of the 1935–36 season. It was an impressive start for the rookie, but not good enough to unseat the incumbent, Davey Kerr, so Gardiner spent the next three seasons toiling for the Philadelphia Ramblers of the AHL.

However, in the spring on 1939, Gardiner was recalled when Kerr was injured in the opening game of the playoffs against Boston. Kerr had suffered a separated shoulder in the third overtime period of the game that ended when Mel Hill, who had been cut by Lester Patrick a few years earlier, scored the game-ending goal for the Bruins.

With only one game of NHL experience under his belt, Gardiner played well in the second game, making 35 saves but, once again, the contest went into overtime and, once again, Hill scored—this time at the 8:48 mark of the first extra session. Boston won the third game, this time in regulation, and it appeared that the Blueshirts were on their way to an early summer. But they roared back by winning the next three games, one of them in overtime, to even the series and set up a dramatic seventh game.

It was the first Game Seven in the playoffs since 1919 because the league had just changed from a best three-of-five to a four-of-seven format. Once again, the two teams battled to a tie at the end of regulation time and once again it was Mel "Sudden Death" Hill who scored the game-winner at the eight-minute mark of the third overtime period. It was Hill's fourth goal and third game-winner of the series. To this day, Hill is the only player to score three overtime goals in the same series.

Overall, the teams battled for 533 minutes and eight seconds—the equivalent of almost nine regulation hockey games. Boston's manager Art Ross requested that the start of the Finals—in which the Bruins were to meet the Maple Leafs two days after the Rangers marathon—be pushed back a few days. The extra rest seemed to help Boston, who beat the Leafs four games to one to win their second Stanley Cup. Hill, who notched four goals in the Rangers series, scored two more in the Finals.

Gardiner played well in the series, posting a 3–3 record and a 1.66 GAA. He was traded to the Montreal Canadiens in April 1940, and played 52 games for the Habs over the next two seasons.

He was then loaned to the Black Hawks for the 1942–43 season and became their everyday netminder. The next season, however, he was traded to Boston for cash and the right to repurchase him if needed. Bert played 41 games for the Bruins in 1943–44 and retired at the end of the season.

Regular Season

Season	Team	GP	W	L	T	GA	GAA	SO	MIN	G	A	PTS	PIM
1935–36	NYR	1	1	0	0	1	1.00	0	60	0	0	0	0
1940–41	MTL	42	13	23	6	119	2.75	1	2600	0	0	0	0
1941–42	MTL	10	1	8	1	42	4.06	0	620	0	0	0	0
1942–43	CBH	50	17	18	15	180	3.58	1	3020	0	0	0	0
1943–44	BOS	41	17	19	5	212	5.17	1	2460	0	1	1	0
NYR Totals	-	1	1	0	0	1	1.00	0	60	0	0	0	0
Career	-	144	49	68	27	554	3.79	3	8760	0	1	1	0

Playoffs

Season	Team	GP	W	L	T	GA	GAA	SO	MIN	G	A	PTS	PIM
1938–39	NYR	6	3	3	-	12	1.66	0	434	0	0	0	0
1940–41	MTL	3	1	2	-	8	2.24	0	214	0	0	0	0
NYR Totals	-	6	3	3	-	12	1.66	0	434	0	0	0	0
Career	-	9	4	5	-	20	1.85	0	648	0	0	0	0

Uniform Numbers: Frank Patrick, brother of Rangers patriarch Lester Patrick, is credited with introducing a numbering system in the family-owned Pacific Coast Hockey Association in 1911. In the days of seven-man hockey, the players were numbered from the goal out: Goal, No. 1; Point, No. 2; Coverpoint, No. 3; Rover, No. 4; Left Wing, No. 5; Center, No. 6; and Right Wing, No. 7. The numbering system also aided in making travel arrangements, with the lower numbers being assigned lower berths on trains, which is one of the reasons that goaltenders wore number 1—teams didn't want to see their netminder falling out of an upper berth if the train came to a sudden stop. Originally worn on armbands, the numbers were eventually moved to first the front and then the back of the players' sweaters, which in those days were just that—sweaters.

CHAPTER TWO

The War Years

On December 7, 1941, the day Japan bombed Pearl Harbor, the Rangers beat Boston, 5–4. Over the next season and a half, ten of the fourteen Rangers in the lineup that evening joined the armed forces. Muzz and Lynn Patrick were among the first to enlist. Even though they were both born in Canada, they were naturalized American citizens and joined the US Army. Goaltender Sugar Jim Henry enlisted in the Canadian Army. Art Coulter joined the Coast Guard, as did Alex Shibicky and Neil and Mac Colville.

The Rangers finished at the top of the NHL standings in 1941–42 but fell to last place the next season with an 11–31–8 record. In fact, from 1942–43 through 1944–45, the Blueshirts posted an overall 27–99–23 record for only 77 out a possible 300 points.

The loss of their best players certainly hurt the Rangers, but they were also victimized by several poor decisions by Lester Patrick who was the architect of the team's previous success.

Patrick thought that the league would cease operations during the war, so he sold off all the players from his top farm club, the Philadelphia Ramblers. But the league didn't miss a game and the Rangers were left with little NHL-caliber talent. He was also leery of wartime border crossing restrictions and loaned Phil Watson, the center on the Rangers' top line with Bryan Hextall on the right and Lynn Patrick on the left, to Montreal in exchange for Charlie Sands, Fern Gauthier, Dutch Hiller, John Mahaffy, and future considerations which turned out to be Tony Demers. Watson got his name on the Stanley Cup that season, while the Rangers finished in the cellar. Patrick wanted to suspend operations after the 1942–43 season but when the Brooklyn Americans dropped out of the league, the NHL's Board of Governors talked him out of it.

The 1943–44 season was the low point of the war years for the Rangers. They opened the season with a record-setting eleven-game losing streak, which was eventually broken by a 2–2 tie with Montreal.

They then proceeded to lose their next four in a row and finished the 50-game season with a 6–39–5 record for 17 points, 26 points out of a playoff spot. They managed to score 162 goals but gave up a whopping 310. No Rangers team would give up more than 300 goals until the 76-game 1975–76 season (333).

The 1943–44 Blueshirts were shut out five times and surrendered 10 or more goals seven times during the season including a franchise worst 15–0 loss to Detroit on January 23 at the Olympia. Despite the lopsided score goalie Ken "Tubby" McAuley made 43 saves that night. The Wings almost scored a 16th goal but it came right at the final buzzer and was not allowed. The Rangers could only muster nine shots on Detroit's Connie Dion, handing the Wings' own wartime replacement goaltender his only NHL shutout.

The fact that McAuley was their goaltender that season is another example of the Rangers' poor planning. When they opened training camp for the 1942–43 season Patrick did not have a goaltender under contract to replace Jim Henry, so they had to scramble to find a capable netminder. Four goalies played for the Rangers in 1942–43: Bill Beveridge, Lionel Bouvrette, Jimmy Franks, and the infamous Steve Buzinski (the puck goes in-ski), each with little success. In all fairness, however, it should be noted that although most of the goaltenders employed by the Rangers during this period were not of NHL caliber, they each did the best they could considering the inferior team in front of them.

Frank McCool, a lanky, twenty-five-year-old goaltender from Calgary, attended the Rangers training camp in the fall of 1943 and made the team. Unfortunately, he was forced to leave due to ulcers and returned home to Calgary where he worked as a sportswriter. The next season, however, McCool signed with the Maple Leafs and had a tremendous season, leading the league in games played and shutouts, winning the Calder Trophy as the NHL's Rookie of the Year and posting four shutouts in the playoffs while backstopping the Leafs to the Stanley Cup.

After McCool left camp at the beginning of the 1943–44 season the Rangers signed McAuley, who had only senior-league experience, and hoped for the best. Ken finished the season with a 6.20 goals-against average, giving up 310 goals. But the guy really deserved a medal. He played in all 50 games; his only relief came when he was injured and replaced for one period by Harry Lumley, Detroit's spare goaltender.

The Blueshirts had no one else to turn to for the 1944–45 season so they re-signed McAuley who was able to lower his GAA to 4.94.

The 1943–44 Blueshirts set a franchise record for the most rookies used during the season (20). One of those youngsters was Don "Bones" Raleigh who was only seventeen years old when he made his Ranger debut. Raleigh recorded two goals and two assists in 15 games before he was sidelined with a broken jaw. Raleigh would return a few years later to enjoy a memorable 10-year career with the Rangers.

Bryan Hextall led the team in scoring with 21 goals and 33 assists, but he received little help from the rest of the forwards. It got so bad that Frank Boucher, who had been named coach in 1939, laced up the skates again at age forty-two and played 15 games. Although his legs and stamina were gone, he still managed to notch four goals and added 10 assists for 14 points, outscoring nineteen other players they tried that season.

The Blueshirts finished the season pretty much the same way they started it with a 21-game winless streak, going 0–17–4 from January 27 to the end of the season on March 19.

The Rangers also finished last in each of the next two seasons and Patrick resigned as GM in 1946. He was replaced by Boucher, who also remained as coach. Boucher rebuilt the farm system that would eventually produce stars such as Andy Bathgate, Harry Howell, and Allan Stanley in the 1950s. But the damage had been done and the Blueshirts didn't make the playoffs again until 1947–48 and only five times in the next fourteen seasons.

Rule Changes:

1941–42: Penalty shots were classified into minor and major categories. Minor penalty shots were taken from a line 28 feet from the goal. Major penalty shots were awarded when a player was tripped with only the goaltender to beat. The player was permitted to skate right at the goalkeeper and shoot from point-blank range. Standby minor-league goaltenders were employed by the NHL as emergency substitutes during the playoffs.

1942–43: Because of wartime restrictions on train scheduling, regular-season overtime was discontinued on November 21, 1942. Regular season overtime would not return to the NHL until the 1983–84 season.

1943–44: The center ice red line was introduced to speed up the game and reduce offside calls. This rule is considered to mark the beginning of the modern era in the NHL.

Sugar Jim Henry
Born: October 23, 1920 in Winnipeg, Manitoba
Died: January 21, 2004
5-9, 165lb
Caught: Left
Rangers Debut: November 1, 1941 at Toronto Maple Leafs
Uniform #1, 20
Seasons with Rangers 4, 1941–42, 1945–46 to 1947–48
All-Star selections: 1951–52 (Second Team)

Jim Henry had some pretty big skates to fill in 1941, as he was being asked to replace Davey Kerr, who had retired at the end of the previous season.

"Sugar Jim," who got his nickname from his love for brown sugar as a baby, began his junior career with the Brandon Elks of the MJHL. He then moved up to the Regina Rangers of the SJHL, leading them to an Allen Cup victory in 1941 where he caught the eye of Rangers coach Frank Boucher.

The twenty-one-year-old rookie came through for the Blueshirts, leading them to a first-place finish. His total of 29 victories not only led the league but also set a Ranger record for rookie netminders that would stand until broken by Henrik Lundqvist sixty-four years later. Henry surprisingly lost out to teammate Grant Warwick in that season's Calder Trophy voting for the NHL Rookie of the Year.

Unfortunately, before the start of the following season World War II escalated and many players including Henry enlisted in the Armed Forces, both in the United States and Canada. Henry joined the Canadian military and later transferred to the Navy. He was based in Canada and played for the Ottawa Commandos club that captured the Allan Cup in 1942–43 and later for Red Deer in Calgary.

When Henry returned to the Rangers in 1945, he discovered that they had signed Chuck Rayner as a free agent after the Brooklyn Americans folded. Coach Frank Boucher still had confidence in "Sugar Jim" and instituted a two-goalie system that was years ahead of its time, switching between Henry and Rayner in alternate games and even shift-by-shift by some reports. Through it all "Sugar Jim" and "Bonnie Prince Charlie" became the best of friends and even started a hunting and fishing business together.

Henry's Ranger career ended in October 1948 when he was dealt to Chicago in exchange for Alex Kaleta and a diminutive goalkeeper named Emile Francis.

He played one lackluster season for a weak Black Hawks team and was part of a nine-player trade that sent him and Metro Prystai, Gaye Stewart, and Bob Goldham to Detroit for Harry Lumley, Jack Stewart, Al Dewsbury, Pete Babando, and Don Morrison in July 1950.

Henry never played a game for Detroit, however, spending the next two seasons in the minors. In September 1951 he was sent to Boston for cash but was badly burned in a fire, placing his playing career in doubt. Ignoring doctor's orders, Henry made it to Bruins training camp. He was able to regain his form, was named to the 1951–52 All-Star team and led Boston to the Stanley Cup finals in 1953. But after playing in 210 consecutive games for the Bruins he suffered a broken jaw in 1955 which forced him out of the NHL. "Sugar Jim" then continued to play for local senior teams and retired in 1960.

Regular Season

Season	Team	GP	W	L	T	GA	GAA	SO	MIN	G	A	PTS	PIM
1941–42	NYR	48	29	17	2	143	2.90	1	2960	0	0	0	0
1945–46	NYR	10	1	7	2	39	4.16	1	563	0	0	0	0
1946–47	NYR	2	0	2	0	9	4.50	0	120	0	0	0	0
1947–48	NYR	48	17	18	13	152	3.17	2	2879	0	0	0	0
1948–49	CBH	60	21	31	8	211	3.52	0	3600	0	0	0	0
1951–52	BOS	70	25	29	16	173	2.47	7	4200	0	0	0	0
1952–53	BOS	70	28	29	13	170	2.43	8	4200	0	0	0	0
1953–54	BOS	70	32	28	10	178	2.54	8	4200	0	0	0	0
1954–55	BOS	27	8	13	5	75	2.92	1	1542	0	0	0	0
NYR Totals	-	108	47	44	17	343	3.16	4	6522	0	0	0	0
Career	-	405	161	174	69	1150	2.84	28	24,264	0	0	0	0

Playoffs

Season	Team	GP	W	L	T	GA	GAA	SO	MIN	G	A	PTS	PIM
1941–42	NYR	6	2	4	-	13	2.17	1	360	0	0	0	0
1951–52	BOS	7	3	4	-	17	2.28	1	447	0	0	0	0
1952–53	BOS	9	4	4	-	26	3.06	0	510	0	0	0	0
1953–54	BOS	4	0	4	-	16	4.00	0	240	0	0	0	0
1954–55	BOS	3	1	2	-	8	2.62	0	183	0	0	0	0
NYR Totals	-	6	2	4	-	13	2.17	1	360	0	0	0	0
Career	-	29	11	18	-	81	2.79	2	1741	0	0	0	0

Steve Buzinski
Born: October 15, 1917, in Dunblane, Saskatchewan
Died: February 20, 1992
5-8, 140lb
Caught: Left
Rangers Debut: October 31, 1942 at Toronto Maple Leafs
Uniform #1
Seasons with Rangers: 1, 1942–43

Steve Buzinski's nickname, "The puck goes-inski," says it all about this Ranger wartime netminder.

Rangers GM Lester Patrick signed Buzinski sight unseen in October 1942, based on a glowing recommendation by a scout in Western Canada. The twenty-five-year-old native of Dunblane, Saskatchewan, was the first of a long line of goaltenders the Blueshirts hoped could replace Sugar Jim Henry, who had enlisted in the military at the beginning of World War II. Buzinski had spent the previous five seasons playing for the amateur Swift Current Indians of the Saskatchewan Intermediate Hockey League.

In his book, *When the Rangers Were Young*, former Rangers player, coach, and GM Frank Boucher described the scene the first time he laid eyes on Buzinski.

"I was out on the ice with the players, when suddenly out of the corner of my eye I was distracted by a movement near a gate in the corner that led to the playing surface. It was a black football helmet and it was on a skinny, scrawny guy all dressed up in a Ranger uniform and goaltenders pads, a little short fellow who was, so help me, the most bow-legged goaler I ever saw in my life. I said to myself, "My God, no it can't be." But it was, Steve Buzinski! Well when he finally did get into the net, he was marvelous. We just couldn't seem to get the puck past him. We tried everything, and he kicked out pucks like Davey Kerr."

That was apparently the high point of Steve's Ranger career and the last time he was ever mentioned in the same sentence as Davey Kerr. He tried his best and was well liked by his teammates, but he just wasn't an NHL-caliber goaltender, not even in wartime.

"We all enjoyed him tremendously, he was a fine little fellow," Boucher once told an interviewer. "But he had a problem though; he couldn't stop the puck. He played nine games for us and allowed 55 goals. We had to let him go."

What the 5-foot-8, 140-pound Buzinski lacked in ability he made up for in confidence. After making a glove save on a high shot by Carl Liscombe of the Red Wings, Steve shouted to teammate Bryan Hextall, "Like pickin' cherries," even though Detroit already had a 7–1 lead and Liscombe was on his way to scoring a hat trick and adding four assists in the contest. Later in that same game, Buzinski gloved another high shot and attempted to toss the puck behind the net. Unfortunately, he misjudged his position and threw the puck into his own goal instead.

"One night in Toronto Steve was knocked flat in a melee, apparently slammed with a stick by Bob Davidson a hard-nosed winger," related Boucher. "From the bench I could see Steve flat on his back. Then he was sitting upright, then flat on his back again. Lynn Patrick came skating from the goalmouth pileup to the bench, laughing so hard he was shaking.

What in the world is going on I asked?

You'll never believe this Lynn gasped, tears rolling down his cheeks. We thought that Steve had been knocked out. We were yelling for a penalty to Davidson for high-sticking. Davidson said 'Hell I didn't belt him. He got hit on the head by a stick.'

That's when Steve lying there cold as a mackerel sat straight up and said to the referee 'that's a damn lie! He high-sticked me.' And fell flat on his back again with his eyes closed."

Buzinski's place in NHL history was assured when he surrendered Maurice "Rocket" Richard's first NHL goal in a 10–1 defeat by the Canadiens on November 8, 1942. Two nights later Steve was in goal as the Rangers beat Chicago, 5–3, in overtime (in those days overtime was a 10-minute period that did not end when a goal was scored). It was Steve's second and last victory as a Ranger and the last regular-season overtime game played for over 40 years. They were eliminated eleven days later by NHL President Frank Calder as part of wartime cutbacks.

Steve played only nine games for the Rangers at the start of the 1942–43 season, allowing 55 goals and posting a 2–6–1 record with a 5.89 GAA, the highest of any Rangers netminder who played in more than three games. He was replaced on the roster by Jimmy Franks, but Lester Patrick liked Buzinski and kept him on the payroll as a member of the public relations department.

He played cards with Patrick and kept him company until one day the Rovers, the Blueshirts' farm team, needed some players for a scrimmage. Patrick suggested that Buzinski take the opportunity to get some ice time, but Steve declined, telling Patrick that he had some letters to write. The next day Buzinski was on a train back to Swift Current.

"We were sorry to see him go," said Boucher. "We kind of missed the little guy. He was a lovely little fellow, earnest and sincere, and we all liked him tremendously, but that simply doesn't stop pucks. Granted he was one of the worst goalies in NHL history, but he was also one of the funniest."

Following his brief stint with the Rangers, Steve enlisted in the armed forces and later returned to Swift Current, retiring after the 1952–53 season. He then coached at the intermediate level for six years before beginning a career as a plant breeder for Agriculture Canada.

Regular Season

Season	Team	GP	W	L	T	GA	GAA	SO	MIN	G	A	PTS	PIM
1942–43	NYR	9	2	6	1	55	5.89	0	560	0	0	0	0
Career	NYR	9	2	6	1	55	5.89	0	560	0	0	0	0

Jimmy Franks
Born: November 8, 1914 in Melville, Saskatchewan
Died: February 12, 1994
5-11, 155lb
Caught: Left
Rangers Debut: November 26, 1942 at Chicago Black Hawks
Uniform #1
Seasons with Rangers: 1, 1942–43

Once it became apparent that Steve Buzinski was not the answer to the Rangers' goaltending problems, GM Lester Patrick arranged to borrow Jimmy Franks from the Detroit Red Wings organization for the remainder of the 1942–43 season.

Franks played his junior hockey with the Regina Pats of the SJHL and later played senior hockey with the Prince Albert Mintos. He turned pro with the Pittsburgh Hornets of the AHL and moved up to the NHL with the Detroit Red Wings in 1937, appearing in one game in place of injured starter Norm Smith. He then spent the next seven seasons in the minors before being loaned to the Rangers.

Franks got off to a good start in New York, winning two of his first three games. Unfortunately, he was only able to win three more in the next 20 games. His season ended early when he suffered a broken wrist in January and was replaced by Bill Beveridge for the remainder of the year.

Franks was returned to Detroit following the season but stirred up quite a bit of controversy the next year when he was suspended for refusing to report to the minor leagues. The situation was resolved when it was decided that Franks would split the season with Connie Dion, with Dion playing home games while Franks played on the road. Franks also played in one game for the Bruins that season as an emergency replacement for Bert Gardiner. That proved to be his last NHL appearance. He spent the following year in the AHL and retired at the end of the 1944–45 season.

Regular Season

Season	Team	GP	W	L	T	GA	GAA	SO	MIN	G	A	PTS	PIM
1937–38	DET	1	1	0	0	3	3.00	0	60	0	0	0	0
1942–43	NYR	23	5	14	4	103	4.48	0	1380	0	0	0	0
1943–44	TOT	18	6	9	3	75	4.17	1	1080	0	0	0	0
1943–44	DET	17	6	8	3	69	4.06	1	1020	0	0	0	0
1943–44	BOS	1	0	1	0	6	6.00	0	60	0	0	0	0
NYR Totals	-	23	5	14	4	103	4.48	0	1380	0	0	0	0
Career	-	42	12	23	7	181	4.31	1	2520	0	0	0	0

Playoffs

Season	Team	GP	W	L	T	GA	GAA	SO	MIN	G	A	PTS	PIM
1936–37	DET	1	0	1	-	2	4.06	0	30	0	0	0	0
Career	DET	1	0	1	-	2	4.06	0	30	0	0	0	0

Bill Beveridge
Born: July 1, 1909 In Ottawa, Ontario
Died: February 13, 1995
5-8, 170lb
Caught: Left
Rangers Debut: January 28, 1943 at Chicago Black Hawks
Uniform #1
Seasons with Rangers: 1, 1942–43

Bill Beveridge was a pretty good goaltender who had the misfortune of playing for some pretty bad teams during his NHL career.

He made his NHL debut with the Detroit Cougars in 1929 and performed well for a weak team that missed the playoffs. He then joined the Ottawa Senators but was sent to the minors in favor of incumbent Alex Connell. The Senators suspended operations in 1931 and Bill wound up in Providence, where he led the Can-Am league with 23 victories. Ottawa resumed operations the next season and Bill posted five shutouts for the cash-strapped team. During the next two seasons Bill led the league in games played, appearing in all of his team's 48 games, the first year with Ottawa and then with the Eagles when the Senators finally folded and moved to St. Louis.

In 1935, Bill moved to the Montreal Maroons, who were the defending Stanley Cup champions. He had his best NHL season with Montreal, recording five shutouts and a 2.16 GAA in 32 games. But when the playoffs rolled around, the Maroons elected to play Lorne Chabot instead and were knocked out in the first round by Detroit. Bill then played for two more seasons with the Maroons before landing back in the minors in 1938.

He was then loaned to the Rangers by Cleveland of the AHL in 1942–43 as a replacement for the injured Jimmy Franks and thus became one of four goalies who played between the pipes that year for the last-place Rangers.

Following his stint with the Blueshirts, Beveridge played a few games for the Ottawa Commandos of the QSHL and retired after the 1945 season.

Regular Season

Season	Team	GP	W	L	T	GA	GAA	SO	MIN	G	A	PTS	PIM
1929–30	DTC	39	14	20	5	109	2.71	2	2410	0	0	0	0
1930–31	OTS	9	0	8	0	32	3.69	0	520	0	0	0	0
1932–33	OTS	33	7	19	7	89	2.59	5	2063	0	0	0	0
1933–34	OTS	48	13	29	6	143	2.86	3	3000	0	0	0	0
1934–35	STE	48	11	31	6	144	2.89	3	2990	0	0	0	0
1935–36	MTM	32	14	13	5	71	2.16	1	1970	0	0	0	0
1936–37	MTM	21	12	6	3	47	2.19	1	1290	0	0	0	0
1937–38	MTM	48	12	30	6	149	3.00	2	2980	0	0	0	0
1942–43	NYR	17	4	10	3	89	5.24	1	1020	0	0	0	0
NYR Totals	-	17	4	10	3	89	5.24	1	1020	0	0	0	0
Career	-	297	87	166	42	879	2.87	18	18,375	0	0	0	0

Playoffs

Season	Team	GP	W	L	T	GA	GAA	SO	MIN	G	A	PTS	PIM
1936–37	MTM	5	2	3	-	11	2.20	0	300	0	0	0	0
Career	MTM	5	2	3	-	11	2.20	0	300	0	0	0	0

Lionel Bouvrette
Born: June 10, 1914 in Hawkesbury, Ontario
Died: February 8, 2000
5-9, 165lb
Caught: Left
Rangers Debut: March 18, 1943 at Montreal Canadiens
Uniform #1
Seasons with Rangers: 1, 1942–43

Lionel Bouvrette played the final game of the 1942–43 season for the Rangers, replacing Bill Beveridge, who had been loaned to the Blueshirts by the Cleveland Barons of the AHL. However, late in the season when the Barons wanted Beveridge back for their playoff run, it left the Blueshirts without a netminder for their season finale against the Montreal Canadiens. So the thirty-year-old Bouvrette, who was the property of the Canadiens, was recalled from the Quebec Aces and loaned to the Rangers. The Canadiens, who were fighting for the final playoff spot, won the contest, 6–0, beating out the Chicago Black Hawks for fourth place by a single point.

The game was Bouvrette's only NHL appearance. He returned to the Aces and retired after the 1947 season.

Regular Season

Season	Team	GP	W	L	T	GA	GAA	SO	MIN	G	A	PTS	PIM
1942–43	NYR	1	0	1	0	6	6.00	0	60	0	0	0	0
Career	NYR	1	0	1	0	6	6.00	0	60	0	0	0	0

Ken McAuley
Born: January 9, 1921 in Edmonton, Alberta
Died: June 18, 1992
5-10, 190lb
Caught: Right
Rangers Debut: October 30, 1943 at Toronto Maple Leafs
Uniform #1
Seasons with Rangers: 2, 1943–44 to 1944–45

Following the 1942–43 season that saw the Rangers employ four goaltenders and surrender a league worst 253 goals, (62 more that their nearest competitor) on their way to an 11–31–8 last-place finish, the Blueshirts brought in Ken "Tubby" McAuley in hopes of upgrading the goaltending position. Unfortunately, it didn't quite work out that way.

McAuley was a twenty-two-year-old goaltender from Edmonton who played senior hockey with the Edmonton Maple Leafs. He missed most of the 1942–43 season due to a head injury suffered while playing for Regina in the Saskatchewan Senior League and wore a helmet in goal during his career with the Rangers to protect the injury.

He made his NHL debut on October 30, 1943 in a 5–2 opening night loss to Toronto. The Blueshirts then lost their next ten games before gaining a tie against the Canadiens on November 28, which at that point had to be considered a moral victory. The season didn't get any better from there on.

The Rangers allowed 10 or more goals seven times that year and a total of 310 over the 50-game season as McAuley finished with a 6.24 GAA. He did, however, lead the league in games played.

Their worst outing was a 15–0 drubbing at the hands of the Detroit Red Wings that could have been worse had time not run out before the Red Wings scored their 16th goal right after the final buzzer. McAuley made 43 saves in the game while his counterpart in the Red Wings net, rookie Connie Dion, only had to stop nine shots to rack up his only NHL shutout. Detroit's Gordie Howe led the scoring attack with three goals and two assists as every Red Wing except for defenseman Colby Simon and goaltender Dion recorded at least one point in the lopsided contest. Ranger GM Lester Patrick was behind the Ranger bench that night subbing for coach Frank Boucher who was away at his brother's funeral.

Having no other options, McAuley was brought back the next season and improved his GAA to 4.93 with one shutout in 46 games but the Blueshirts still finished in last place, a point behind the Chicago Black Hawks.

The next season with the war over, the Rangers used a tandem of Charlie Rayner and Jim Henry and McAuley returned to Edmonton where he played senior hockey until 1950. He then coached the Edmonton Oil Kings for four seasons and led them to the Memorial Cup final in 1954.

He then became very active in the local sports scene and was president and co-founder of the Edmonton Old-timers Hockey League and managed the Edmonton Mortons team that won the Western Canadian ladies fastball championships seven times. He also served as president of the Big Seven Baseball League, the North Edmonton Community League, and the Edmonton District Fastball Association. He also organized the first charity golf tournament in Alberta. Ken was inducted into the Edmonton Sports Hall of Fame in 1975 and inducted into the Alberta Amateur Fastball Hall of Fame in 1988.

Regular Season

Season	Team	GP	W	L	T	GA	GAA	SO	MIN	G	A	PTS	PIM
1943–44	NYR	50	6	39	5	310	6.24	0	2980	0	0	0	0
1944–45	NYR	46	11	25	10	227	4.93	1	2760	0	0	0	0
Career	NYR	96	17	64	15	537	5.61	1	5740	0	0	0	0

Harry Lumley
Born: November 11, 1926 in Owen Sound, Ontario
Died: September 13, 1998
6-0, 195lb
Caught: Left
Rangers Debut: December 23, 1943 at Detroit Red Wings
Uniform #1
Seasons with Rangers: 1, 1944–45
Stanley Cup: Detroit, 1949–50
Vezina Trophy: 1953–54 (with Toronto)
Hockey Hall of Fame: 1980
All-Star selections: 1953–54 and 1954–55 (First Team)
All-Star Games: 3, 1951, 1954, and 1955

Seventeen-year-old Harry "Apple Cheeks" Lumley became the youngest goaltender in Rangers history on December 23, 1943, when he was called upon to replace the injured Ken McAuley in Detroit. McAuley had been struck in the jaw by a shot and was unable to play the third period. Lumley, who had already made his NHL debut with the Red Wings earlier that season, giving up 13 goals in two games, was seated in the stands and loaned to the Rangers on an emergency basis. The youngster shut out the Red Wings for the final 20 minutes of a 5–3 loss.

Lumley went on to become one of the NHL's best goaltenders over a 16-year Hall-of-Fame career with Detroit, Chicago, Toronto, and Boston. He beat the Rangers in a tough seven-game series to win the Stanley Cup in 1950 and was awarded the Vezina Trophy in 1953. He also led the league in wins, games played, and goals-against average numerous times and was a perennial All-Star.

Regular Season

Season	Team	GP	W	L	T	GA	GAA	SO	MIN	G	A	PTS	PIM
1943–44	DET	2	0	2	0	13	6.50	0	120	0	0	0	0
1943–44	NYR	1	0	0	0	0	0.00	0	20	0	0	0	0
1944–45	DET	37	24	10	3	119	3.22	1	2220	0	0	0	0
1945–46	DET	50	20	20	10	159	3.18	2	3000	0	0	0	6
1946–47	DET	52	22	20	10	159	3.06	3	3120	0	0	0	4
1947–48	DET	60	30	18	12	147	2.46	7	3592	0	0	0	8
1948–49	DET	60	34	19	7	145	2.42	6	3600	0	0	0	12
1949–50	DET	63	33	16	14	148	2.35	7	3780	0	0	0	10
1950–51	CBH	64	12	41	10	245	3.88	3	3785	0	0	0	4
1951–52	CBH	70	17	44	9	237	3.40	2	4180	0	0	0	2
1952–53	TOR	70	27	30	13	164	2.34	10	4200	0	0	0	18
1953–54	TOR	69	32	24	13	128	1.86	13	4140	0	0	0	6
1954–55	TOR	69	23	24	22	132	1.91	8	4137	0	0	0	9
1955–56	TOR	59	21	28	10	157	2.67	3	3526	0	0	0	2
1957–58	BOS	24	11	10	3	70	2.92	3	1440	0	0	0	2
1958–59	BOS	11	8	2	1	27	2.45	1	660	0	0	0	0
1959–60	BOS	42	16	21	5	146	3.48	2	2518	0	0	0	12
NYR Totals	-	1	0	0	0	0	0.00	0	20	0	0	0	0
Career	-	803	330	329	142	2206	2.75	71	48,044	0	0	0	9

Playoffs

Season	Team	GP	W	L	T	GA	GAA	SO	MIN	G	A	PTS	PIM
1944–45	DET	14	7	7	-	31	2.13	2	871	0	0	0	0
1945–46	DET	5	1	4	-	16	3.10	1	310	0	0	0	0
1947–48	DET	10	4	6	-	30	3.00	0	600	0	0	0	10
1948–49	DET	11	4	7	-	26	2.15	0	725	0	0	0	2
1949–50	DET	14	8	6	-	28	1.85	3	908	0	0	0	0
1953–54	TOR	5	1	4	-	14	2.62	0	321	0	0	0	0
1954–55	TOR	4	0	4	-	13	3.26	0	240	0	0	0	0
1955–56	TOR	5	1	4	-	13	2.57	1	304	0	0	0	2
1957–58	BOS	1	0	1	-	5	5.00	0	60	0	0	0	0
1958–59	BOS	7	3	4	-	20	2.75	0	436	0	0	0	4
Career	-	76	29	47	-	196	2.46	7	4778	0	0	0	18

Fast Fact: Harry Lumley was the first of six emergency goaltenders to be used by the Rangers. The other five were Bob DeCourcy, Julian Klymkiw, Joe Schaefer (twice), Dan Olesevich, and Dave Dryden.

Doug Stevenson
Born: April 6, 1924 in Regina, Saskatchewan
Died: November 9, 1975
5-8, 170lb
Caught: Left
Rangers Debut: February 11, 1945 vs. Montreal Canadiens
Uniform #1
Seasons with Rangers: 1, 1944–45

Doug Stevenson played junior hockey with the Edmonton Athletic Club and signed with Chicago to be their spare goaltender in 1942–43. Two seasons later he was signed as a free agent by the Rangers, who were in desperate need of help in goal.

Stevenson played in four games during the 1944–45 season, lost them all, and wound up with a 5.00 GAA. He played 20 games for the New York Rovers, the Rangers' Eastern League affiliate, and was loaned to Chicago in March to replace injured starter Mike Karakas. He played two games for the Black Hawks that season and two more the following year before returning to the minors. He spent the remainder of his career playing for teams in the PCHL and WHL, retiring in 1956.

Regular Season

Season	Tm	GP	W	L	T	GA	GAA	SO	MIN	G	A	PTS	PIM
1944–45	NYR	4	0	4	0	20	5.00	0	240	0	0	0	0
1944–45	CBH	2	1	1	0	7	3.50	0	120	0	0	0	0
1945–46	CBH	2	1	1	0	12	6.00	0	120	0	0	0	0
NYR Totals	-	4	0	4	0	20	5.00	0	240	0	0	0	0
Career	-	8	2	6	0	39	4.88	0	480	0	0	0	0

CHAPTER THREE

Postwar Recovery

At the end of World War II, nearly fifty players returned to their respective NHL teams including key Rangers such as Muzz and Lynn Patrick, Alex Shibicky, Alf Pike, and Mac Colville, whose brother Neil had returned during the previous season. Unfortunately, after three or four years away from the league, these men were now past their prime. The Patricks as well as Shibicky gave it one last try and retired following the 1945–46 season.

After two decades at the helm of the Rangers, Lester Patrick resigned as general manager in February of 1946, leaving his successor, coach Frank Boucher, the monumental task of rebuilding the franchise from the ashes of the war years. Boucher's first priority was restoring the Rangers' farm system that Patrick had decimated when he mistakenly thought that the league would shut down during the war. Patrick had sold off most of his minor-league players and kept only the New York Rovers of the ECHL as a farm club. Boucher traveled across Canada that summer and signed deals with junior teams in Lethbridge, Alberta; Prince Albert, Saskatchewan; Winnipeg and Flin Flon, Manitoba; and Verdun, Quebec. He also resurrected the Guelph Biltmores of the OHA which would eventually produce future Rangers stalwarts such as Andy Bathgate, Harry Howell, Lou Fontinato, Ron Murphy, Jean Ratelle, Rod Gilbert, and many others. Boucher also signed working agreements with minor pro clubs in Tacoma, Vancouver, St. Paul, and Saskatoon.

In 1945–46, the Blueshirts won only two more games than the previous season and finished last in every statistical category for the third straight year. Bryan Hextall missed most of the season with a liver ailment but twenty-six-year-old Edgar Laprade scored 15 goals with 19 assists and skated away with the Calder Trophy as the NHL's Rookie of the Year.

The next season the league increased the schedule from 50 to 60 games and the Rangers won nine more of those contests but still wound up out of the money in fifth place.

In 1947–48, the Blueshirts managed to finish in fourth place to make the playoffs for the first time in six seasons. They were led by center Buddy O'Connor, who Boucher had acquired from Montreal the previous August along with defenseman Frankie Eddolls for Hal Laycoe, Joe Bell, and George Robertson. O'Connor, who had won two Stanley Cups with Montreal, led the Rangers in scoring with 24 goals and 36 assists and won both the Hart Trophy as the NHL's MVP and the Lady Byng Trophy as the league's most gentlemanly player. The Blueshirts lost in the semifinals to the Red Wings four games to two, but for the first time since the beginning of the war it looked like better days were ahead.

Unfortunately, just before the start of the 1948–49 campaign, Buddy O'Connor, Frankie Eddolls, Edgar Laprade, and Bill Moe were involved in a serious automobile accident and missed the beginning of the season. As a result, the Blueshirts got off to a 3–11–5 start and never recovered, falling back to last place in the final standings, a full 10 points out of a playoff spot. Lynn Patrick was brought in from New Haven to coach midway through the season, allowing Boucher to spend more time tending to his GM responsibilities. With the move, the Patricks became the first father and son duo to coach the same team. Lynn's brother Muzz also ran the team as coach and general manager in the 1950s and years later, Lynn's son Craig would also become GM and coach in the early 1980s, making the Rangers the only team in the NHL that has been coached by three generations of the same family.

The Rangers bounced back in 1949–50 led by Laprade's 22 goals and the solid goaltending of Chuck Rayner. They finished in fourth place and beat Montreal in the semifinals. However, by the time the finals began, the circus had chased the Blueshirts out of the Garden and team president John Reed Kilpatrick lost a power struggle to Detroit owner James Norris and the Rangers were allowed only two neutral site games in Toronto while the rest of the seven-game series was to be played in the Detroit Olympia.

The series went the full seven games and ended when Detroit's Pete Babando beat Rayner at 8:31 of the second overtime session. Although it appeared that the Rangers were finally on the right track, less than two weeks after the season ended Patrick resigned as coach, saying that he didn't want to raise his family in New York. He accepted an offer to coach a team in Victoria that was owned by his father. However, before the next season started, Lynn got a call and a tremendous offer from Art Ross to become coach of the Boston Bruins. It proved to be an offer he couldn't refuse.

Neil Colville was then hired to coach the team but the Blueshirts got off to a slow start, winning only five of their first 31 games. Grasping at straws, looking for ways to snap the team out of their doldrums as well as a gimmick to put people in the seats, Boucher took the advice of the team's publicist Stan Saplin and brought in Dr. David Tracy, a New York City hypnotist who claimed that he could restore the team's confidence by putting them in a trance.

So, prior to a mid-November game against the Bruins, the good doctor stood in the middle of the Rangers dressing room and put several players under his spell. Tracy then gave an inspirational message and snapped his fingers to wake them up. Unfortunately, some of the players had fallen asleep and needed more than a gentle finger snapping to roust them out of their trance.

The Rangers played well that night, holding onto a 3–3 tie in the third period until Boston defenseman Bill Quackenbush launched a long shot that found its way through the legs of Chuck Rayner in the final minute to give the Bruins a 4–3 victory.

Dr. Tracy was stunned by the loss and said that the next time he would concentrate on Rayner, who he thought seemed a little tense. He never got the chance, however, as the Rangers didn't ask him to come back.

They then tried a mysterious concoction developed by Gene Leone, who owned the famed theater district restaurant Mamma Leone's and was a big Rangers fan and good friend of Boucher's.

"Leone's Magic Elixir" which was supposed to restore the Rangers confidence was delivered to Boucher in mid-December 1950 in a large black bottle with a note attached that read, "Drink it and Win!" "I told the boys this was a magic brew, a new liquid vitamin discovery," Boucher wrote in *When the Rangers Were Young*. "We passed it around in paper cups from the washroom. I told the writers, as seriously as I could, that Gene had just provided the Rangers with the key to a glowing future."

Even though the ingredients of Leone's brew were a closely guarded secret at the time, it has been said that the elixir was a simple mixture of warmed up orange juice and ginger ale, with a little honey. There was nothing magical about it, but it gave the Blueshirts the psychological lift they needed.

The results were amazing. After drinking the elixir, the Rangers began winning and by early January, had lost only twice in a stretch of 11 games. But the big test would come on January 6 when the Rangers traveled to Toronto, where they hadn't won since December of 1947, to meet the Maple Leafs, who were the best team in the league and eventual Stanley Cup champions.

But first there was a major logistical problem that needed to be overcome.

The Rangers were in Toronto and Leone, who was in New York, insisted on mixing the concoction as close to game time as possible. To overcome this problem the Blueshirts enlisted the help of longtime beat reporter Jim Burchard, who had been following the farce of the magic elixir for readers of the *New York World-Telegram*. Once the brew was ready, it was given to Burchard who was scheduled to fly to Toronto that afternoon and present the bottle to the Rangers right before game time.

But Burchard would first have to get the bottle through customs and as it turned out, the Maple Leafs had gotten wind of the Rangers plan and arranged for border officials to seize the bottle, which was stored in a sealed bag and kept warm by three hot water bottles.

At this point, a photographer from the *Toronto Globe and Mail* named Harold Robinson stepped in and saved the day. Robinson, who had been assigned to cover the arrival of the magic potion by sportswriter Al Nickleson, distracted the customs agents by bribing them with cigars and Burchard was able to slip through. Robinson then sped Burchard to Maple Leaf Gardens where the Rangers quaffed the magic brew and beat the Leafs, 4–2.

The Blueshirts played better hockey for another few weeks but eventually whatever real or imagined effect the elixir had on them wore off and they won only four of their last 16 games and finished in fifth place.

Bill Cook, Frank Boucher, Muzz Patrick, and Phil Watson then each took their turn coaching the Blueshirts who didn't qualify for the post-season again until 1955–56 when they finished in third place under Watson. They finished fourth the next season and climbed to second the year after that but lost in the opening round each spring.

Rule Changes:

1947–48: A goal was awarded when a player with the puck has an open net to shoot at and a thrown stick prevents the shot on goal. A major penalty was given to any player who threw his stick in any zone other than defending zone. If a stick is thrown by a player in his defending zone but the thrown stick is not considered to have prevented a goal, a penalty shot is awarded.

1949–50: The league made it mandatory for clubs to paint the ice surface white. Major penalties incurred by goaltenders were to be served by a member of the goaltender's team instead of resulting in a penalty shot.

1950–51: Each team was required to provide an emergency goaltender in attendance with full equipment at each game for use by either team in the event of illness or injury to a regular goaltender.

1951–52: The goal crease was enlarged from 3 x 7 feet to 4 x 8 feet.

Chuck Rayner—Franchise Goaltender
Born: August 11, 1920 in Sutherland, Saskatchewan
Died: October 6, 2002
5-11, 190lb
Caught: Left
Rangers Debut: November 3, 1945 at Toronto Maple Leafs
Uniform #1
Seasons with Rangers: 8, 1945–46 to 1952–53
Hart Trophy: 1949–50
Hockey Hall of Fame: 1973
All-Star selections: 1948–49, 1949–50, 1950–51 (Second Team)
All-Star Games: 4, 1949 through 1952

Public Domain

Despite never winning a Stanley Cup or setting any records, Chuck Rayner more than earned the title of franchise goaltender by providing the Rangers with eight seasons of solid play as they tried to rebuild from the rubble of the World War II years.

Claude Earl Rayner, or "Chuck" as he had been known since childhood, played junior hockey for the Kenora Thistles of the Manitoba Junior Hockey League, leading them to the Memorial Cup finals in 1939–40 where they lost to the Oshawa Generals.

The following season at the age of twenty, Chuck signed his first pro contract with the Springfield Indians, but after a year was sold to the New York Americans who were in dire need of help between the pipes. Rayner played a total of 48 games over the next two seasons, compiling a 3.60 goals-against average for the defensively challenged Americans, before joining the Royal Canadian Navy where he served until the end of World War II.

While in the Navy, Chuck became the only goaltender on record to skate the length of the ice and score a goal. It happened while he was playing for the Royal Canadian Armed Forces team. After blocking a shot with his chest and with the rest of the players scattered behind his net, Rayner snared the loose puck and took off down the ice. Always a strong skater, he sped quickly through center ice and continued directly towards the goalmouth where he fired a low shot past Art Jones, the astonished opposing netminder.

When the war was over, the now Brooklyn Americans (they changed their name but still played their home games at Madison Square Garden) had folded and Chuck, then twenty-five years old, signed with the Rangers as a free agent. Unfortunately, their roster was decimated by the war and they managed to gain a playoff berth only twice during Chuck's tenure. But that doesn't mean that the 5-foot-11, 205-pound, bushy-haired Rayner wasn't a big man in the nets for the Rangers.

In 1946–47 Chuck led the NHL with five shutouts and posted a 3.05 GAA. However, the next season the Rangers brought back Sugar Jim Henry, who had tended goal for them in 1941–42 but had spent most of the past three seasons in the minors. The two netminders happened to be good friends and business partners off the ice. For a while coach Frank Boucher alternated the two netminders first by games and then by five-minute intervals, switching them like forwards.

"Frank switched us every third line change or so," Chuck later explained. However, the Rangers only had one pair of goalie gloves. "When I skated off to the bench and 'Sugar Jim' came on the ice, we would meet at the blueline so we could exchange gloves in front of 15,000 fans."

The experiment ended for two reasons: The Blueshirts' minor-league team needed help in goal and the Rangers needed offense and couldn't afford the luxury of two goaltenders instead of an extra forward. However, shortly thereafter, Rayner suffered a double fracture of the cheekbone and Henry played the rest of the regular season. The Blueshirts managed to make the playoffs after a six-year absence and Rayner was back in the crease when the Rangers met the Red Wings in the first round. At the beginning of the 1948–49 season Henry was traded to Chicago for winger Alex Kaleta and another goalkeeper by the name of Emile Francis.

The innovative Boucher recognized Rayner's offensive talents and used him on the point during power plays in a few games in the late 1940s. "That was Frank's idea all the way. I used to do a lot of skating and shooting in practice, so he decided to try it in a game," Rayner said. "I'd only come out halfway up to the blueline. It only happened four or five times."

But on February 1, 1947, Chuck took it a step further. After making a stop late in a 2–1 loss in Montreal he rushed the puck up ice into the Canadiens zone and tried to score the tying goal. He went on to try it a couple more times, each to no avail.

In 1950, Chuck led the Blueshirts into the Stanley Cup Finals against Detroit, prompting many sportswriters to dub the team the "New York Rayners" in honor of his heroic performance in goal. The Blueshirts pushed the series to the seventh game but lost when Pete Babando scored in the second overtime period. Chuck was awarded the Hart Trophy as the NHL's Most Valuable Player for his efforts that season, becoming only the second goaltender to receive the honor (Roy Worters was the first).

Given the nickname "Bonnie Prince Charlie" by the press, Rayner became a fan favorite with his acrobatic style and courageous play. Many longtime Rangers fans remember the night Chuck stopped a point-blank shot with his forehead and had to be carried off the ice, leaving a long stream of blood from the crease to the bench. Remember, this was in the days before teams were required to carry a backup goaltender, so 10 minutes later, a stitched-up Rayner returned to the ice with a white turban of bandages wrapped around his head. "Back when I was playing," Rayner once recalled, "they gave you ten minutes to get stitched. One night I was getting sewn up by the doctor when the referee, King Clancy, opened the door and yelled, 'Time.' I went back out with a towel around my head."

Chuck played in four All-Star games and was voted the Rangers MVP three times. His 24 shutouts tie him with both Gump Worsley and Mike Richter for fifth place on the Rangers all-time whitewash list behind Henrik Lundqvist, Ed Giacomin, Davey Kerr, and John Ross Roach. Not bad considering the teams he had in front of him.

Chuck retired after the 1952–53 season due to knee problems. He played a handful of games for the Saskatoon Quakers of the WHL and Nelson Maple Leafs of the WIHL and later coached senior hockey in Nelson, BC, minor pro in Edmonton, and intermediate and junior hockey in Kenora, Ontario. Rayner was elected to the Hockey Hall of Fame in 1973 and passed away on October 6, 2002, at the age of eighty-two.

The fans loved Chuck Rayner and he loved being a Ranger. "New York was a great part of my life," he once said. "I will never forget my days as a New York Ranger."

Regular Season

Season	Team	GP	W	L	T	GA	GAA	SO	MIN	G	A	PTS	PIM
1940–41	NYA	12	2	7	3	44	3.42	0	773	0	0	0	0
1941–42	BRO	36	13	21	2	129	3.47	1	2230	0	0	0	0
1945–46	NYR	41	12	21	7	151	3.72	1	2437	0	0	0	6
1946–47	NYR	58	22	30	6	177	3.05	5	3480	0	0	0	0
1947–48	NYR	12	4	7	0	42	3.65	0	691	0	0	0	0
1948–49	NYR	58	16	31	11	168	2.90	7	3480	0	0	0	2
1949–50	NYR	69	28	30	11	181	2.62	6	4140	0	0	0	6
1950–51	NYR	66	19	27	20	185	2.82	2	3940	0	0	0	6
1951–52	NYR	53	18	25	10	156	2.94	2	3180	0	0	0	4
1952–53	NYR	20	4	8	8	58	2.90	1	1200	0	0	0	2
NYR Totals	-	377	123	179	73	1118	2.98	24	22,548	0	0	0	26
Career	-	425	138	207	77	1294	3.03	25	25,551	0	0	0	26

Playoffs

Season	Team	GP	W	L	T	GA	GAA	SO	MIN	G	A	PTS	PIM
1947–48	NYR	6	2	4	-	17	2.83	0	360	0	0	0	0
1949–50	NYR	12	7	5	-	29	2.25	1	774	0	0	0	0
Career	NYR	18	9	9	-	46	2.43	1	1134	0	0	0	0

Bob DeCourcy
Born: June 12, 1927 in Toronto, Ontario
Died: March 25, 2012
5-11, 160lb
Caught: Right
Rangers Debut: November 12, 1947 vs. Boston Bruins
Uniform #1
Seasons with Rangers: 1, 1947–48

Bob DeCourcy was a twenty-year-old backup netminder for the EHL's New York Rovers when he was called into service as an emergency goaltender for the Rangers.

In the days before teams were required to dress two netminders, it was customary for the home team to have an emergency goaltender on hand in case either team's netminder was injured and could not continue. That was DeCourcy's role as one of the 14,691 spectators in Madison Square Garden on the night of November 12, 1947, as the Rangers hosted the Boston Bruins.

Midway through the second period with the Bruins leading, 2–1, Chuck Rayner was struck under the right eye by a shot from Boston's Jack Crawford. The shot knocked Rayner out and six players were needed to carry him to the dressing room, where Dr. Vincent Nardiello stitched the big goalie up but would not allow him to return to the game. In the meantime, DeCourcy had made his way down to the Rangers locker room and got ready to take Rayner's place in the net.

The Rangers protected their young netminder well and neither team scored for the remainder of the second period. However, the Blueshirts opened their game up in the third period and Boston's Milt Schmidt scored at the 2:04 mark. Buddy O'Connor put a shot past the

Bruins' Frankie Brimsek to bring the Rangers back within a goal. But sensing DeCourcy's inexperience, the Bruins pressured the Rangers defense and shot the puck from every angle, putting four goals past the rookie in a five-minute span, making it an 8–2 rout for the Bruins.

The game marked DeCourcy's only NHL appearance. In 29 minutes of play the young netminder surrendered six goals which equals a 12.41 GAA, the highest of any Rangers' goaltender. DeCourcy returned to the Rovers for the remainder of that season. He then spent three years in the USHL before playing senior hockey with St. Michael's and retiring at the end of the 1950–51 season.

Regular Season

Season	Team	GP	W	L	T	GA	GAA	SO	MIN	G	A	PTS	PIM
1947–48	NYR	1	0	1	0	6	12.29	0	29	0	0	0	0
Career	NYR	1	0	1	0	6	12.29	0	29	0	0	0	0

Emile "The Cat" Francis
Born: September 13, 1926 in North Battleford, Saskatchewan
5-6, 145lb
Caught: Left
Rangers Debut: December 19, 1948 vs. Montreal Canadiens
Uniform #1, 16
Seasons with Rangers: As Player: 4, 1948–49 to 1951–52 As Coach: 10, 1965–66 to 1974–75 As GM: 11, 1965–66 to 1975–76
Hockey Hall of Fame (as a builder): 1982

Public Domain

Emile "The Cat" Francis is well known as the longtime general manager and coach of the Rangers, but he also played 22 games for the Blueshirts in the late 1940s and early 1950s, mostly as a backup to Chuck Rayner.

Francis began his playing career with the hometown North Battleford Beavers of the Saskatoon Junior Hockey League in 1941.

Two years later he made his way to the East Coast, playing for both the Philadelphia Falcons and Washington Lions of the EAHL.

After a year in the Canadian Armed Forces, Emile returned to Saskatchewan to play for the Moose Jaw Canucks. It was while he was with the Canucks that he earned the nickname that would stick with him for the rest of his career. The Canucks were in the midst of an 18-game undefeated streak and Emile's play so impressed Scotty Melville, a local sportswriter, that he wrote "The Moose Jaw Canucks unveiled a new goalkeeper named Emile Francis and he's as quick as a cat."

Francis made his NHL debut with the Black Hawks at the age of twenty in 1946 and he played 73 games over two seasons with Chicago.

"The guy that gave me the most trouble was Gordie Howe," recalled Francis. "I'll never forget him. I broke into the league in January the year before and now we're playing in Detroit in October and I see this guy coming down the right wing and I knew I'd never seen him before. So I move out to the edge of the crease and I say 'Okay I've got you exactly where I want you now' because John Mariucci, a veteran and captain of the team was right in the middle of the ice and I knew he couldn't cut around. I knew he had to shoot. But guess what he did? He switched hands on me going from shooting left to right which gave him an extra two feet on my right side and put the puck right inside the post. Well as he skated around the net I turned around and looked at him and turned to Mariucci and said 'Who the hell is that guy?' 'Some kid they just brought in from Omaha last week,' he tells me. He stayed in the league for about fifty-two years. But I never had anybody do that to me before or after. He was a great player and a mean guy. We used to put two guys on him. We'd put our toughest defenseman on the left side and our best checker. And it was only a matter of time before one of them would come back to the bench with his nose going from one side to another. He had great elbows and he would shake those checkers."

Francis became a favorite of Black Hawks coach Charlie Conacher but was eventually traded by team owner Bill Tobin to the Rangers in October 1948 for Sugar Jim Henry and Alex Kaleta.

The deal didn't sit well with Francis and he let his feeling be known the first time he played against his former team.

"So the Rangers made a change," Emile remembered. "Frank Boucher stepped down as coach and brought in Lynn Patrick who was coaching in New Haven. And I was playing for Patrick in New Haven. So Chuck Rayner got hurt and the next game was in Chicago and they called me up to play. So it was Lynn Patrick's first game coaching the Rangers and we beat them, 3–2. Now Bill Tobin always sat in the corner to the right of the visiting net. So when the game ended I took my thumb and I went 'Up your ass' towards Tobin. So the next day I got a call from the president of the league 'We got a complaint, did you do this, did you do that?' I said yes I did. So he says well, it's gonna cost you $500. God, I think I was only making about $5,000 back then so it was a lot of money."

Emile played sporadically for the Rangers, filling in occasionally for Chuck Rayner when he was either tired or injured. His longest stretch with the Blueshirts was late in the 1951–52 season playing 14 games when Rayner was forced to undergo knee surgery.

Francis spent the 1952–53 season with Vancouver of the WHL where he was named the league's Most Valuable Player. His rights were then traded to the Cleveland Barons of the AHL in June 1953 for another goalie, twenty-nine-year-old Johnny Bower.

Francis was an innovator. While he was with the Black Hawks, he forever changed the way netminders played their position by developing the forerunners of the modern-day goalie gloves.

Having played a lot of baseball in the offseason, he asked the team's trainer to take a first baseman's mitt to the shoemaker and have him sew the cuff of a regular hockey glove onto it.

Francis used that glove for about a season and a half before anyone questioned him about it. But then one night, Jack Adams, Detroit's GM and coach, noticed the glove and complained to referee King Clancy about it.

"Clancy comes over and says, 'Let me see that glove you're wearing,'" remembers Emile. "So Clancy says, 'You can't use that, it's too big.'"

So I told him it was a trapper mitt, George McQuinn model, he played for the Yankees. I put a cuff on it."

Clancy still insisted that Francis couldn't use the glove. But when Emile explained that it was the only glove he had with him, King relented and ordered him to see NHL president Clarence Campbell and have him decide whether the glove could be used or not.

"So I had to go see Campbell, and he had been a Colonel in the army and on the Nuremberg trials," continued Francis. "He was questioning me like I was on trial for killing people. 'Where did you get that glove, how much did you pay for it, who put that cuff on.' He questioned me for an hour. He asked me, 'Why did you want this kind of glove?' I told him, 'Look at the goalkeepers gloves, they're stupid, they've got this little web between your thumb and forefinger so you're catching everything in the palm of your hand, I won't last two seasons playing goal with those kind of gloves. I need something to protect my hand.'

"But what I didn't tell him was that when I got that puck in that trapper mitt, it didn't get out. I played baseball as a shortstop, but I knew that the trapper would hold the puck. Goalkeepers used to knock the puck down. Not me. With that first baseman's mitt it stayed in there. The mistake I made was that two days after my meeting with Campbell, word got out and within thirty days CCM and Rawlings came out with trapper mitts designed after what I had done. I should have put a patent on it, but I never thought about it. I was just trying to prove my point because I was small and my glove hand was the biggest part of my game. I probably didn't even know what a patent was in those days."

But Emile didn't stop there. His next innovation was an early prototype of the blocker glove. Working with Black Hawks trainer Eddie Froelich, who was also a trainer with the New York Yankees during the Joe McCarthy era, they began to try different ways of padding the stick hand. Through a process of trial and error, they concluded that the best protection would be to attach the kneecap from a shin guard to sponge padding and felt and strap it to the back of a glove.

"That's what we came up with and I used that all the years that I played," Francis said. "Now it wasn't nearly as good as what they have now, but it was still better than what we had before. And the league didn't give me any problems. I guess they figured after the first go around they better leave me alone."

Francis was small (5-foot-6, 150 pounds) but he was quick and gained a reputation as a feisty, tenacious competitor who had the mental and physical toughness needed to play hockey's most demanding position. During his career he had suffered multiple broken noses, torn ligaments in both knees, separated shoulders, and needed over 250 stitches to close various wounds. In *When the Rangers were Young*, Frank Boucher related a couple of stories which demonstrated Emile's toughness. Boucher was the Rangers GM and he was in New Haven watching his top farm club play Providence when Emile was hit in the face with a shot from the point.

> *He was a little fellow, five seven or so and weighing 155 pounds and his view was blocked by a big defenseman named Jerry Claude, six-two and burly. He didn't see the shot from the point which Claude could have blocked but ducked at the last instant. The puck hit Cat in the mouth and nose. It loosened six teeth and cut his nose badly. I went down to the dressing room to see how he was. He was the only New Haven goaltender so he knew he would have to go back into the net when the doctor was finished patching him up. "Has anyone got any brandy?" I asked. Someone produced a bottle and I poured a stiff slug for Emile. He downed it, shook his head, climbed to his feet and went back into the padded cell.*
>
> *There was another night in New York when the puck tore his lip so badly that it curled around his nose. Our club doctor Vincent Nardiello did the stitching with Emile sprawled on his back in the dressing room. I knew from experience that the most painful part of the body stitching was around the nose and lips and eyes. Emile kept saying "Doc, doc for the love of Mike, hurry up!" He was really suffering, but he just laid there telling the doctor to get the damned job done. Emile had more guts than most. He lost eighteen teeth during his career, had his nose broken five times and needed something like 250 stitches to close up the cuts. He had ligaments torn in both knees and required surgery on his right ankle. Dr. Kazuo Yanagisawa, another Ranger doctor operated on his shoulder in 1951 because of chronic pain following a shoulder separation.*

Emile played seven more years of pro hockey before retiring in 1960. In 1961, he was named head coach of the Blueshirts' junior team in Guelph, Ontario. Two seasons later he was back in New York, first as Muzz Patrick's assistant GM before succeeding Patrick in October 1964. He then presided over one of the most successful eras in Rangers history before being dismissed in 1976. Francis moved on to the St. Louis Blues and later the Hartford Whalers. He was elected to the Hockey Hall of Fame in 1982.

Regular Season

Season	Team	GP	W	L	T	GA	GAA	SO	MIN	G	A	PTS	PIM
1946–47	CBH	19	6	12	1	104	5.47	0	1140	0	0	0	0
1947–48	CBH	54	19	30	5	183	3.39	1	3240	0	0	0	6
1948–49	NYR	2	2	0	0	4	2.00	0	120	0	0	0	0
1949–50	NYR	1	0	1	0	8	8.00	0	60	0	0	0	0
1950–51	NYR	5	1	2	1	14	3.23	0	260	0	0	0	0
1951–52	NYR	14	4	7	3	41	3.00	0	840	0	0	0	0
NYR Totals	-	22	7	10	4	67	3.14	0	1280	0	0	0	0
Career	-	95	31	52	11	354	3.75	1	5660	0	0	0	6

Lorne Anderson
Born: July 26, 1931 in Renfrew, Ontario
Died: March 20, 1984
5-11, 165lb
Caught: Right
Rangers Debut: March 19, 1952 vs. Boston Bruins
Uniform #1
Seasons with Rangers: 1, 1951–52

In 1951–52, Lorne "Lefty" Anderson was the third-string netminder behind Charlie Rayner and Emile Francis on the Rangers' depth chart, but he earned a place in Blueshirts history when he was called up to play the final three games of another losing season.

Anderson began moving up the hockey ladder at the age of seventeen when he played two games for the Atlantic City Sea Gulls of the EHL in 1947–48. He then returned to his native Ontario and played for the Renfrew Lions of the NOJHA for the next two seasons. In 1950, he returned to Atlantic City and then moved to the Rangers-owned New York Rovers in 1951, playing a career-high 61 games, posting a 25–34–2 record with one shutout and a 3.75 GAA.

Late in the 1951–52 season the Rangers lost the services of starter Chuck Rayner to a knee injury. Rayner had suffered the injury in December but continued to play until February when he underwent surgery. Rayner was replaced by Emile "The Cat" Francis, who filled in admirably.

But by the last week of the season the Blueshirts were firmly ensconced in fifth place with no chance of making the playoffs. So Francis was sent to the Cincinnati Mohawks of the AHL to help in their playoff run and the Rangers signed the twenty-year-old Anderson to play the final three games of the season. Anderson won his first game, 6–4, over Boston but lost the second, 6–3, to Detroit.

A mere 3,254 fans showed up for the season finale on March 23 at the Garden as the Rangers hosted the sixth place Chicago Black Hawks. In those days it would have been called a "brother-in-law" game, with both teams far out of playoff contention and finishing the season, so nobody wanted to get hurt. In fact, referee George Gravel did not call a single penalty during the entire contest.

The Rangers were leading, 6–2, early in the third period on the back of Ed Slowinski's hat trick. But that lead proved to be short-lived. At 6:09 Chicago's captain Bill Mosienko, a speedy 5-foot-6 winger, took a pass from Gus Bodnar in front of the net and shot the puck past Anderson. Bodnar then won the ensuing center ice faceoff and passed again to the streaking Mosienko, who beat Anderson from the wing at 6:20.

Again, Bodnar won the center ice faceoff and moved the puck to George Gee on the left wing. Gee carried the puck over the blue line and passed to Mosienko, who was breaking towards the net. He scored once again at 6:30, giving him 31 goals for the season and three within 21 seconds, a record that still stands today. Chicago's Sid Finney later scored a pair of goals to give Chicago a 7–6 victory.

The game marked the end of Anderson's brief NHL career. He returned to Ontario and had a lengthy amateur career playing for Pembroke, Renfrew, North Bay, and Sudbury, where he backstopped the Wolves to the Allan Cup championship in 1953.

Regular Season

Season	Team	GP	W	L	T	GA	GAA	SO	MIN	G	A	PTS	PIM
1951–52	NYR	3	1	2	0	18	6.00	0	180	0	0	0	0
Career	NYR	3	1	2	0	18	6.00	0	180	0	0	0	0

CHAPTER FOUR

No Direction

The Rangers spent the fourteen seasons between their Stanley Cup Finals appearance in 1950 to the dismissal of GM Muzz Patrick in 1964 wandering through the NHL's wilderness.

Neil Colville was replaced as coach by former captain Bill Cook midway through the 1951–52 season. Cook lasted until the end of the following season when general manager Frank Boucher stepped back behind the bench for 40 games before replacing himself with Muzz Patrick. Patrick, the third member of the Rangers' royal family to coach the team, remained behind the bench until the end of the 1954–55 season when Boucher, who had been with the organization since their inception in 1926, was fired after missing the playoffs for the fifth consecutive year.

Following in the footsteps of his father Lester, Muzz Patrick became the general manager and immediately brought in Phil Watson as coach. "Fiery Phil" benefitted from the maturing of the many young players such as Andy Bathgate, Dean Prentice, Lou Fontinato, and Harry Howell, who came up through the Guelph pipeline and the rest of the farm and development system that Boucher had restored following the war. Watson took the team to third-, fourth-, and second-place finishes but lost in the first round of the playoffs each year.

But late in the 1958–59 season, with the Blueshirts in fourth place, Watson began to lose control of the team. On February 15, 1959, the Rangers were protecting a slim 1–0 lead over the Montreal Canadiens with 10 minutes remaining in the third period. Montreal suddenly erupted for five unanswered goals and skated away with a 5–1 victory. Watson was so incensed by the loss that he ordered every player except for goaltender Gump Worsley back onto the ice and put them through a grueling 45-minute workout consisting of strenuous skating drills. It was both humiliating and exhausting for the players and from that point on the Rangers went 5–8–2 through the rest of the season.

They had a seven-point lead over fifth place Toronto with five games left but proceeded to lose four of those five matches while the Maple Leafs won all of their final five games and finished in fourth place, one point ahead of the Rangers.

Watson was fired when the Rangers got off to a bad start the following season and few were sad to see him go. His replacement, Alf Pike, lasted until the 1961–62 season when Patrick acquired All-Star defenseman Doug Harvey from Montreal for Lou Fontinato and made him a player-coach. Harvey brought them to a fourth-place finish but once again they lost in the opening round.

The perception of the Rangers around the NHL during that time was so bad that many of the better players in the league didn't want to come to New York. In 1960, Patrick made a deal with Detroit that would have brought Leonard "Red" Kelly and Billy McNeill to the Rangers in exchange for Bill Gadsby and Eddie Shack. Kelly, thirty-three, an eight-time All-Star who had already won four Stanley Cups and the Norris Trophy as the league's best defenseman, in addition to multiple Lady Byng Trophies as the league's most gentlemanly player with the Red Wings, refused to report and retired. McNeill also refused to report and was suspended for the remainder of the season by the Wings and the deal was voided. Maple Leafs coach George "Punch" Imlach eventually stepped in and sent Marc Reaume to the Red Wings for Kelly, who gladly unretired and won another four Stanley Cups with Toronto. McNeill was claimed by the Rangers in the intra-league draft that June but later sold back to Detroit for cash in January of 1961 without ever playing a game for the Blueshirts.

Shack was eventually traded to Toronto for Pat Hannigan and Johnny Wilson in November 1960 and won four Stanley Cups while with the Leafs. Gadsby was dealt to Detroit in June 1961 for minor leaguer Les Hunt, who never played a game for the Rangers, or in the NHL for that matter. Of the three principals in the original deal, Gadsby was the only one who played his entire career without being on a Stanley Cup-winning team.

Patrick later made two moves that did not change the Rangers' fortunes nor sit well with the paying customers. In June 1963 he sent goalie Lorne "Gump" Worsley, a fan favorite, along with Dave Balon, Leon Rochefort, and Len Ronson to Montreal for netminder Jacques Plante, Donnie Marshall, and Phil Goyette. Marshall and Goyette played very well and were major contributors to the rebuilding of the franchise that was to come, but Plante, the centerpiece of the deal who was supposed to be the next Rangers savior, was a bust.

Patrick then traded team captain Andy Bathgate, another fan favorite, and Don McKenney to Toronto in February 1964 for Bob Nevin, Dick Duff, Rod Seiling, Arnie Brown, and Billy Collins. The deal eventually paid off as Nevin, Seiling, and Brown became key players in the rebuilding process but Patrick would unfortunately not be around to reap those rewards.

After missing the playoffs for three consecutive seasons, it was clear that the Rangers needed a change. Garden management as well as the fans were losing patience with Patrick. Attendance was down especially on weeknights and the fans that did show up began chanting "Muzz Must Go" and releasing balloons with the same "Muzz Must Go" slogan, imprinted on them in both French and English.

Patrick's fate was sealed early in the 1964–65 season when Plante was sent down to the Rangers' Baltimore farm team. The goaltender blasted the Rangers' management, coaches, and training conditions in a wire service story that was buried in the sports pages of the *New York Herald-Tribune*. However, Stan Fischler, then a reporter for the *New York Journal-American*, contacted Plante in Baltimore to validate the story. When Plante continued to ridicule Patrick, coach Red Sullivan, and everything else associated with the Blueshirts, Fischler wrote his own story which subsequently made headlines, attracting the attention of the Rangers.

An irate Patrick called Plante back to New York for an explanation and later at the ensuing news conference got into a heated exchange with Fischler, twice calling him a "prick." The episode greatly embarrassed new team president William Jennings and Muzz resigned as general manager the next day, October 30, 1964, and was bumped upstairs and put in charge of the upcoming move to the new Madison Square Garden.

Rule Changes:

1956–57: Players serving a minor penalties were now allowed to return to the ice when a goal was scored by the opposing team. Previously it was not uncommon for teams like the Montreal Canadiens to score multiple goals during a single power play.

Gump Worsley—Franchise Goaltender
Born: May 14, 1929 in Montreal, Quebec
Died: January 27, 2007
5-7, 180lb
Caught: Left
Rangers Debut: October 9, 1952 at Detroit Red Wings
Uniform #1
Seasons with Rangers: 10, 1952–53 to 1962–63
Calder Trophy: 1952–53
Stanley Cups: 4, Montreal (1964–65, 1965–66, 1967–68, 1968–69)
Vezina Trophy: 1965–66 (Montreal, shared with Charlie Hodge) and 1967–68 (with Montreal, shared with Rogie Vachon)
Hockey Hall of Fame: 1980
All-Star selections: 1965–66 (Second Team), 1967–68 (First Team)
All-Star Games: 4, 1961, 1962, 1965, 1972

Public Domain

Lorne "Gump" Worsley was one of the most beloved characters to ever don a Rangers sweater. The Montreal native began his hockey journey in 1946 with the Rangers-sponsored Verdun Cyclones of the QJHL, playing against the likes of Jacques Plante with the Quebec Citadelles, Bernie Geoffrion with the Montreal Concordia Civics, and Jean Beliveau, who was just starting out with the Victoriaville Panthers.

Worsley, who was tagged with the nickname "Gump" thanks to his childhood resemblance to the cartoon character Andy Gump, was invited to the Rangers training camp in 1949 and assigned to the New York Rovers of the EAHL. He also saw action with the New Haven Ramblers of the AHL that season, appearing in two games and winning both. But it was during a Rovers road trip that Worsley's apprehension about flying grew into all-out fear. The team was returning home from Milwaukee when one of the engines of their twin engine plane caught fire, forcing the pilot to make an emergency landing. Thankfully there were no injuries, but Gumper never overcame his fear after that.

In 1950–51 Worsley turned pro with the St. Paul Saints of the USHL where he was named Rookie of the Year and won the Charlie Gardiner Award as the top goaltender in the league. He was then moved to the Saskatoon Quakers of the PCHL, where he once again excelled.

Gump's NHL career was like a roller-coaster ride with more than a few peaks and valleys along the way. He began the 1952–53 season with the Rangers subbing for the injured Chuck Rayner and made his NHL debut on Opening Night, October 9, 1952, in a 5–3 loss in Detroit. He stayed with the Rangers until mid-November while Rayner worked himself into shape. Gumper was then sent back to Saskatoon, but was recalled at midseason when Rayner severely injured his knee. The twenty-three-year-old netminder wound up playing 50 games for the sixth-place Rangers and was awarded the Calder Trophy as the NHL's top rookie despite posting a 13–29–8 record.

But during the offseason the Rangers acquired veteran minor-league goaltender Johnny Bower from the Cleveland Barons of the AHL and Gumper once again found himself in the minors, this time in Vancouver of the WHL. The official party line at the time was that Rangers management feared that Worsley at 5-foot-7 and 180 pounds was too small to withstand the rigors of a full NHL season and that Bower at 5-foot-11, 189 would be a sturdier option. But, of course, there was more to it than that.

Gump discussed the demotion with author Dick Irvin in his book *In the Crease*. "I was playing In Saskatoon in '52–53 when Charlie Rayner got hurt and they called me up. He screwed up his knee and never played again. I played the last fifty games and won the rookie of the year. The next year I asked for a $500 raise and ended up in Vancouver. Everybody thinks Johnny Bower beat me out of a job, but it had to be the money. The next year, Camille Henry won the rookie award with the Rangers and he asked for a $500 raise. I got news for you: He ended up in Providence for most of the year."

While Bower had a good year in New York, Worsley had an outstanding season for Vancouver in 1953–54 earning league MVP honors and finishing with the best goals-against average in the WHL. So at the start of the next season Bower was in Vancouver and Gumper was back in New York, this time for good.

Worsley came back strong. On January 19, 1955, he posted a 2–0 shutout against the powerful Detroit Red Wings, stopping 51 shots, which is believed to be the most saves made by any Rangers goaltender in a shutout. The blanking came during one of the best stretches in Worsley's Rangers career when he allowed only eight goals in a six-game span that also included a scoreless tie and a 2–0 shutout, both against the Bruins.

During his time in New York, Worsley was often asked which team gave him the most trouble. His response was always an emphatic, "The Rangers!" and for good reason. Worsley was one of the few bright spots on some mediocre Ranger teams during the 1950s. He didn't set many records while with the Rangers, but he earned the distinction of being a franchise goaltender. He was a warrior; his main accomplishment was surviving 10 long seasons in the Blueshirts shooting gallery. Gump took a beating in the Rangers net, having to be carried off the ice on a number of occasions. His most serious injury as a Ranger occurred on February 17, 1960, when Chicago's Bobby Hull accidentally skated over his hand, severing two tendons. He required surgery and missed the rest of the season.

Worsley played for seven coaches while with the Rangers, including Phil Watson, who had been his coach while with the Rovers. The Blueshirts made the playoffs three times with Watson behind the bench but it was clear that "Fiery Phil" didn't like Worsley and as far as Gump was concerned, the feeling was mutual. Watson was the kind of coach who would take all the credit for a victory but blame a loss on the players. Gump was one of Watson's favorite whipping boys, constantly getting on him about his "beer belly," to which Worsley calmly replied, "Beer is the poor man's champagne. I'm strictly a VO [rye] man."

Worsley may not have looked very athletic, but the pudgy little netminder was extremely agile. He could scramble back to his feet very quickly and emphatically swat rebounds out of harm's way with a one-handed golf swing in which after making contact with the puck, the blade of his goalie stick would wind up over his left shoulder.

Quotable and always quick with a quip, Gumper was a favorite of the press as well as the fans. Even though the Rangers only made the playoffs four times in Gump's 10 seasons on Broadway, he was recognized as one of the top netminders in the league. In 1955–56 he played every minute of every game, becoming the last Rangers goaltender to do so. He also set a team record with 32 victories, which stood until Ed Giacomin racked up 36 in 1967–68. He led the NHL in games and minutes played in 1962–63 and played in two All-Star games while with the Blueshirts. Worsley also was selected as the Rangers MVP in 1960–61 and 1962–63 and given the Frank Boucher Trophy as the most popular Ranger in 1955–56 and again in 1962–63.

Gump's Ranger career came to an end on June 4, 1963, when he was traded with Dave Balon, Leon Rochefort, and Len Ronson to the Canadiens for Jacques Plante, Phil Goyette, and Donnie Marshall. Gumper, who had played for the Rangers for 10 years, never got a call from GM Muzz Patrick informing him of the deal and only heard about it when a neighbor told him to turn on the radio.

Worsley spent most of the next seven seasons playing for Montreal, where he collected four Stanley Cups and two Vezina Trophies (1965–66 shared with Charlie Hodge and 1967–68 shared with Rogie Vachon).

Gumper may have been a fan favorite while with the Blueshirts but when he returned to the Garden wearing the "Bleu, Blanc et Rouge" of the Canadiens, he became a target just like the rest of his Montreal teammates. In March 1967 Worsley was hit in the temple by an egg that was thrown from the balcony at the old Madison Square Garden. As reported in the *Montreal Gazette*, "The Gumper was hit flush on the right temple by the egg which was thrown from about 100 feet away. The egg-tosser, a twenty-five-year-old fan who had a bag of them when caught by Garden police, got off lucky when Worsley refused to press charges." Gump took part in a voluntary practice the next day but complained of dizziness and wound up being sidelined for six weeks.

Playing for a team like the Canadiens brought with it a different kind of pressure; the pressure to win every game and a Stanley Cup every year. Add to that the extra air travel brought on by the NHL's expansion and by November 1968 Gump was ready to pack it in. After a particularly bumpy flight into Chicago on the first leg of a western road trip, he abruptly quit the Canadiens, informing team captain Jean Beliveau of his decision and taking a train back home. Montreal GM Sam Pollack didn't want to lose the Gumper, so he arranged for him to see a psychiatrist on a daily basis to talk about his problems and in about two months, he was back on the ice and Montreal won another Stanley Cup that spring.

Gump was ready to retire again during the 1969–70 season but was talked out of it by Minnesota GM Wren Blair who had worked out a deal to acquire the forty year old to help stabilize the North Star's goal-tending situation and back up Cesare Maniago. The pair became good friends and were known as "Mutt and Jeff" owing to Maniago's 6-foot-3 stature compared to Gump's 5-foot-7 frame. Maniago even talked

Gump into donning a mask for the first time during the final season of his 21-year NHL career.

Worsley finally retired for good in the spring of 1974 at the age of forty-five and spent the next ten years scouting for the North Stars.

Worsley played in 581 games with the Rangers, placing him behind only Henrik Lundqvist and Mike Richter on the team's all-time list. He was inducted into the Hockey Hall of Fame in 1980 and passed away in January 2007 at the age of seventy-seven.

Regular Season

Season	Team	GP	W	L	T	GA	GAA	SO	MIN	G	A	PTS	PIM
1952–53	NYR	50	13	29	8	151	3.02	2	3000	0	0	0	2
1954–55	NYR	65	15	33	17	195	3.00	4	3898	0	0	0	4
1955–56	NYR	70	32	28	10	198	2.83	4	4198		0	0	2
1956–57	NYR	68	26	28	14	216	3.18	3	4078	0	0	0	19
1957–58	NYR	37	21	10	6	86	2.32	4	2220	0	0	0	0
1958–59	NYR	66	26	29	11	193	2.94	2	3938	0	0	0	10
1959–60	NYR	39	7	23	8	135	3.52	0	2299	0	0	0	12
1960–61	NYR	59	20	29	8	190	3.29	1	3469	0	0	0	10
1961–62	NYR	60	22	27	9	172	2.92	2	3531	0	0	0	12
1962–63	NYR	67	22	34	10	217	3.27	2	3979	0	0	0	14
1963–64	MTL	8	3	2	2	22	2.98	1	444	0	0	0	0
1964–65	MTL	19	10	7	1	50	2.78	1	1080	0	0	0	0
1965–66	MTL	51	28	13	6	114	2.36	2	2898	0	1	1	4
1966–67	MTL	18	6	6	2	47	3.18	1	887	0	0	0	4
1967–68	MTL	40	21	7	8	73	1.98	6	2211	0	0	0	10
1968–69	MTL	30	19	5	4	64	2.26	5	1702	0	0	0	0
1969–70	MTL	6	3	1	2	14	2.33	0	360	0	0	0	0
1969–70	MNS	8	5	1	1	20	2.65	1	453	0	0	0	0
1970–71	MNS	24	4	10	8	57	2.50	0	1367	0	0	0	10
1971–72	MNS	34	16	10	7	68	2.12	2	1924	0	1	1	2
1972–73	MNS	12	6	2	3	30	2.88	0	624	0	1	1	22
1973–74	MNS	29	8	14	5	86	3.23	0	1597	0	0	0	0
NYR Totals	-	581	204	270	101	1753	3.04	24	34,610	0	0	0	85
Career	-	860	333	348	149	2398	2.87	43	50,157	0	3	3	137

Playoffs

Season	Team	GP	W	L	T	GA	GAA	SO	MIN	G	A	PTS	PIM
1955–56	NYR	3	0	3	-	14	4.68	0	180	0	0	0	2
1956–57	NYR	5	1	4	-	21	4.01	0	314	0	0	0	0
1957–58	NYR	6	2	4	-	28	4.61	0	365	0	0	0	0
1961–62	NYR	6	2	4	-	21	3.28	0	384	0	0	0	0
1964–65	MTL	8	5	3	-	14	1.68	2	501	0	0	0	0
1965–66	MTL	10	8	2	-	20	1.99	1	602	0	0	0	0
1966–67	MTL	2	0	1	-	2	1.50	0	80	0	0	0	0
1967–68	MTL	12	11	0	-	21	1.88	1	672	0	0	0	10
1968–69	MTL	7	5	1	-	14	2.27	0	370	0	0	0	5
1969–70	MNS	3	1	2	-	14	4.67	0	180	0	0	0	0
1970–71	MNS	4	3	1	-	13	3.25	0	240	0	0	0	0
1971–72	MNS	4	2	1	-	7	2.16	1	193	0	0	0	0
NYR Totals	-	20	5	15	-	84	4.05	0	1243	0	0	0	2
Career	-	70	40	26	-	189	2.78	5	4081	0	0	0	17

Johnny Bower
Born: November 8, 1924 in Prince Albert, Saskatchewan
Died: December 26, 2017
5-11, 189lb
Caught: Left
Rangers Debut: Oct. 8, 1953 at Detroit Red Wings
Uniform #1
Seasons with Rangers: 3, 1953–54, 1955–56, 1956–57
Stanley Cups: 4, Toronto (1961–62, 1962–63, 1963–64, 1966–67)
Vezina Trophy: 1960–61 (with Toronto) and 1964–65 (Toronto, shared with Terry Sawchuk)
Hockey Hall of Fame: 1976
All-Star selections: 1960–61 (First Team)
All-Star Games: 4, 1961 through 1964

After toiling for eight seasons with the Cleveland Barons of the American Hockey League, Johnny Bower finally got a crack at the NHL in 1953 at age twenty-nine.

The Saskatchewan native had been acquired by the Rangers in exchange for Emile Francis and Neil Strain in June 1953. Bower, who had changed his last name from Kiszkan to Bower to make it easier for sportswriters, was scouted by the Rangers' Carson Cooper, who told everyone that Bower belonged in the NHL.

Bower was brought up when Gump Worsley, who had won the league's Rookie of the Year Award in 1952–53, asked for a $500 raise. Rangers GM Frank Boucher balked and Gumper found himself in Vancouver of the WHL while Bower spent the season in New York. Johnny had a great rookie season for the fifth-place Rangers, playing all 70 games and recording five shutouts and a 2.60 GAA, the lowest average by any Rangers goaltender in the previous 14 seasons.

While in New York, Johnny was mentored by former Ranger goaltender Chuck Rayner who taught him the fine art of the poke check. He was popular with the press, who called him the "veteran rookie" and with the fans, who awarded him the Frank Boucher Award as the most popular Ranger.

"Bower's a good goalie. I don't think there was much of a choice between us in training camp," Worsley once told reporters. "He got the call and has done fine. He's been everything the Rangers expected."

The next season Gump had a better camp and Johnny was sent to the Rangers farm club in Vancouver but played in seven more games for the Blueshirts over the next two seasons filling in for the injured Worsley. Bower and Gump eventually wound up being good friends; their families even went on cruises together. Whenever they played against each other, they would wish the other good luck.

In 1956 he was assigned to Providence of the AHL, where he became friendly with the Lamoriello family, whose son Lou went on to become general manager of the New Jersey Devils, Toronto Maple Leafs, and New York Islanders.

The next season, the Rangers wanted to move Marcel Paille who they considered their goaltender of the future from the Cleveland Barons to the Providence Reds. However, Cleveland GM Jim Hendy pointed out a clause in Paille's contract that stated that he could not play for any other AHL team besides the Barons. So in order to move Paille and appease Hendy, Bower was traded to Cleveland for Ed MacQueen and cash.

Finally, in 1958 at the age of thirty-four, Bower was claimed by Toronto in the inter-league draft. Nicknamed "The China Wall," Johnny went on to become a franchise goaltender in Toronto and one of the best NHL netminders of his era, winning the Vezina Trophy twice (sharing one with Terry Sawchuk) and four Stanley Cups.

Bower retired following the 1969–70 season at the ripe old age of forty-six and became a much-loved ambassador for the game. He was inducted into the Hockey Hall of Fame in 1978 and passed away in December 2017 at the age of ninety-three.

Regular Season

Season	Team	GP	W	L	T	GA	GAA	SO	MIN	G	A	PTS	PIM
1953–54	NYR	70	29	31	10	178	2.54	5	4200	0	0	0	0
1954–55	NYR	5	2	2	1	13	2.60	0	300	0	0	0	0
1956–57	NYR	2	0	2	0	6	3.01	0	120	0	0	0	0
1958–59	TOR	39	15	17	7	106	2.72	3	2339	0	0	0	2
1959–60	TOR	66	34	24	8	177	2.69	5	3954	0	0	0	4
1960–61	TOR	58	33	15	10	145	2.50	2	3480	0	0	0	0
1961–62	TOR	59	31	18	10	151	2.56	2	3540	0	1	1	4
1962–63	TOR	42	20	15	7	109	2.60	1	2520	0	0	0	2
1963–64	TOR	51	24	15	11	106	2.11	5	3008	0	0	0	4
1964–65	TOR	34	14	13	7	81	2.38	3	2039	0	0	0	6
1965–66	TOR	35	18	10	5	75	2.25	3	1995	0	1	1	0
1966–67	TOR	27	11	8	3	63	2.64	2	1427	0	0	0	0
1967–68	TOR	43	13	17	8	84	2.25	4	2239	0	1	1	14
1968–69	TOR	20	6	4	3	37	2.85	2	777	0	0	0	0
1969–70	TOR	1	0	1	0	5	5.00	0	60	0	0	0	0
NYR Totals	-	77	31	35	11	197	2.56	5	4620	0	0	0	0
Career	-	552	250	192	90	1336	2.51	37	31,989	0	3	3	36

Playoffs

Season	Team	GP	W	L	T	GA	GAA	SO	MIN	G	A	PTS	PIM
1958–59	TOR	12	5	7	-	38	3.05	0	746	0	0	0	0
1959–60	TOR	10	4	6	-	31	2.88	0	645	0	0	0	0
1960–61	TOR	3	0	3	-	8	2.67	0	180	0	0	0	2
1961–62	TOR	10	6	3	-	20	2.07	0	579	0	0	0	0
1962–63	TOR	10	8	2	-	16	1.60	2	600	0	1	1	0
1963–64	TOR	14	8	6	-	30	2.12	2	850	0	0	0	0
1964–65	TOR	5	2	3	-	13	2.43	0	321	0	0	0	0
1965–66	TOR	2	0	2	-	8	4.03	0	119	0	0	0	0
1966–67	TOR	4	2	0	-	5	1.63	1	184	0	0	0	2
1968–69	TOR	4	0	2	-	11	4.33	0	152	0	0	0	0
Career	TOR	74	35	34	-	180	2.47	5	4376	0	1	1	4

Gordie Bell
Born: March 13, 1925 in Portage La Prairie, Manitoba
Died: November 3, 1980
5-10, 164lb
Caught: Left
Rangers Debut: March 22, 1956 at Montreal Canadiens (playoffs)
Uniform #1
Seasons with Rangers: 1, 1955–56 (playoffs)

Gordie Bell was a journeyman goaltender bouncing around the minor leagues when he was signed as a free agent by the Rangers to fill in for the injured Gump Worsley during the 1956 semifinals against Montreal. Bell got his start with the local Portage Terriers of the Manitoba Junior Hockey League in 1941 and climbed the hockey ladder until he made his NHL debut with the Maple Leafs in 1945, appearing in eight games and posting a 3–5–0 record with a 3.88 GAA. He then spent the next 10 seasons in the minor leagues until he was signed by the Rangers in March 1956.

Bell and Worsley both saw action in the opener, which the Blueshirts lost, 7–1. Bell started the next game and played very well, coming away with a 4–2 victory. It was the Rangers' first win in the Montreal Forum since January 1954. Montreal eventually won the series four games to one, outscoring the Rangers by a combined total of 24–9.

Bell was released following the series and spent the rest of his career in the minors. He joined the Bellville McFarlands of the Eastern Ontario Hockey League and represented Canada at the 1959 World Championships. Bell went 5–1–0 during the tournament and captured the gold medal. He retired following the 1959–60 season.

Regular Season

Season	Team	GP	W	L	T	GA	GAA	SO	MIN	G	A	PTS	PIM
1945–46	TOR	8	3	5	0	31	3.87	0	480	0	0	0	0
Career	TOR	8	3	5	0	31	3.87	0	480	0	0	0	0

Playoffs

Season	Team	GP	W	L	T	GA	GAA	SO	MIN	G	A	PTS	PIM
1955–56	NYR	2	1	1	-	9	4.50	0	120	0	0	0	0
Career	NYR	2	1	1	-	9	4.50	0	120	0	0	0	0

Marcel Paille
Born: December 8, 1932 in Shawinigan Falls, Quebec
Died: October 7, 2002
5-8, 175lb
Caught: Left
Rangers Debut: October 31, 1957 at Boston Bruins
Uniform #1, 23
Seasons with Rangers: 7, 1957–58 to 1962–63, 1964–65.

Joseph Marcel Rejean Paille was born and raised in Shawinigan Falls, Quebec, the same small Canadian town that produced the legendary Jacques Plante. He began his junior hockey career at the age of seventeen with the Quebec Citadelles of the QJHL in 1949 and later moved to the Mantane Red Rockets (LSLHL) and then the North Bay Trappers (NOHA). It was while he was with North Bay that he was scouted and later signed by the Chicoutimi Sagueneens (QHL) where he earned Rookie of the Year honors in 1956.

However, like many netminders of the pre-expansion era, Paille had the great misfortune of trying to break into the NHL during what many consider to be the golden age of goaltending. Those were the days of the Original Six, when each team carried only one goalkeeper and five of the incumbents, Johnny Bower, Glenn Hall, Jacques Plante, Terry Sawchuk, and Gump Worsley were eventually inducted into the Hockey Hall of Fame.

The Rangers selected Paille from Chicoutimi in the 1956 interleague draft and sent him to the Cleveland Barons of the AHL. Marcel had a great year in Cleveland, posting a 34–25–3 record with seven shutouts and a 3.20 GAA, was named a Second Team All-Star, and led the Barons to the Calder Cup championship that spring. At that point, the Rangers considered Marcel to be their goaltender of the future and moved him to their Providence Reds farm club while trading the rights to thirty-two-year-old Johnny Bower to the Barons.

Paille made his NHL debut on the night of October 31, 1957, shutting out the Bruins, 5–0, in Boston. He played a total of 33 games for the Blueshirts that season, posting an 11–15–7 record with a 3.09 GAA while sharing the Rangers' netminding workload with Gump Worsley.

While with the Rangers that season, Marcel experimented with an odd-looking white fiberglass mask that was manufactured by the Brunswick-Balke Collender Company in Toronto and featured a wide Plexiglass eye shield. The contraption was heavy, however, and offered little ventilation. Perspiration from Marcel's forehead ran down into his eyes and the Plexiglass shield became foggy. The experiment ended after a single practice, but Marcel donned a more traditional mask while with Providence in the early 1970s.

Over the next seven seasons Marcel bounced between the Rangers and their various farm clubs in Providence, Springfield, Buffalo, Baltimore, and Vancouver, being recalled whenever Worsley was injured or in need of a rest. Paille made a place for himself in AHL history when he joined the Springfield Indians in 1959 and backstopped them to three consecutive Calder Cup titles. Marcel's 47 victories in 1960–61 set an AHL record and he won the Harry "Hap" Holmes Award in 1961 and 1962 for posting the lowest goals-against average in the league. Paella went 107–54–8 with 12 shutouts in 169 games overall with Springfield.

In 1964–65, when Emile Francis was growing tired of Jacques Plante's diva-like behavior, Marcel was brought up to New York and played in 39 games, posting a 10–21–7 record with a 3.58 GAA.

"Paille was a standup goalkeeper," recalled Francis. "He played his angles very well and gave up very few rebounds. He was a very calm guy with a lot of poise. He never got excited. We were playing against the Chicago Black Hawks and Paille had a pompadour haircut. Bobby Hull came down the wing, outside the blue line, and he took a slap shot and the puck split his hair! I damn near passed out on the bench. I could see the puck go right through his hair. If it hit him, it would've killed him."

Paille played well considering the team that he had in front of him, but the Rangers were in a rebuilding mode and he was traded to Providence that spring as part of the deal that brought Ed Giacomin to the Rangers. In parts of seven seasons with the Rangers, Marcel saw action in 107 games, going 32–52–22 with two shutouts and a 3.42 GAA. Marcel then spent the next seven seasons in Providence where he became a fan favorite both on and off the ice.

In 1972, at the age of forty, Marcel signed with the Philadelphia Blazers of the WHA who had acquired his rights from the Chicago Cougars. The Blazers doubled the salary that the Reds were paying him, so it was an offer he couldn't refuse, but it was not a good experience for Marcel. He was backing up Bernie Parent, which meant he didn't play that often, sometimes going more than a month between starts. And there were also times, on the road, that he didn't even get a chance to practice. His coach, Phil Watson, treated him with disdain and when he was given a chance to play, he was rusty. He finished the season with a 2–8–0 record and a 4.81 GAA. When Marcel tried to hook up with another club the following season, he found that Watson had blackballed him, telling everyone that his reflexes were gone and that he was washed up. Paille eventually caught on with the Richmond Robins of the AHL and retired at the end of the 1973–74 season.

Marcel played for 15 seasons in the American Hockey League and set many records that still stand today including games played by a goaltender (765), minutes played (45,300), Calder Cup playoff games (87), playoff minutes played (5,368), Calder Cup games won (49), and longest playoff shutout streak (207:27). He also placed second in career victories (349) behind Johnny Bower (359) and posted 36 career AHL shutouts, placing him fifth on the all-time list.

Marcel was inducted into the Springfield Hockey Hall of Fame in 1997. He passed away in 2002 and was inducted posthumously into the American Hockey League Hall of Fame in 2010.

"He was a good goalkeeper," said Francis. "Hey, when there are only six teams and you make it to the NHL you must be pretty good. And the American Hockey League was no different, all the teams in professional hockey carried only one goalkeeper. When I played in the American League it was the same thing, they only had eight teams and out on the West Coast they only had eight teams so that was all you had. There weren't that many places a goalkeeper could play."

Regular Season

Season	Team	League	GP	W	L	T	GA	GAA	SO	MIN	G	A	PTS	PIM
1957–58	NYR	NHL	33	11	15	7	102	3.09	1	1980	0	0	0	0
1958–59	NYR	NHL	1	0	0	1	4	4.00	0	60	0	0	0	0
1959–60	NYR	NHL	17	6	9	2	67	3.94	1	1020	0	0	0	0
1960–61	NYR	NHL	4	1	2	1	16	4.00	0	240	0	0	0	0
1961–62	NYR	NHL	10	4	4	2	28	2.80	0	600	0	0	0	0
1962–63	NYR	NHL	3	0	1	2	10	3.33	0	180	0	0	0	0
1964–65	NYR	NHL	39	10	21	7	135	3.58	0	2260	0	1	1	2
1972–73	PHB	WHA	15	2	8	0	49	4.81	0	611	0	0	0	0
NYR Totals	-	NHL	107	32	52	22	362	3.42	2	6340	0	1	1	2
Career	-	NHL	107	32	52	22	362	3.42	2	6340	0	1	1	2
Career	-	WHA	15	2	8	0	49	4.81	0	611	0	0	0	0

Playoffs

Season	Team	League	GP	W	L	T	GA	GAA	SO	MIN	G	A	PTS	PIM
1972–73	PHB	WHA	1	-	-	-	5	11.11	0	27	0	0	0	0
Career	PHB	WHA	1	-	-	-	5	11.11	0	27	0	0	0	0

Some statistics on the WHA are not available.

Fast Fact: Hal Winkler, John Ross Roach, Marcel Paille, and Antti Raanta are the only netminders to post a shutout in their first game with the Rangers.

Julian Klymkiw
Born: July 16, 1933 in Winnipeg, Manitoba
5-11, 180lb
Caught: Right
Rangers Debut: October 12, 1958 at Detroit Red Wings
Uniform #1
Seasons with Rangers, 1, 1958–59

Julian Klymkiw was a twenty-five-year-old assistant trainer and practice goaltender for the Detroit Red Wings when he was called upon to replace Gump Worsley on October 12, 1958. Worsley had been tripped and crashed into the net, pulling a tendon in his left leg, early in the third period with the Wings leading, 1–0. Klymkiw played the remaining 19 minutes and surrendered two goals as the Blueshirts lost, 3–0.

As a junior, Klymkiw, a native of Winnipeg, Manitoba, played with the Brandon Wheat Kings of the MJHL and led the league with 23 wins and an impressive 3.36 GAA in 1953. In 1953–54 he played 57 games for three different IHL teams then returned to Brandon for a year of senior hockey.

While playing for the WHL's Winnipeg Warriors in the late 1950s Klymkiw took on the additional role of trainer and eventually got a job with the Red Wings as their practice goaltender and assistant trainer.

Klimkiw's brief experience with the Rangers was his only NHL appearance and he finished his career with a 6.32 GAA.

Regular Season

Season	Team	GP	W	L	T	GA	GAA	SO	MIN	G	A	PTS	PIM
1958–59	NYR	1	0	0	0	2	6.37	0	19	0	0	0	0
Career	NYR	1	0	0	0	2	6.37	0	19	0	0	0	0

Bruce Gamble
Born: May 24, 1938 in Port Arthur, Ontario
Died: December 30, 1982
5-9, 200lb
Caught: Left
Rangers Debut: February 11, 1959 vs. Boston Bruins
Uniform #1
Seasons with Rangers: 1, 1958–59
All-Star Games: 1, 1968

The Rangers signed Bruce Gamble as a free agent in June 1958 following an impressive junior career with the Port Arthur North Stars, Guelph Biltmores, and the Hull-Ottawa Canadiens, backstopping all three teams to the Memorial Cup playoffs.

Gamble turned pro with the Vancouver Canucks of the WHL in 1958 and was called up to the Rangers to fill in for the injured Gump Worsley. He appeared in only three games but played well behind the porous Ranger defense.

In June 1959 Gamble was selected by the Bruins in the intra-league draft and after a year with Providence of the AHL took over the starting job in Boston, playing 61 games in 1960–61. Gamble then spent most of the next few seasons in the minors and in 1964 refused a demotion to Springfield of the AHL and was suspended for the remainder of the season. He was then traded to the Toronto Maple Leafs where he backed up Johnny Bower and Terry Sawchuk. Gamble remained with the Leafs until midway through the 1970 season when he was traded to Philadelphia with Mike Walton and Toronto's first-round draft pick in 1971 for Bernie Parent and the Flyers' second-round pick in 1971.

Unfortunately, his career came to a sudden end when he suffered a heart attack during a game against Vancouver on February 9, 1972. Gamble later suffered a fatal heart attack in Niagara Falls, Ontario, on December 30, 1982, at the age of forty-four.

Regular Season

Season	Team	GP	W	L	T	GA	GAA	SO	MIN	G	A	PTS	PIM
1958–59	NYR	3	0	3	0	11	3.67	0	180	0	0	0	0
1960–61	BOS	52	12	33	7	193	3.71	0	3118	0	0	0	14
1961–62	BOS	28	6	18	4	121	4.32	1	1680	0	0	0	4
1965–66	TOR	10	5	2	3	21	2.51	4	502	0	0	0	0
1966–67	TOR	23	5	10	5	67	3.40	0	1181	0	0	0	0
1967–68	TOR	41	20	14	2	85	2.32	5	2194	0	0	0	2
1968–69	TOR	61	28	20	11	161	2.81	3	3439	0	0	0	2
1969–70	TOR	52	19	24	9	156	3.06	5	3054	0	1	1	0
1970–71	TOR	23	6	14	1	83	3.89	2	1280	0	0	0	0
1970–71	PHI	11	3	6	2	37	3.37	0	658	0	0	0	0
1971–72	PHI	24	7	8	2	58	2.94	2	1184	0	0	0	2
NYR Totals	-	3	0	3	0	11	3.67	0	180	0	0	0	0
Career	-	328	111	152	46	993	3.23	22	18,470	0	1	1	24

Playoffs

Season	Team	GP	W	L	T	GA	GAA	SO	MIN	G	A	PTS	PIM
1968–69	TOR	3	0	2	-	13	9.08	0	86	0	0	0	0
1970–71	PHI	2	0	2	-	12	6.01	0	120	0	0	0	0
Career	-	5	0	4	-	25	7.29	0	206	0	0	0	0

Joe Schaefer
Born: December 21, 1924 in Long Island, New York
Died: December 27, 2000
5-8, 165lb
Caught: Left
Rangers Debut: February 17, 1960 vs. Chicago Black Hawks
Uniform #1
Seasons with Rangers: 2, 1959–60 to 1960–61

When asked to name the Rangers' first American-born goaltender, fans of a certain age often guess 1960 Olympian Jack McCartan. It's a good guess but the wrong answer. McCartan played his first game as a Ranger on March 6, 1960, but Joe Schaefer made his Ranger debut less than a month earlier on February 17, 1960.

Joe who? Exactly!

Schaefer, a Long Island native, managed an office supply company and worked part-time at Madison Square Garden as the Rangers' practice goalie, statistician, penalty-clock timekeeper, and goal judge. It seemed that whatever the Rangers needed, Schaefer was willing to do it. If they had asked him to clean the ice and play the organ, he probably would have given it a try.

Schaefer also became the Garden's emergency goaltender. In the years before the NHL mandated that teams had to dress two goaltenders for a game (1965–66), each home team was required to have an emergency goaltender in the stands to be used if either team's netminder was injured and could not continue to play in the game. The Canadian teams usually had a promising junior netminder sitting in the stands as their "house goalie," but in the States the teams had to do the best they could with what was available.

Schaefer was first called to duty on the night of February 17, 1960, when Bobby Hull of the Chicago Black Hawks accidentally skated over Gump Worsley's stick hand, ripping through the goaltender's glove and tearing tendons in his hand in the first minute of the second period.

The game was delayed for 23 minutes as the thirty-five-year-old Schaefer, whose experience was limited to playing goal for the Sands Point Tigers of the amateur Metropolitan Hockey League and a few games in the minors, raced down to the Rangers locker room to get ready to take Worsley's place. The Rangers held a 1–0 lead when Schaefer, 5-foot-8, 165 pounds, entered the game. Facing Hull and the rest of the hard-shooting Hawks, Joe made 17 saves but ended up losing the game, 5–1. The *New York Times* reported that "Schaefer had little to offer except courage."

Schaefer made his second emergency appearance on March 8, 1961. Once again, Worsley was the injured netminder and Hull was the culprit. With the score tied, 1–1, midway through the first period, Worsley tore a thigh muscle while attempting to stop Hull's wrist shot. As Schaefer made his way to the dressing room, the Gumper was being carried off the ice on a stretcher. Schaefer made 27 saves, but the Rangers lost, 4–3. However, one Hawk goal deflected off a Rangers defenseman and another came on a two-on-one breakaway. Following the game, a still shaking and sweating Schaefer visited Worsley in the hospital and left him with these immortal words, "Stay healthy Gumpy, will you please?"

Each game appearance put Schaefer in a rather unique situation. From a performance standpoint he was severely overmatched and could only perform to the best of his abilities. Basically, he was there so that the game could continue; no one really expected game-saving stops from him. It was also a bit of a financial windfall for Schaefer, who earned one hundred dollars for each game he played, a hefty increase from the ten dollars a game he made as an off-ice official. He also had quite a story to tell the next day at the office.

Schaefer also played a small part in NHL history on the night of November 1, 1959, when Andy Bathgate's well-placed backhand shot caught Montreal's Jacques Plante in the face and forced him to leave the game for repairs. Plante told coach Toe Blake that he would not return to the game unless he was allowed to wear his mask. No netminder had worn a mask in an NHL game since Clint Benedict three decades earlier and Blake was against it.

But faced with the choice of using Schaefer or thirty-three-year-old Arnee Nocks (who also served as a Rangers practice goalie and later went on to direct *The Soupy Sales Show*) or letting Plante wear the mask, Blake wisely chose Plante and the mask.

After his second Ranger appearance, Schaefer was never again called upon to suit up for a game. He continued as a statistician until 1986 when he retired and moved to South Carolina. Schaefer passed away in December of 2000 at the age of seventy-six.

Regular Season

Season	Tm	GP	W	L	T	GA	GAA	SO	MIN	G	A	PTS	PIM
1959–60	NYR	1	0	1	0	5	7.57	0	40	0	0	0	0
1960–61	NYR	1	0	1	0	3	3.64	0	49	0	0	0	0
Career	NYR	2	0	2	0	8	5.39	0	89	0	0	0	0

Fast Fact: Joe Schaefer was the Rangers' first American-born goaltender. He was also the first New Yorker to stop pucks for the Blueshirts. The Rangers have used eight American-born netminders; three were from New York (Schaeffer, Guy Hebert, and Mike Dunham), two from Michigan (John Vanbiesbrouck and Brandon Halverson) and one each from Massachusetts (Steve Baker), Minnesota (Jack McCartan), and Pennsylvania (Mike Richter).

Al Rollins
Born: October 9, 1926 in Vanguard, Saskatchewan
Died: July 27, 1996
6-2, 175lb
Caught: Left
Rangers Debut: February 20, 1960 at Montreal Canadiens
Uniform #1
Seasons with Rangers: 1, 1959–60
Stanley Cup: Toronto, 1950–51
Vezina Trophy: 1950–51 (with Toronto)
Hart Trophy: 1953–54 (with Chicago)
All-Star Games: 1, 1954

On February 17, 1960, Chicago's Bobby Hull inadvertently skated over Gump Worsley's hand, slicing two tendons and putting the Rangers netminder out of commission for the remainder of the season. Worsley was replaced for the rest of that game by Joe Schaefer, the Rangers' emergency goaltender, but to fill the void for the rest of the season Muzz Patrick arranged to borrow Al Rollins from the Chicago Black Hawks organization in exchange for minor-league goaltender Ray Mikulan, future considerations, and cash.

Rollins had seen action as a seventeen year old with the New York Rovers and bounced around hockey's minor leagues for more than seven seasons before he was signed by Conn Smythe of the Maple Leafs in 1949. He took over for the legendary Turk Broda in 1950–51, winning the Vezina Trophy and leading the Leafs to a Stanley Cup victory, allowing only six goals in the four games he played.

In September 1952, Al was sent to Chicago with Gus Mortson, Cal Gardner, and Ray Hannigan for goaltender Harry Lumley. Rollins played for five seasons with the Black Hawks, winning the Hart Trophy as the league's MVP in 1954.

Rollins lost his starting job to Glenn Hall in 1957–58 and was sent to the Calgary Stampeders of the WHL. He stayed in the minors until loaned to the Rangers during the 1959–60 season.

Rollins retired at the end of the 1961–62 season and coached the University of Calgary hockey team as well as clubs in Spokane, Salt Lake City, Houston, Tulsa, and Phoenix. As a coach he enjoyed a good measure of success, including an Allan Cup victory with Spokane in 1970.

Regular Season

Season	Team	GP	W	L	T	GA	GAA	SO	MIN	G	A	PTS	PIM
1949–50	TOR	2	1	1	0	4	2.40	1	100	0	0	0	0
1950–51	TOR	40	26	6	7	70	1.77	5	2367	0	0	0	0
1951–52	TOR	70	29	24	16	152	2.19	5	4170	0	0	0	4
1952–53	CBH	70	27	28	15	175	2.50	6	4200	0	0	0	0
1953–54	CBH	66	12	47	7	212	3.21	5	3958	0	0	0	20
1954–55	CBH	44	9	27	8	150	3.41	0	2640	0	0	0	0
1955–56	CBH	58	17	30	11	171	2.95	3	3479	0	0	0	10
1956–57	CBH	70	16	39	15	224	3.20	3	4198	0	1	1	9
1959–60	NYR	10	3	4	3	31	3.10	0	600	0	0	0	0
NYR Totals	-	10	3	4	3	31	3.10	0	600	0	0	0	0
Career	-	430	140	206	82	1189	2.77	28	25,712	0	1	1	43

Playoffs

Season	Team	GP	W	L	T	GA	SO	MIN	G	A	PTS	PIM
1950–51	TOR	4	3	1	-	6	0	210	0	0	0	0
1951–52	TOR	2	0	2	-	6	0	120	0	0	0	0
1952–53	CBH	7	3	4	-	18	0	425	0	0	0	0
Career	-	13	6	7	-	30	0	755	0	0	0	0

Jack McCartan
Born: August 5, 1935 in St. Paul, Minnesota
6-1, 195lb
Caught: Left
Rangers Debut: March 6, 1960 vs. Detroit Red Wings
Uniform #1
Seasons with Rangers: 2, 1959–60 to 1960–61

Public Domain

Jack McCartan is best remembered for leading the surprising Team USA squad to the gold medal at the 1960 Winter Olympics, but he also had a brief NHL career with the Rangers.

McCartan began playing organized hockey as a high school freshman in his hometown of St. Paul, Minnesota. He then went on to star in hockey as well as baseball at the University of Minnesota, earning All-American honors in both sports. In fact, McCartan once told a reporter, "Baseball was my No. 1 sport. If I had concentrated on baseball, I could have turned pro."

Following graduation, Jack enlisted in the Army and represented the US in the World Championships in Prague in 1959. He then led the United States hockey team past the powerful Canadian, Russian, and Czechoslovakian squads to capture the gold medal at the 1960 Winter Olympics at Squaw Valley, California. For his efforts, he was named the All-World goaltender of the Winter Games.

After the Olympics, Rangers GM Muzz Patrick signed Jack to a five-game tryout contract. Many thought the move was a publicity stunt meant to sell tickets to the remaining games of another dismal season, but a few days later Jack made his NHL debut, beating the Detroit Red Wings, 3–1, at the Garden.

McCartan's biggest save in that game came on the first shot he faced, when Detroit's Gordie Howe deked around Rangers defenseman Bill Gadsby and came in one-on-one on the rookie netminder. "I hugged the near post, and he faked a shot to the far corner while still holding the puck," McCartan later told reporters. "Gordie wanted to pull me out of the net and put it behind me. But I was ready for him, and when he took a wrist shot low, I dove at the puck and got my body in front of it for my big first save."

McCartan played well in his next three starts, going 1–1–2 overall with a 1.75 GAA in four games. He returned to the Blueshirts the next season but clearly wasn't an NHL-caliber goaltender, especially for a team like the Rangers that needed an extraordinary performance between the pipes every night just to compete with the rest of the league. McCartan spent most of that season with the Kitchener-Waterloo Beavers of the EPHL and appeared in only eight games for the Blueshirts, posting a 1–6–1 record with one shutout and a 4.77 GAA.

McCartan wasn't ready for NHL shooters or the rough stuff that came with the territory. One night after a scuffle with Chicago's Reggie Fleming, he bent over to pick up his gloves when Reggie floored him. "Fleming suckered me with a punch to the head," McCartan lamented. "That was it ... I saw stars."

McCartan was claimed by Chicago in the 1963 intra-league draft and remained in the minor leagues, mostly in the old Western Hockey League playing for the Los Angeles Blades, San Francisco Seals, and San Diego Gulls. In 1972, he signed with the Minnesota Fighting Saints of the WHA and mentored a young Mike Curran who had won a silver medal at that year's Winter Olympics.

McCartan retired at the end of the 1974–75 season and scouted for the Hartford Whalers when they were in the WHA and later the Vancouver Canucks. He was inducted into the United States Hockey Hall of Fame in 1983.

Regular Season

Season	Team	League	GP	W	L	T	GA	GAA	SO	MIN	G	A	PTS	PIM
1959–60	NYR	NHL	4	1	1	2	7	1.75	0	240	0	0	0	0
1960–61	NYR	NHL	8	1	6	1	35	4.77	1	440	0	0	0	0
1972–73	MFS	WHA	38	15	19	1	129	3.58	1	2160	0	0	0	19
1973–74	MFS	WHA	2	-	-	-	5	7.14	0	42	0	0	0	0
1974–75	MFS	WHA	2	1	-	-	5	4.92	0	61	0	0	0	0
NYR Totals	-	NHL	12	2	7	3	42	3.71	1	680	0	0	0	0
Career	-	NHL	12	2	7	3	42	3.71	1	680	0	0	0	0
Career	-	WHA	42	16	19	1	139	3.69	1	2263	0	0	0	0

Playoffs

Season	Team	League	GP	W	L	T	GA	SA	SO	MIN	G	A	PTS	PIM
1972–73	MFS	WHA	4	-	-	-	14	130	0	213	0	1	1	0
Career	-	WHA	4	-	-	-	14	130	0	213	0	1	1	0

Dan Olesevich
Born: September 16, 1937 in Port Colborne, Ontario
Died July 15, 1983
6-0, 170lb
Caught: Left
Rangers Debut: October 21, 1961 at Detroit Red Wings
Uniform #1
Seasons with Rangers: 1, 1961–62

Danny Olesevich was a twenty-four-year-old assistant trainer/practice goaltender for the Detroit Red Wings when he was called into service for the Rangers after Gump Worsley was injured. Olesevich was the second Red Wings assistant trainer to replace Worsley as Julian Klymkiw filled the same role three years earlier.

Olesevich had previously played with the Hamilton Tiger Cubs of the OHA for four seasons. He also spent a season in the Eastern Hockey League playing for the Charlotte Checkers and Johnstown Jets and later saw action with the Windsor Bulldogs of the NOHA. However,

Olesevich realized that he would never be more than a backup, so when the Red Wings offered him a job as trainer/practice goalie in the summer of 1959 he jumped at the chance.

Worsley's injury occurred on the night of October 21, 1961, in Detroit when he was struck in the forehead by a shot by the Red Wings' Ed Litzenberger. Gumper fell backwards, smacking his head on the ice and was knocked unconscious. He was carried off the ice on a stretcher and taken to Detroit's Osteopathic Hospital where he was diagnosed with a severe concussion.

Since this was in the days before teams were required to carry two goaltenders, the Rangers had little choice but to use Olesevich. Worsley left the game about midway through the second period with the Rangers leading, 3–2. The game was halted at that point and the teams were sent to their dressing rooms, with the remaining time tacked on to the third period.

When play resumed, Gordie Howe and Allan Johnson scored late second-period goals against Olesevich to put the Wings up, 4–3. However, Jean Guy Gendron scored early in the third and Olesevich and the Blueshirts held on for a 4–4 tie.

In his only NHL appearance, Olesevich played 29 minutes for the Blueshirts that night, made 17 saves, and finished with a 4.14 GAA.

Regular Season

Season	Team	GP	W	L	T	GA	GAA	SO	MIN	G	A	PTS	PIM
1961–62	NYR	1	0	0	1	2	4.12	0	29	0	0	0	0
Career	NYR	1	0	0	1	2	4.12	0	29	0	0	0	0

Dave Dryden
Born: September 5, 1941 in Hamilton, Ontario
6-1, 185lb
Caught: Left
Rangers Debut: February 3, 1962 at Toronto Maple Leafs
Uniform #1
Seasons with Rangers: 1, 1961–62
All-Star Games: 1

Public Domain

Dave Dryden's long professional career began on February 3, 1962, when as a twenty-one year old he was loaned to the Rangers to replace the injured Gump Worsley in Toronto. Dryden was in his first season with the Toronto Marlboros of the Ontario Hockey Association when summoned from the stands as an emergency replacement for Worsley, who had injured his elbow while falling to the ice, making a save on a shot by Dave Keon 27 seconds into the second period. Dryden made 24 saves in his NHL debut but allowed three goals as the Rangers lost, 4–1, to the Maple Leafs.

Dave, the older brother of Hall of Fame goalie Ken Dryden, signed with Chicago in 1965 and played 11 games for the Black Hawks that season. He then spent the next few seasons bouncing around the Chicago organization. In 1969, he was suspended for refusing a demotion to the minors and subsequently traded to Pittsburgh for cash. The Penguins turned around and sent him to Buffalo, where he played for four seasons.

The most memorable moment of Dave Dryden's career came on the evening of March 20, 1971, when he and his brother Ken faced each other for the first time. But the matchup almost didn't happen. Buffalo coach Punch Imlach had announced that Dave would be his starting goaltender, assuming that Ken would be in net for Montreal. The Canadiens started Rogie Vachon, however, so Imlach pulled Dryden and played Joe Daley instead. Fate intervened in the second period when Vachon was injured and had to be replaced by Ken Dryden. This prompted Imlach to switch back to Dave Dryden. Following the 5–2 Montreal victory, the two brothers met and embraced at center ice.

In 1974, Dave Dryden jumped to the Chicago Cougars of the WHA and was later traded to the Edmonton Oilers where he finished his career in 1979–80 when the Oilers became part of the NHL.

Regular Season

Season	Team	League	GP	W	L	T	GA	GAA	SO	MIN	G	A	PTS	PIM
1961–62	NYR	NHL	1	0	1	0	3	4.55	0	40	0	0	0	0
1965–66	CBH	NHL	11	3	3	0	23	3.04	0	454	0	1	1	0
1967–68	CBH	NHL	27	9	9	2	69	3.27	1	1266	0	0	0	0
1968–69	CBH	NHL	30	12	11	2	79	3.21	3	1475	0	1	1	0
1970–71	BUF	NHL	10	3	3	0	22	3.23	1	408	0	1	1	0
1971–72	BUF	NHL	20	3	9	5	68	3.98	0	1025	0	0	0	0
1972–73	BUF	NHL	37	14	13	7	89	2.65	3	2015	0	0	0	0
1973–74	BUF	NHL	53	23	20	8	148	2.98	1	2977	0	1	1	4
1974–75	CHC	WHA	45	18	26	1	176	3.87	1	2728	0	1	1	4
1975–76	EDO	WHA	62	22	34	5	235	3.95	1	3567	0	2	2	2
1976–77	EDO	WHA	24	10	13	0	77	3.26	1	1416	0	2	2	0
1977–78	EDO	WHA	48	21	23	2	150	3.49	2	2578	0	1	1	0
1978–79	EDO	WHA	63	41	17	2	170	2.89	3	3531	0	8	8	0
1979–80	EDM	NHL	14	2	7	3	53	4.29	0	741	0	0	0	0
NYR Totals	-	NHL	1	0	1	0	3	4.55	0	40	0	0	0	0
Career	-	NHL	203	69	76	27	555	3.20	9	10,401	0	4	4	4
Career	-	WHA	242	112	113	10	808	3.51	8	13,820	0	14	14	6

Playoffs

Season	Team	League	GP	W	L	T	GA	GAA	SO	MIN	G	A	PTS	PIM
1965–66	CBH	NHL	1	0	0	-	0	0.00	0	8	0	0	0	0
1972–73	BUF	NHL	2	0	2	-	9	4.53	0	119	0	0	0	0
1975–76	EDO	WHA	3	-	-	-	15	5.00	0	180	0	0	0	0
1977–78	EDO	WHA	2	-	-	-	6	3.96	0	91	0	0	0	0
1978–79	EDO	WHA	13	-	-	-	42	3.67	0	687	0	1	1	0
Career	-	NHL	3	0	2	-	9	4.23	0	127	0	0	0	0
Career	-	WHA	18	-	-	-	63	3.95	0	958	0	1	1	0

Marcel Pelletier
Born: December 6, 1927 in Drummondville, Quebec
Died: May 13, 2017
5-11, 180lb
Caught: Right
Rangers Debut: October 28, 1962 vs. Chicago Black Hawks
Uniform #1
Seasons with Rangers: 1, 1962–63

Marcel Pelletier was a true journeyman goaltender, playing for 17 teams in seven leagues during his 20-year career. He was a pretty good minor-league goaltender who unfortunately had the misfortune of getting his shot at the NHL with some pretty poor teams.

Pelletier came up through the Quebec Junior League and played senior hockey in both Ontario and Quebec. In 1950–51, he was playing for the Milwaukee Seagulls of the USHL when he was loaned to the Chicago Black Hawks to replace an injured Harry Lumley for six games. Chicago finished last that season and was a poor defensive team, surrendering 280 goals, the most in the league. With little help in front of him, the twenty-four-year-old Pelletier gave up 28 goals for a 4.73 GAA and a 1–5–0 record.

Marcel then bounced around the minor leagues for the next 11 years, picking up numerous honors and awards along the way. He was a First Team All-Star in the QMHL in 1952–53 and was named to the WHL's first or second All-Star squads for three consecutive seasons from 1956 to 1958. He was also given the WHL's Outstanding Goaltender Award in 1958.

He signed with the Rangers as a free agent in 1962 and made two brief appearances for the fifth-place Blueshirts that season. In both cases he replaced an injured Gump Worsley in the third period of losing causes. In a total of 39 minutes of play, Pelletier gave up three goals and came away with a 4.62 GAA and an 0–1–0 record.

Pelletier was then returned to the minors where he continued to move from team to team until his retirement in 1969 at the age of fourty-one. Pelletier played for 13 professional teams during his career, six of which won league championships.

After twenty years as a player, Marcel then became a scout and goaltending consultant for the expansion Philadelphia Flyers.

Regular Season

Season	Team	GP	W	L	T	GA	GAA	SO	MIN	G	A	PTS	PIM
1950–51	CBH	6	1	5	0	28	4.73	0	355	0	0	0	2
1962–63	NYR	2	0	1	0	3	4.62	0	39	0	0	0	0
NYR Totals	-	2	0	1	0	3	4.62	0	39	0	0	0	0
Career	-	8	1	6	0	31	4.72	0	394	0	0	0	2

Jacques Plante
Born: January 17, 1929 in Shawinigan Falls, Quebec
Died: February 27, 1986
6-0, 175lb
Caught: Left
Rangers Debut: October 9, 1963 at Chicago Black Hawks
Uniform #1
Seasons with Rangers: 2, 1963–64 to 1964–65
Stanley Cups: 6, Montreal (1952–53, 1955–56, 1956–57, 1957–58, 1958–59, 1959–60)
Vezina Trophy: 7, 1955–56, 1956–57, 1957–58, 1958–59, 1959–60, 1961–62 (with Montreal), and 1968–69 (St. Louis, shared with Glenn Hall)
Hart Trophy: 1961–62 (with Montreal)
Hockey Hall of Fame: 1978
All-Star selections: 1955–56, 1958–59, 1961–62 (First Team); 1956–57, 1957–58, 1959–60, 1970–71 (Second Team)
All-Star Games: 8, 1956–60, 1962, 1969–70

Jacques Plante was one of the greatest goaltenders to ever strap on a pair of pads. But when he came to the Rangers in a blockbuster 1963 trade it became all too apparent that on most nights, he like any other goaltender is only as good as the team in front of him.

After a four-year apprenticeship with the Montreal Royals in the Quebec Senior League and two more years with AHL's Buffalo Bisons, Plante spent the first 11 years of his NHL career with the fabled Montreal Canadiens where he won six Stanley Cups and six Vezina

Trophies. He also revolutionized the art of goaltending by becoming the first netminder to wear a mask during a game.

Plante began wearing the mask in practice in 1956 following an operation on his sinuses. On the evening of November 1, 1959, Plante was struck in the face by Andy Bathgate's well-placed backhand shot. Earlier in the game Plante had bloodied Bathgate with a high stick and the backhander was Andy's way of retaliating. After getting stitched up, Plante refused to return to the game unless coach Toe Blake allowed him to wear the mask. Blake's decision was to either use one of the Rangers house goaltenders, Joe Schaefer or Arnee Nocks, or go with Plante and the mask. He chose the latter and the fate of goaltenders changed for the better.

Plante was traded to the Rangers on June 4, 1963, along with Donnie Marshall and Phil Goyette for Gump Worsley, Dave Balon, Leon Rochefort, and Len Ronson. Jacques was shocked by the deal, but he had worn out his welcome with coach Toe Blake as well as his teammates. Blake thought he was a hypochondriac and could no longer depend on him due his many injuries and illnesses, either real or imagined. And his teammates were not sad to see him go either. "It might have been a surprise when he was traded," said Henri Richard, "but nobody complained."

The Rangers had high hopes for Plante, who was thirty-four years old at the time, and gave him a $24,000 a year contract that ranked near the top of the NHL pay scale in those days. It was certainly much more than he made in Montreal. Plante was also given special privileges, like staying at a different hotel if one of his many allergies kicked in. The Rangers also said that, if necessary, they would book flights that would get Jacques to road games two hours before the opening faceoff and allow him to skip practices when he felt he needed a rest.

At his first press conference as a Ranger, Plante claimed that he still "had it" and blamed much of his problems on the pressure of playing in Montreal, where he was expected to "win every game." He also blamed his many health problems on the harsh Montreal winters saying that the milder New York climate would be good for him. Unfortunately, his bitterness began to show as he took the opportunity to take digs at his former team.

"The Rangers are on their way up and the Canadiens are on their way down," Plante proclaimed. "[Bernie] Geoffrion doesn't have as hard a shot as he used to. [Jean] Beliveau has been sick, Henri Richard loses too many scoring chances trying to pull the goalie out of position and [J. C.] Trembley shoots off the wrong foot."

Emile Francis, the Rangers' assistant general manager at the time, was at that first press conference and couldn't believe what Plante was saying. "The Canadiens never forgot that, it was like committing suicide."

Plante made his Rangers debut on October 9, 1963, in Chicago making 40 saves in a 3–1 defeat. Two nights later the Rangers traveled to Montreal to face Plante's former teammates who were looking forward to the encounter to say the least. The Canadiens fired 59 shots at Plante and won, 6–2. Geoffrion scored on a slap shot and skated by the crease to ask Plante, "Hey Jacques, if my shot is so slow, how come you can't see it anymore?"

At the home opener Jacques notched a 34-save, 3–0 shutout over Detroit in front of 15,240 fans, the largest opening night crowd in sixteen years. It was his 59th career shutout. He also shut out the Bruins eight days later.

From there on the 1963–64 season was a series of winless streaks interrupted here and there by a few victories. And as the losses mounted the bloom soon began to fall off Plante's rose. "He drove our trainer Frank Paice crazy," said Francis. "He had forty-two pieces of equipment. He had a pad for everything. You name it, he had a piece of equipment for it."

The highlight of Plante's season was the night of March 8 when he shut out the Canadiens (0–0) at Madison Square Garden.

Plante was an intelligent but complicated individual who enjoyed painting and knitting toques in his spare time. While in New York he had an efficiency apartment at the Coliseum House on West 71st Street and was intrigued by the city's subway system. He also enjoyed wandering around the campuses of Columbia and Fordham Universities as well as Brooklyn College, admiring the architecture.

Plante also had a keen eye when it came to the architecture of the piece of real estate he was paid to protect. When he was a member of the Canadiens, he noticed that the goals in Madison Square Garden were wider than the six-foot by four-foot nets set forth in the NHL rule book. He complained to league president Clarence Campbell who then notified GM Muzz Patrick. Muzz dismissed Plante's claim but asked Herb Goren, the Rangers' publicist, to check it out. Goren assigned the task to his assistant, Hal Bock, and the Garden's superintendent, Dick Donopria, who measured the nets and found that they were indeed three inches too wide. "When we reported back to Muzz with the details, he put his finger to his mouth and said 'Shhh,'" recalled Bock, who went on to work for the Associated Press and author numerous books on hockey and other sports. Patrick told Campbell that the nets were regulation size but promptly ordered a new set, without anyone being the wiser, except of course, Mr. Plante.

It should come as no surprise that Plante faced more shots as a Ranger than he did in Montreal. In 1963–64 he saw an average of 38 shots a game, the most in the league and a full 10 shots more per game than the year before. Over the 70-game season that amounted to 700 more shots than Jacques was used to seeing as a member of the Canadiens.

The Rangers finished the season with a 22–38–10 record, 17 points behind fourth-place Detroit but only six points ahead of the sixth-place Bruins. More telling was that they allowed 242 goals that season, the most in the league and nine more than the previous season without Plante.

Due to a sore knee Plante began the 1964–65 season with the Baltimore Clippers of the AHL and stirred up trouble when he complained about the Rangers to a local reporter. Plante's comments, in which he blasted the Rangers management, coaches, and training conditions, appeared in a wire service story that was buried in the back of the *New York Herald-Tribune*. Stan Fischler, then a reporter for the *New York Journal-American*, saw the story and contacted Plante in Baltimore to validate his comments. When Plante continued to ridicule Patrick, coach Red Sullivan, and everything else associated with the Blueshirts, Fischler wrote his own story which subsequently made headlines, attracting the attention of the Rangers.

An irate Patrick called Plante back to New York for an explanation and later at the ensuing news conference exchanged harsh words with Fischler and greatly embarrassed new team president William Jennings. Patrick was asked to resign and was put in charge of the Rangers' upcoming move to the new Garden. He was replaced as GM by his assistant, Emile Francis.

Francis had seen and heard enough of Plante to know that he was not the kind of goaltender that he wanted to build a team around. "Plante was a loner," said Francis. "He didn't mingle with the players. He was never going to be the kind of goalkeeper that the players would work their butts off for."

Marcel Paille took over in goal for the Rangers, but Jacques was recalled on an emergency basis on November 7 in Toronto after Paille suffered a twisted knee in practice. Plante came through in the clutch, shutting out the Maple Leafs, 1–0, and earning first star of the game honors. From that point on he and Paille shared the netminding duties for the rest of the season. In 33 games with the Rangers that season, Plante posted a 10–17–5 record with a 3.37 GAA and two shutouts. Paille played in 39 games, going 10–21–7 with a 3.58 GAA. But the Rangers finished out of the playoffs once again, 22 points behind the fourth-place Maple Leafs.

By then it was obvious that Plante's days as a Ranger were numbered and his fate was sealed when Francis acquired Eddie Giacomin in May 1965. At that point the plan was to keep Plante and gradually work Giacomin into the number one spot. Plante, however, perhaps reading the handwriting on the wall, had other ideas. He telephoned Francis in early June, telling him that he was going to retire, citing health issues and his desire to spend more time with his family. Plante then said that he planned to make the announcement to the press in two days, giving Francis just 48-hours to swing a deal for an experienced netminder before the rest of the GMs in the league knew that he was dealing from a disadvantage.

Francis first tried to get veterans Johnny Bower or Terry Sawchuk from Toronto but was rebuffed by Maple Leafs GM Punch Imlach. He then turned to Montreal where he struck a deal with GM Sam Pollock, acquiring Cesare Maniago. Later that same day he also claimed thirty-four-year-old netminder Don Simmons from Toronto in the intra-league draft.

But that was not the end of the Rangers' connection to Jacques Plante. In 1967, Bert Olmstead, the coach of the expansion Oakland Seals, hired Plante to be his goaltending consultant. Plante took it a step further, signing a tryout contract and appearing in an exhibition game in Port Huron. Since Plante's NHL rights still belonged to the Rangers, Francis tried to make a deal with the Seals for Plante. But when an agreement could not be reached, Jacques left training camp and returned home. The next season Plante told Francis that he wanted to come out of retirement so he was left exposed in the interleague draft and selected by the St Louis Blues where he shared the Vezina Trophy in 1968–69 with teammate Glenn Hall.

But Plante's role in Rangers history didn't end there either. When the Blueshirts acquired Tim Horton from Toronto for Denis Dupere in March 1970, the Rangers were still owed an unnamed player from St. Louis to complete an earlier trade. Francis had that "player to be named later" transferred to the Leafs as part of the Horton deal. That player was Plante, who was going to be left unprotected by the Blues anyway.

Plante went on to play for Toronto and Boston before moving on to the WHA with Edmonton. He retired in 1975 and was inducted into the Hockey Hall of Fame in 1978. He died of stomach cancer in February of 1986 at the age of fifty-seven.

Jacques Plante may not have had his best years on Broadway, but he was a character—innovative, colorful, and controversial and proof that although they might "steal" a game once in a while, a goaltender is really only as good as the team in front of him.

Regular Season

Season	Team	League	GP	W	L	T	GA	GAA	SO	MIN	G	A	PTS	PIM
1952–53	MTL	NHL	3	2	0	1	4	1.33	0	180	0	0	0	0
1953–54	MTL	NHL	17	7	5	5	24	1.41	5	1020	0	0	0	0
1954–55	MTL	NHL	52	33	12	7	109	2.12	5	3079	0	0	0	2
1955–56	MTL	NHL	64	42	12	10	119	1.86	7	3840	0	0	0	10
1956–57	MTL	NHL	61	31	18	12	122	2.00	9	3658	0	0	0	16
1957–58	MTL	NHL	57	34	14	8	119	2.11	9	3386	0	0	0	13
1958–59	MTL	NHL	67	38	16	13	144	2.16	9	4000	0	1	1	11
1959–60	MTL	NHL	69	40	17	12	175	2.54	3	4140	0	0	0	2

Season	Team	League	GP	W	L	T	GA	GAA	SO	MIN	G	A	PTS	PIM
1960–61	MTL	NHL	40	23	11	6	112	2.80	2	2400	0	0	0	2
1961–62	MTL	NHL	70	42	14	14	166	2.37	4	4200	0	0	0	14
1962–63	MTL	NHL	56	22	14	19	138	2.49	5	3320	0	1	1	2
1963–64	NYR	NHL	65	22	36	7	220	3.39	3	3898	0	1	1	6
1964–65	NYR	NHL	33	10	17	5	109	3.38	2	1938	0	1	1	6
1968–69	STL	NHL	37	18	12	6	70	1.96	5	2138	0	0	0	2
1969–70	STL	NHL	32	18	9	5	67	2.19	5	1838	0	2	2	0
1970–71	TOR	NHL	40	24	11	4	73	1.89	4	2323	0	0	0	2
1971–72	TOR	NHL	34	16	13	5	86	2.63	2	1962	0	0	0	2
1972–73	TOR	NHL	32	8	14	6	87	3.05	1	1713	0	0	0	0
1972–73	BOS	NHL	8	7	1	0	16	2.00	2	480	0	2	2	2
1974–75	EDO	WHA	31	15	14	1	88	3.32	1	1592	0	1	1	2
NYR Totals	-	NHL	98	32	53	12	329	3.38	5	5836	0	2	2	12
Career	-	NHL	837	437	246	145	1960	2.38	82	49,513	0	8	8	92
Career	-	WHA	31	15	14	1	88	3.32	1	1592	0	1	1	2

Playoffs

Season	Team	League	GP	W	L	T	GA	GAA	SO	MIN	G	A	PTS	PIM
1952–53	MTL	NHL	4	3	1	-	7	1.75	1	240	0	0	0	0
1953–54	MTL	NHL	8	5	3	-	14	1.75	2	480	0	0	0	0
1954–55	MTL	NHL	12	6	3	-	29	2.72	0	640	0	0	0	0
1955–56	MTL	NHL	10	8	2	-	18	1.80	2	600	0	0	0	2
1956–57	MTL	NHL	10	8	2	-	17	1.66	1	614	0	0	0	4
1957–58	MTL	NHL	10	8	2	-	20	1.94	1	618	0	0	0	2
1958–59	MTL	NHL	11	8	3	-	26	2.33	0	669	0	0	0	0
1959–60	MTL	NHL	8	8	0	-	11	1.35	3	489	0	0	0	0
1960–61	MTL	NHL	6	2	4	-	16	2.33	0	412	0	0	0	2
1961–62	MTL	NHL	6	2	4	-	19	3.17	0	360	0	0	0	2
1962–63	MTL	NHL	5	1	4	-	14	2.80	0	300	0	0	0	0
1968–69	STL	NHL	10	8	2	-	14	1.43	3	589	0	1	1	0
1969–70	STL	NHL	6	4	1	-	8	1.49	1	323	0	0	0	2
1970–71	TOR	NHL	3	0	2	-	7	3.16	0	133	0	0	0	0
1971–72	TOR	NHL	1	0	1	-	5	5.00	0	60	0	0	0	0
1972–73	BOS	NHL	2	0	2	-	10	5.00	0	120	0	0	0	0
Career	-	NHL	112	71	36	-	235	2.12	14	6647	0	1	1	14

Gilles Villemure
Born: May 30, 1940 in Trois-Rivieres, Quebec
5-8, 185lb
Caught: Right
Rangers Debut: November 20, 1963 vs. Boston Bruins
All-Star Games: 3, 1971–73
Uniform #1, 30
Seasons with Rangers: 8, 1963–64, 1967–68 to 1968–69, 1970–71 to 1974–75
Vezina Trophy: 1970–71 (shared with Ed Giacomin)

Courtesy of Jay Moran

Gilles Villemure grew up in Trois-Rivieres, Quebec, where the local hockey rink was right next to the fairgrounds racetrack, and so his two passions became hockey and horse racing. Luckily for him he was able to pursue both these interests professionally.

Gilles began playing goal at the age of fourteen when the net-minder on his local team was injured. He had a brief tryout with the Troy (Ohio) Bruins of the IHL and played his junior hockey with the famed Guelph Biltmores of the OHA where his teammates were Jean Ratelle and Rod Gilbert. He was scouted by Yvan Prud'homme and at sixteen signed a "C" form and received a one hundred dollar signing bonus from the Rangers, with the promise of $500 when he turned pro. Following a season in Guelph, he played for the New York Rovers (1960–61) and the Long Island Ducks (1961–62) and signed with the Rangers as a free agent in 1962.

According to Villemure, "I took Eddie Giacomin's job with the New York Rovers. He went up to Providence and I took over with the Rovers. Then I played for the Long Island Ducks. Lots of traveling. We played in Nashville, Knoxville, places like that. We used to play five, six games on the road with 15, 16-hour bus trips. But we didn't know any better. We just played. But I was happy to be there. I was making $165 a week and I had to pay for my rent and things like that. We got four dollars a day meal money."

Unfortunately for Villemure, back then there were only six goal-tending jobs in the NHL and most of the incumbents were future Hall of Famers. So Gilles's road to the big leagues was a long one, spending most of next nine years playing for Rangers farm clubs in Vancouver,

Buffalo, and Baltimore. It was while playing for the Baltimore Clippers in 1966 that Gilles started wearing the mask with the famous grin that would become his trademark. He also got a brief taste of the NHL, making his Rangers debut during the 1963–64 season when he played five games in place of the injured Jacques Plante. He also saw action with the Rangers during the 1967–68 and 1968–69 seasons.

Gilles excelled at every stop along his minor-league trail, being named the WHL's Rookie of the Year in 1962–63, winning the AHL's Les Cunningham Award as the league's MVP twice (1968–69 and 1969–70) and the Harry "Hap" Holmes Award for the lowest GAA in the AHL those same years. During the 1969–70 season Villemure's goaltending took the Buffalo Bisons of the AHL to regular-season and playoff championships. He posted eight shutouts, was named a First Team All-Star and was considered by many to be the best goaltender outside of the NHL.

Villemure finally made it to the Rangers on a full-time basis in 1970–71, going 14–1–3 in his first eighteen games.

Villemure said, "I thought I was ready because the last two years in Buffalo I was the MVP of the league and I thought I was playing well. But you never know, the minors and the NHL are two different things. But Emile Francis gave me a chance."

Teamed with Ed Giacomin, the duo gave up a combined 173 goals for a 2.22 GAA, edging out their nearest competitor, the Chicago Black Hawks (2.33 GAA) to earn the Vezina Trophy. It was the Rangers' first Vezina win since Davey Kerr in 1940. The pair also combined for a total of 12 shutouts (Giacomin eight, Villemure four) the most since John Ross Roach recorded thirteen blankings in 1928–29.

Regarding sharing time with Giacomin, Villemure said, "At first Eddie didn't like it because I was taking half his playing time. But once I started playing in the NHL, when I was thirty, I was winning, so Emile had no choice but to play me, and Eddie and I got along very well. Winning the Vezina was special. Eddie played that last game against Detroit and I came on the ice and he lifted my arm up. I'll never forget that. I still have a picture of that on my desk. Team trophies are better, but the individual trophies stay with you. You remember them."

Both were selected to the All-Star Game in 1971 and 1973, the first time two goaltenders from the same team had played in the midseason exhibition match. During Villemure's Rangers career, he appeared in three All-Star games (1971, 1972, and 1973) and set a record for the longest recorded shutout streak at 79 minutes, 21 seconds. In a total of 88 minutes in three All-Star Game appearances Gilles surrendered only one goal. His 0.68 All-Star Game GAA is still the lowest of any netminder who has made at least two appearances.

Looking back, Villemure says, "In those years, the 1970s, the game was not the same as it is today. Now it's wide open, but back then we played a regular game with low scores, now they're 9–8, 10–8, whatever. It's all offense now, nobody wants to get hurt."

Villemure and Giacomin had vastly different styles. Where Giacomin was acrobatic, Villemure was a classic stand-up goaltender who played his angles extremely well. There was also another difference between the two netminders which Emile Francis used to the Rangers' advantage. "It was great when I had Villemure and Giacomin because Eddie caught with his left hand and Gilly with his right and the other team was always all screwed up as to where they should shoot," Francis once said. "They were both great goaltenders. But I had to keep telling the reporters, 'We don't have a number one goalie and we don't have a number two goalie. They're both number one goalies.'"

Gilles was very low key, self-deprecating and perhaps the most underrated goaltender in team history. He could have been a starter for any team in the league. But as Ed Giacomin often noted, "I think way down deep Gilles Villemure's first love was horses. But what made the rotation so special for him was that he happened to have a guy who liked to play a lot, so he could devote more time to studying the racing forms."

Villemure concurred. "It didn't bother me. If I played, I played, if not, it didn't bother me one way or the other. Whatever was best for the team."

Often asked the eternal question, Gilles knows exactly why the Rangers of the Francis era never won a Stanley Cup.

"Jean Ratelle got hurt at the wrong time [late in the 1971–72 season]. He was the best player we had. Rod Gilbert has said that many times, 'Jean was the best.' We went to the sixth game of the finals against

Boston in 1972, I played the last two games because Eddie got hurt. We won the fifth game in Boston, 3–2, and lost game six at home, 3–0. But losing Ratelle was the big thing."

During the offseason Villemure pursued his other passion—harness racing. He began driving horses at the age of seventeen and eventually raced locally at Roosevelt, Monticello, Freehold and the Meadowlands racetracks.

"When I was a kid I had a chance to be a goalie or a harness driver. But I chose hockey. But I was that good as a driver. I was doing that well back home in the summertime. I did both, I think it helped my reflexes. It's all timing. Emile Francis didn't know that I was driving the horses and one day he was at Roosevelt Raceway and he sees me in the race and he says what the hell are you doing there Gilly? He didn't even know I was racing. But he never bothered me about it. Never said you can't do that," Villemure said.

The Giacomin-Villemure partnership lasted through the 1974–75 season when injuries began to catch up with both veteran netminders. During the summer of 1975, the Rangers had obtained young goaltender John Davidson from the St. Louis Blues and were in the process of revamping the team. Reading the handwriting on the wall, Villemure, who was going through a divorce, asked Francis for a trade and was sent to Chicago for defenseman Doug Jarrett on October 28, 1975.

The deal came as no surprise to Villemure. "I was having problems at home and I said to Emile, if you want to trade me, just trade me. And the next day I was gone. There was a big turnover there. I don't know why or who was behind it. You hear different stories. But everybody was being moved."

Gilles stayed in Chicago until the end of the 1976–77 season, seeing spot duty as Tony Esposito's backup. At that point John Ferguson tried to get him back for the Rangers, who needed a steadying influence in goal. Villemure remembered that. "I was traded back to New York when John Ferguson came in. However, the third-string goalie in Chicago got hurt and I had to go back."

Former teammate Glen Sather, who by then was coach of the WHA's Edmonton Oilers, also offered Gilles a job, but he didn't want to take his children out of school and disrupt his family life, so he retired.

Villemure enjoyed his years with the Rangers and still lives in the area. He also has many fond memories of his Ranger teammates and the camaraderie they shared. "The team, the players we had were all unbelievably nice guys. That's what I remember the most really. We were very close. On the road after the game we would all go out for a beer. Everybody was there and that's an amazing thing right there, because usually you have your own way to go. But we stuck together like that all the time. It was incredible. Even at home after practice we would all go out to lunch together. I don't think I was ever mad at anybody on the team. No one ever fought off the ice, everyone got along very well. That's what I remember. We were all on the same page."

Regular Season

Season	Team	GP	W	L	T	GA	GAA	SO	MIN	G	A	PTS	PIM
1963–64	NYR	5	0	2	3	18	3.60	0	300	0	0	0	0
1967–68	NYR	4	1	2	0	8	2.40	1	200	0	0	0	0
1968–69	NYR	4	2	1	1	9	2.25	0	240	0	0	0	0
1970–71	NYR	34	22	8	4	78	2.30	4	2036	0	0	0	0
1971–72	NYR	37	24	7	4	74	2.09	3	2127	0	2	2	6
1972–73	NYR	34	20	12	2	78	2.30	3	2035	0	0	0	2
1973–74	NYR	21	7	7	3	62	3.53	0	1053	0	0	0	0
1974–75	NYR	45	22	14	6	130	3.16	2	2465	0	0	0	2
1975–76	CBH	15	2	7	5	57	4.30	0	796	0	0	0	0
1976–77	CBH	6	0	4	1	28	5.41	0	312	0	0	0	0
NYR Totals	-	184	98	53	23	457	2.62	13	10,456	0	2	2	10
Career	-	205	100	64	29	542	2.81	13	11,562	0	2	2	10

Playoffs

Season	Team	GP	W	L	T	GA	GAA	SO	MIN	G	A	PTS	PIM
1968–69	NYR	1	0	1	-	4	4.00	0	60	0	0	0	0
1970–71	NYR	2	0	1	-	6	4.50	0	80	0	0	0	0
1971–72	NYR	6	4	2	-	14	2.33	0	360	0	0	0	0
1972–73	NYR	2	0	1	-	2	1.97	0	61	0	0	0	0
1973–74	NYR	1	0	0	-	0	0.00	0	1	0	0	0	0
1974–75	NYR	2	1	0	-	6	3.83	0	94	0	0	0	0
Career	NYR	14	5	5	-	32	2.93	0	656	0	0	0	0

CHAPTER FIVE

Rangers Practice and Emergency Goaltenders

Prior to the 1965–66 season when the NHL ruled that teams had to dress two netminders for every game, many teams often employed amateurs and lower minor leaguers to serve as practice and emergency goaltenders. These goaltenders were happy to share the ice with the pros and make a few bucks on the side. They provided relief for the regular netminder when he was injured or needed a day off and also allowed the team to hold a split-squad scrimmage with two real goalies instead of using a sheet of plywood, nicknamed "Woody" with holes cut in it, to cover one of the nets.

These goaltenders came from various walks of life and for many it was more of an avocation than an occupation. For example, Donald Summerville, the former mayor of Toronto, served as a practice goalie for the Maple Leafs in the 1930s while Jacques Beauchamp, a sports editor in Montreal, traveled with the Canadiens as their practice-substitute goaltender in the 1950s.

Often the team's trainer doubled as their practice goaltender. The Detroit Red Wings had three trainers through the years that not only donned the pads in practice but also got into NHL games as emergency goaltenders. Ross "Lefty" Wilson had a brief minor-league career and served as the Wings trainer from 1950 to 1982 and for several years was also their practice goaltender. Wilson also saw action in three games, but only once for the Red Wings.

On October 10, 1953, Wilson replaced Terry Sawchuk during a 4–1 loss to the Montreal Canadiens. On January 22, 1956, he was loaned to the Maple Leafs to replace Harry Lumley and faced his own club briefly in the third period of a 4–1 Red Wings triumph. Wilson's final NHL appearance came on December 29, 1957, when he played 52 minutes for the Bruins, replacing Don Simmons in a 2–2 tie.

In total Wilson allowed only one goal in three NHL appearances and finished his career with a 0–0–1 record and a very respectable 0.74 GAA. "There was no way I wanted those guys to score on me," Wilson once told Dick Irvin in his book, *In the Crease*, referring to the Red Wings players he had tended to as a trainer. "It would have been terrible to go to work in the dressing room the next day and have them give me the needle about how many they scored."

Two of Wilson's assistants, Julian Klymkiw and Danny Olesevich, also saw action replacing the injured Gump Worsley for parts of two games in the late 1950s and early 1960s.

The Rangers often called upon a goaltender from the New York Rovers, their Eastern Hockey League farm club and Garden co-tenant, to fill the void. Records of the names and dates of these practice goalies are sketchy at best. Sometimes these men would show up in a team picture, but most often not. And so below is a list of known New York Rangers practice goaltenders in mostly chronological order. Some of the names you will recognize but most you will not.

Courtesy of Michael Cosby

Gerry Cosby, founder of the famous sporting goods empire that bears his name, served as a practice goaltender for the Rangers during the late 1930s and early '40s, including the 1940 team that won the Stanley Cup. Cosby had gotten his foot in the door of the hockey business as a teenager working as an office boy and switchboard operator at the Boston Arena, the home of the Boston Tigers of the Canadian-American Hockey League. One day in 1928, Eddie Powers, the manager of the Tigers, fired their netminder because he had a drinking problem and asked Gerry to be their practice goaltender. Even though the nineteen-year-old had never played hockey, let alone tended goal in his life, he went down to the Tigers locker room and gamely donned the pads and oversized skates, willing to give it a shot. But Gerry's eagerness couldn't hide his inexperience and he expected the Tigers to bring in another goalie for their next practice.

But Powers asked him to come back and try it again and each day he improved and eventually caught the eye of Art Ross, the GM and coach of the Boston Bruins, who also practiced at the Arena and soon Gerry was seeing double duty as the practice netminder for both teams. Although Gerry was not getting paid for any of these practice sessions, he was gaining valuable experience and being mentored by Bruins netminder Cecil "Tiny" Thompson, a future Hall of Famer.

Cosby eventually put his experience to good use and made quite a name for himself in the amateur ranks. In 1932, he toured Europe with a group of American hockey players that was organized by Bruins president Walter Brown and a year later played for the United States in the World Championships in Prague, Czechoslovakia. Amazingly, with only five years of experience under his belt, Gerry posted four consecutive shutouts against Switzerland, Poland, Czechoslovakia, and Austria and then beat a heavily favored Canadian team, 2–1, in overtime for the championship. It marked the first time that a Canadian team had been defeated in the World Championships.

In 1935, Cosby played for the Wembley Lions in the English Hockey League where he was voted the league MVP while attending business college in his spare time. A year later he was invited to play on the United States Olympic team but declined because he had just gotten a new job with future US Hockey Hall of Famer Stewart Iglehart's construction business.

Gerry then moved to New York to take a job as a runner on Wall Street, but he didn't want to give up on his hockey career. So he called Rangers general manager and coach Lester Patrick and asked him if he could skate with the team and wound up becoming their practice goaltender.

During the late 1930s and early '40s Gerry was a very busy guy, seeing duty as the backup netminder for the New York Rovers, as well as serving as the practice goaltender for both the Rangers and the New York Americans. During World War II when many players from all levels of hockey were overseas, Cosby was often called upon to tend goal for multiple EHL teams in the same week.

Gerry's involvement in the sporting goods business began while he was with the Rovers, when GM and coach Tom Lockhart asked him to order some sticks. He found a company called Lovell Manufacturing, in Erie, Pennsylvania, that made hockey sticks, mouse traps, and washing machine parts and ordered six dozen at a good price. The sticks were delivered, Lockhart and the players liked them, and soon Gerry was placing orders for gloves and pads and a sporting goods empire was born.

Jack McGill served as the Rangers' practice goaltender in the early 1940s while he was a member of the Rovers. Best remembered for playing with a white towel wrapped around his neck, McGill spent most of his career with the St. Paul Saints of the USHL before retiring in 1951.

Larry Feltham played for various teams in the EHL, Metropolitan Amateur Hockey League, and Atlantic Hockey League and occasionally served as a practice goalie in the early 1940s.

Doug Stevenson was a spare goaltender for the Black Hawks before coming to the Rangers in 1944. He practiced with the Rangers and played 20 games for the Rovers. He saw action in four games with the Blueshirts in 1944–45 and lost then all. In March 1945, he was loaned to Chicago to replace their injured starter Mike Karakas. He played two games for the Black Hawks that season and two more the next before returning to the minors. He spent the remainder of his career playing for teams in the PCHL and WHL and retired in 1956.

Bill McLaughlin served as the Rangers' practice goaltender for a brief time in 1946–47. He was also on the roster of the Los Angeles Monarchs and San Francisco Shamrocks (PCHL) and New York Rovers (EHL) before moving back to the West Coast the following year.

Bob DeCourcy spent part of the 1947–48 season as a practice goaltender for the Rangers and the backup netminder for the Rovers. He would also occasionally serve as the Blueshirts' emergency goaltender who would be called upon to play if either team's netminder was injured and couldn't continue.

Which is exactly what happened on the evening of November 12, 1947, as the Rangers hosted the Boston Bruins. Midway through the second period with the Bruins leading, 2–1, Rangers goaltender Chuck Rayner was felled by a shot from Boston's Jack Crawford. Dr. Vincent Nardiello stitched Chuck up but would not allow him to return to the game. In the meantime, DeCourcy had made his way down to the Rangers locker room to get ready to take Rayner's place in the net. DeCourcy did the best he could but was just overmatched, surrendering six goals in 29 minutes as the Rangers lost, 8–2. DeCourcy returned to the Rovers for the remainder of that season and then spent three years in the USHL before playing senior hockey with St. Michaels and retiring at the end of the 1950–51 season.

Bev Bentley spent the entire 1953–54 season traveling with the Rangers as their backup and practice goaltender. However, Johnny Bower, who was only twenty-nine years old at the time, played every minute of the 70-game schedule that season and Bev, a cousin of NHL stars Max and Doug Bentley, did not get into a game. Bev made three Memorial Cup appearances and played with fourteen teams in seven leagues over the course of 18 seasons. He retired in 1962 and took a job as a trainer for the Knoxville Knights of the EHL in 1965 and appeared in 14 games over two seasons as an emergency replacement for the team's starting netminder.

Bob Popper occasionally served as a practice goaltender in the late 1950s. He was a photographer who often worked with Stan Fischler when they were both with the *New York Journal-American.*

"He shot fashion stuff and lots of models," recalled Fischler. "After the shoots he'd often ask them to come to a Rangers game with him and most accepted.

One day, he finished shooting a comely model and did his usual, 'Would you like to see a Rangers hockey game with me?' He expected what he often got: an enthusiastic response. This model had just one word for Bob: 'Why?' By the time he got over the lockjaw, she was over the horizon."

One of the most interesting stories is that of Brooklyn-native **Arnee Nocks,** who served as the Blueshirts' practice goaltender from 1955 to 1963. Although Nocks didn't even start skating until he was in his twenties, he got his big break in February 1955 while he was watching the Rangers practice. The club's regular spare netminder didn't show up and trainer Frank Paice, who had seen Arnee play recreation league hockey, asked him if he wanted to fill in. Paice didn't have to ask him twice as Arnee jumped at the opportunity to live his dream.

"The day Paice came over to me was the biggest thrill in my life," Nocks once told Stan Fischler. "I was scared yet I knew this was the chance I'd waited for and I was going to go through with it. When I got on the ice my stomach was tied up in a thousand little knots. Then Andy Bathgate fired a shot and to my amazement, I stopped it! After that, one by one the little knots began to untie themselves and I felt like this is what I should have been doing all my life."

By all accounts, Nocks was a pretty good goaltender. In 1958, the thirty-two year old attended Rangers training camp and played so well that coach Phil Watson said that he would have made him the Rangers regular goalie but he was too old.

Nocks accumulated more than 60 stitches during those workouts but kept all his teeth until one day when he tried playing with a mask. A shot by Pat Hannigan struck Arnee's mask at the mouth, shattering it and taking two of his front teeth with it. "Now I'm a real hockey player," he later told friends.

Nocks died of Parkinson's disease in 1992 but he had an interesting life. When he wasn't practicing with the Rangers, he was a player-coach for the New Jersey Rockets of the New York/New Jersey Met League. He was also an accomplished organist and worked for the DuMont network and ABC-TV in New York, directing such shows as *The Kraft Theater*, *Captain Video*, *P.M. New York*, *Eyewitness News*, and *The Soupy Sales Show*. He also directed the first televised open-heart surgery, which earned him an Emmy nomination. And by being in the right place at the right time one cold February morning, he got to live his dream.

Ray Mikulan's 10-year professional career was spent in the minor leagues despite being named the top goaltender of the WHL in

1955–56 while with the Vancouver Canucks. He was brought up to the Rangers as a spare goaltender during the 1957 playoffs when Gump Worsley was nursing an injury and couldn't practice with the team.

Long Island native **Joe Schaefer** managed an office supply company and worked part-time at Madison Square Garden as a statistician, penalty-clock timekeeper, goal judge, and practice goaltender. Schaefer also served as the Blueshirts' emergency goaltender and was called into service on the evening of February 17, 1960, when Bobby Hull of the Chicago Black Hawks accidentally skated over Gump Worsley's stick hand in the first minute of the second period. Hull's skates ripped through Gump's glove and tore tendons in his hand. The thirty-five-year-old Schaefer played the rest of the game, thus becoming the first American-born goaltender in Rangers history. Joe made 17 saves but surrendered five goals in the Black Hawks' 5–1 victory.

Schaefer made his second emergency appearance on March 8, 1961, once again replacing Worsley, who had torn a thigh muscle making a save on Bobby Hull. Joe entered the game midway through the first period with the score tied, 1–1. He made 27 saves, but the Rangers lost, 4–3. However, one Hawks goal deflected off a Ranger defenseman and another came on a two-on-one breakaway.

Schaefer also played a small role in NHL history on the night of November 1, 1959, when Andy Bathgate's well-placed backhand shot caught Montreal's Jacques Plante in the face and forced him to leave the game for repairs. After being stitched up Plante told coach Toe Blake that he would not return to the game unless he could wear his mask. No other netminder had worn a mask in an NHL game since Clint Benedict three decades earlier, and Blake was against it.

But faced with the choice of using Schaefer or allowing Plante to wear the mask, Blake wisely chose the latter and hockey history was made.

Sal Messina served as the Rangers' practice/emergency goalie for two seasons in the early 1960s. Sal played for Metropolitan League teams throughout the New York area and saw some action with the Long Island Ducks, New York Rovers, and Philadelphia Ramblers of the Eastern Hockey League. "We had a pretty decent senior league over in New Jersey and at the time the Rovers had a team and near the end of the season someone got hurt and they needed a goalie," Sal recalled. "Stan Fischler had written a couple of articles about me, so they called me up and I played a few games, a couple of good ones. The Rangers automatically put me on their list and Muzz Patrick signed me to a "C-Form."

"I went to two training camps with the Rangers," Sal continued. "The first was right after they traded Gump [Worsley] to Montreal in 1963. I played in training camp games. I played for the Rangers and against the Rangers."

Sal was able to stick around with the Blueshirts and traveled with the team for two seasons. "I would sit in the stands with Muzz Patrick or Emile Francis, even on the road, and they would announce your name as wearing number 23," said Sal. "They used to have house goalies at that time but by Muzz having me travel with the team I would have gone in instead of the other team's house goalie if our guy got hurt."

"I almost got into a game once. Jacques Plante was hurt or sick. We had taken the train up to Montreal, and that morning we got off the train and Jacques told me that he didn't feel very well. He hadn't beaten the Canadiens all year and the Rangers weren't going to make the playoffs. When we got to the rink, I skated with the guys who weren't playing. But when I got to the rink that night, they had my equipment out and all the guys were giving me the needle. But Jacques came into the dressing room and they made him play. I think they threatened to fine him and so he played and I think they won the game, 3–1. That was the closest I ever got to getting into a game except for training camp."

Sal also continued to play amateur hockey on teams in New Jersey. He was cut by the 1963 US National team but in 1964 played with a USA team from the EHL, which toured in Russia and Czechoslovakia. "That was the highlight of my career. Wearing the USA jersey in Russia and Czechoslovakia was a thrill. We played in Prague, but we didn't do very well because the Russians were better than anybody thought they were."

When his playing career ended, Sal became an off-ice official at the Garden, serving as a goal judge, official scorer, and penalty timekeeper. Then in 1973, he took over as the analyst on Rangers radio broadcasts with play-by-play man Marv Albert who bestowed the nickname "Red Light" on Sal. After nearly three decades behind the mic, Messina retired in 2002 and was given the Foster Hewitt Memorial Award for his outstanding work as an NHL broadcaster.

Last, but not least, is **Frank Brown,** former Rangers beat writer for the *New York Daily News* for many years and Group Vice President for Content Integration for the NHL. Frank was not a typical practice goalie. But he still served a purpose and had a lot of fun doing it. My thanks to Frank for contributing the following story.

> The truth is I was an *after*-practice goalie. On game days, after the starting goalie would leave the morning skate, I would get a wave from the coach (be it Herb Brooks or Tom Webster or Phil Esposito or Michel Bergeron or Roger Neilson) to go in and handle cleanup duties at that end for any of the skaters who were still on the ice. Shooters aren't particular; they always prefer a human target to a sheet of rubberized canvas with holes cut out at the corners and the center of the net. At first, players would take their best shots to see if they could rattle me or get me to flinch given that I was a writer, not a full-time athlete. Once they realized I more or less could handle whatever they had to offer—I knew that, like a lion tamer, I was toast if I showed any fear whatsoever—the routine became somewhat comfortable . . . and I learned a ton about how good these players were, which really helped my writing.
>
> Of course, the shots were hard, and of course—given the state of equipment at the time—some of the shots hurt. Didn't matter to me; I was in the net, facing shots from the New York Rangers! It was a tremendous thrill to do it at the Garden, where in the '70s I had a season ticket (Section 417, Row C, Seat 11). And it was an unimaginable thrill to serve in the same capacity at rinks such as the Montreal Forum, Maple Leaf Gardens and Chicago Stadium. Let me tell you: Walking *up* that long flight of stairs from the dressing room to the ice in Chicago Stadium was *way* easier than walking *down* when you're wearing full equipment.
>
> The whole experience was just a joy. We're talking about the '80s and '90s, so I don't have any selfies to provide, but the memories are burned into my brain. I give credit to every one of the players, because every one of them could have scored easily on every one of their shots if they used their best breakaway dekes on me. Largely, they didn't do that. They had enough respect for me being out there that during any breakaway drills they would do what they had to do without showing me up.

Mostly, though, the shots I faced were slap shots from the blue line or the tops of the circles. Tomas Sandstrom's shot stands out: I could *hear* it coming, like a major-league fastball. In terms of puck rotation and velocity, I probably would credit him with the "heaviest" shot I faced; it would drive my glove backward when I would catch it, drive my leg backward when it struck my pad. He wasn't always the most accurate—if "Boom Boom" Geoffrion was famous for the noise his shots made when they missed the net and hit the boards, I would say Tomas could have been "Clank Clank" Sandstrom for the noise his shots made when they missed my head and blasted into the seamless glass behind the net. There might have been other guys whose shots were faster but didn't drive my hand back if I happened to be lucky enough to catch it.

Other shooters would be so impressive for the way they could shoot without breaking stride, so you never knew when the shot was coming. A lot of goaltending at that time was about timing, angles, reading the puck off the stick and positioning yourself proactively just to have a fighting chance at a save. Guys who could shoot in stride, or even while crossing over, had the element of surprise on their side. I would love to single out individuals for those skills, but for one thing, it was decades ago—and for another thing, I was just trying to survive out there.

Through charity/celebrity games, media games, or morning skates, I can say it was my honor and privilege to be scored on by some of the greatest players ever—Bobby Orr, Phil Esposito, Gordie Howe, Rod Gilbert, and Bob Clarke, to name some. I gave up goals to some of the poorest players, as well. I wasn't any damn good, but I was out there, trying—getting the education of a lifetime. The bumps and bruises were more than worth it, because they meant that even if I was lousy—and I was—at least I stopped a few!

Emergency Backup Goaltenders in the Twenty-First Century

After an absence of more than fifty years the emergency backup goaltender (now called EBUGs) has made a comeback, following a spate of incidents where teams were left scrambling for a local third goaltender when one of their regular netminders was deemed unable to play either before or during a game.

In 2017, a new rule mandated that each team have one EBUG in the stands for every home game. The emergency goaltenders are used when one of the team's primary goalies are not healthy enough to play and it is not possible to bring in a backup from within that team's organization.

As of 2019, the most famous appearance by an emergency backup occurred on March 29, 2018, when the Chicago Blackhawks were forced to use Scott Foster, a thirty-six-year-old accountant from Oak Park, Illinois, in their game against the Winnipeg Jets. With their regular goalie Corey Crawford unavailable due to injury, and after backup Anton Forsberg was hurt in warmups, the Blackhawks started the game with Collin Delia, their third-string goalie, who was making his NHL debut between the pipes. But when Delia was forced to leave the game in the third period due to cramping, Foster got the call. Scott, who had tended goal for Western Michigan University and saw some action with the Petrolia Jets of the Western Ontario Hockey League and still plays recreational league hockey, entered the game with 14 minutes left in the third period and stopped seven Winnipeg shots as the Black Hawks won, 6–2.

The Rangers have yet to call on an emergency backup, but on February 9, 2018, they placed a call to Andrew Margolin of Mahwah, New Jersey, when Ondrej Pavelec injured his knee during the first period of their 4–3 win over the Calgary Flames. Henrik Lundqvist took Pavelec's place in goal but Margolin was there in case anything happened to the Blueshirts' franchise goaltender. The twenty-nine-year-old Margolin, who played goal for Connecticut College, was assigned a jersey with the number 69 and "McBackup" across the shoulders.

CHAPTER SIX

The Emile Francis Era

In 1964, Emile Francis took over virtually every aspect of a hapless Rangers franchise that had not made the playoffs in four years and began to rebuild the organization from the ground up. Francis, a former goaltender, had played professional hockey for 15 years, mostly in the minor leagues. During his playing days, Emile had assembled and managed baseball teams in Western Canada in the offseason, recruiting players from the United States and Cuba and winning seven championships in ten years.

When he retired, it was a natural progression for him to move right into coaching. The Chicago Black Hawks wanted Emile to coach their junior team in Moose Jaw but when GM Tommy Ivan delayed signing him, Muzz Patrick called and offered him a position in the Rangers organization. He took the job as coach of the Guelph Royals of the OHA and two seasons later moved up to New York as Patrick's assistant GM. Then in 1964 when Patrick was asked to resign as GM, Francis took full charge of the Blueshirts.

The team Francis inherited had some very good players but lacked a physical presence on the ice. Francis was aware of the Rangers lack of size; as the assistant GM, he got a call one day from the general manager of the Rangers' developmental team in Kitchener, Ontario. The team's uniforms were old and threadbare so they needed new ones. Francis told him that he'd send them the Rangers uniforms from the previous season, a common practice in those days. They were used, but still in good shape. A few days later Francis got another call from Kitchener—they received the uniforms, but they were too small.

So Francis set out to acquire bigger, tougher players such as Orland Kurtenbach, Reggie Fleming, and Wayne Hillman to protect his smaller, skilled skaters. He desperately needed a goaltender to build the team around, so he acquired Ed Giacomin and Cesare Maniago to battle for the starting job. When he saw that the Rangers needed an inspirational leader, he signed former Montreal Canadien "Boom Boom" Geoffrion.

He also reorganized the franchise from top to bottom. The farm system underwent a much-needed overhaul and expansion to bring the organization up to the level of the rest of the league. For example, successful teams like Toronto and Montreal had as many as sixteen development teams while the Rangers only had four. Within a year, the scouting staff was doubled and many of Patrick's old cronies were let go.

Francis saw that the rosters of the Blueshirts' affiliated clubs in the AHL, WHL, and CHL were clogged with players that were not going to make it to the NHL as Rangers. Yet these players were taking up valuable roster spots that could have been used for prospects with greater potential. Francis and his staff reevaluated each player in the organization and those who were deemed expendable were either let go or thrown into trades for skaters who had a better chance of making it to New York. Francis also strove to have enough depth to create a competition for each position, believing that a team must be competitive among its own players before it can be competitive in the league. He then installed set systems of play, outlining the way he wanted the players to bring the puck up ice and where each player should be positioned. There would be a set way of killing penalties and forechecking. He then had the coaches on each of the Rangers affiliated teams use the same system, thus making the transition easier as players moved up through the ranks.

The changes were ongoing but in 1966–67, two seasons after Francis took charge, the Rangers made the playoffs for the first time in six seasons and continued to qualify for the postseason for the next eight years. And through the years the Rangers continued to get younger, with the additions of Brad Park, Walt Tkaczuk, Billy Fairbairn, and Steve Vickers as well as tougher with the acquisition of players such as Teddy Irvine, Ron Harris, and Tim Horton. Francis also had the foresight to put tough Vic Hadfield on a line with young stars Jean Ratelle and Rod Gilbert to protect them. The line became known as the Goal-A-Game (G-A-G) line and Hadfield became a 50-goal scorer.

Emile's Rangers reached the Stanley Cup Finals once but never attained the ultimate prize. In the eyes of many hockey observers, they were the best team to never win a Stanley Cup.

If Francis had a fault, it was that he was never able to find a suitable coach so that he could dedicate more of his time to his duties as general manager. He hired Bernie Geoffrion and Larry Popien and had to step back behind the bench when each lasted less than a season. His final coaching choice was Ron Stewart in 1975–76, who was hired after former Montreal Canadien John Ferguson turned down the job.

Following an embarrassing loss to the Islanders in the first round of the 1974–75 playoffs it was obvious that changes had to be made. During the summer Francis sent three of the Rangers' toughest players, Ted Irvine, Bert Wilson, and Jerry Butler, to St. Louis for a package that included young goaltender John Davidson. Then when the team got off to a bad start in 1975–76, Francis made a series of moves that broke up the core of the team and saw many fan favorites sent out of town. It was perhaps the most chaotic 10-day stretch in Rangers history, a period in which Francis deconstructed the team he had painstakingly built over the previous ten years.

Surprisingly, the first player to go was Gilles Villemure, who was sent to Chicago for veteran defenseman Doug Jarrett on October 28. Not surprisingly, Jarrett, who had not played for Chicago due to a knee injury, reinjured his knee in his first game with the Blueshirts and sat out the next two weeks. Two days later, Derek Sanderson was sent to St. Louis for a first-round pick in the 1977 draft.

The next to go was Ed Giacomin, who was placed on waivers and claimed by Detroit. The move was a shock to everyone—Eddie, his teammates, as well as the fans. Ironically Eddie's first game with the Red Wings was two nights later against the Rangers at the Garden. The fans paid tribute to Giacomin who had tended goal for the Blueshirts for 10 seasons by chanting "Eddie! Eddie!" throughout warmups, the national anthem, as well as the game. Giacomin's former teammates didn't want to score on Eddie on his night and apologized to him when they did.

But Giacomin was not the last to go. Less than a week later, on November 7, in a deal that shocked the hockey world, Jean Ratelle,

Brad Park, and minor-league defenseman Joe Zanussi were sent to Boston for Phil Esposito and Carol Vadnais. Francis and Boston's GM Harry Sinden had been talking about a trade for more than a month. The deal originally included Espo and defenseman Dallas Smith, but Francis didn't want Smith and insisted on Vadnais instead.

Less than two months later with the Rangers still slumping, Francis himself was fired and replaced by John Ferguson, who took the job this time.

Rule Changes:
1965–66: Teams were now required to dress two goaltenders for each regular-season game.
1967–68: Limit of curvature of a hockey stick blade set at 1½ inches.
1969–70: Limit of curvature of a hockey stick blade set at 1 inch.
1970–71: Limit of curvature of a hockey stick blade set at half an inch.

Ed Giacomin—Franchise Goaltender
Born: June 6, 1939 in Sudbury, Ontario
5-11, 180lb
Caught: Left
Rangers Debut: October 24, 1965 vs. Montreal Canadiens
Uniform #1, 23, 30
Seasons with Rangers 11, 1965–66 to 1975–76
Vezina Trophy: 1970–71 (shared with Gilles Villemure)
Number 1 jersey retired, March 1989
Hockey Hall of Fame: 1987
All-Star selections: 1966–67, 1970–71, (First Team); 1967–68, 1968–69, 1969–70 (Second Team)
All-Star Games: 6, 1967–71, 1973

Courtesy of Tony Accordino

To say that Ed Giacomin's road to the NHL was rocky is an understatement. After being rejected at numerous NHL tryout camps, the native of Sudbury, Ontario, continued to play in "midnight leagues" and finally caught on with the Washington Presidents of the old Eastern League in 1959. The Presidents were dead last in the standings and needed a goaltender for the last few weeks of the season. They really wanted Eddie's brother, Rollie, who was older and had more experience, but couldn't afford to take the time off from work and convinced Eddie to go in his place. Giacomin played the final four games of the season, won them all, and seemed to have a good shot at playing the next season.

Unfortunately, during the summer Eddie suffered severe burns on his legs in a kitchen fire and spent a month in the hospital and later had to undergo therapy while doctors told him to forget about playing hockey. But Eddie wouldn't let his dream die. He reported to the Providence Reds training camp that September, getting to the rink early every morning so he could wrap his legs in bandages before anyone could notice. Eddie played for both the New York Rovers and Clinton Comets that season facing 60 to 70 shots a night while learning his craft. Giacomin finally advanced to the AHL's Providence Reds in 1960 and starred for five seasons before being acquired by Emile Francis on May 18, 1965, in exchange for Marcel Paille, Jim Mikol, Aldo Guidolin, and Sandy MacGregor.

In his first NHL season, Eddie shared the goaltending duties with young veteran Cesare Maniago. Eddie liked to handle the puck and often dashed into the corners or behind the net to pass the disc up to his defensemen. The fans and media loved it, but it often left his teammates out of position and resulted in numerous open-net goals. Eddie was sent to Baltimore of the AHL around midseason but was recalled two weeks later and spent most of the rest of the year watching and learning from the end of the bench.

Giacomin's sophomore season didn't start off any better as Francis alternated the young goaltender with Maniago as he tried to decide who was going to be his number one netminder. Then on November 9, 1966, an odd sequence of events helped Francis make up his mind. In a game against the Bruins at Madison Square Garden, Maniago stopped a Johnny McKenzie shot with his chin and needed to leave the game for repairs. He was replaced by Giacomin but when Maniago came back to the bench Francis wanted him to return to the game, but Cesare begged off, claiming to still be in pain. This constituted an unpardonable sin to Francis, an old goalie himself who withstood five broken noses, torn ligaments in both knees, separated shoulders and needed over 250 stitches to close various wounds in his career. Needless to say, "The Cat" was not very sympathetic.

Meanwhile, on the ice, with the Rangers leading, 3–1, Giacomin, who had blown third-period leads in his last two outings, was being pressured by the Bruins and hearing it from the crowd. First, Boston's Ron Murphy was left unchecked in front of the net and scored with 1:29 remaining in the game to bring the Bruins within a goal. Then Bruins goaltender Gerry Cheevers was pulled for an extra skater and Wayne Connelly scored to tie the game. Boston had scored twice in 89 seconds and the fans were not happy. They booed and jeered and threw all sorts of garbage towards Giacomin, forcing him to take shelter in his own net.

"So the next day I was still pretty mad," Francis remembers. "I went over to Maniago after practice and I said we're in this game as teammates to protect one another. I don't see how you could have been hurt so badly that you couldn't go back into the game. I said, Shit I've gone back with eight broken noses and over 200 stitches and I didn't back down, not one minute. So I said up until now I really didn't know who the hell was going to be the next goalkeeper of the New York Rangers, but now my mind's made up. Eddie Giacomin's gonna be the goalkeeper. And that was in front of the whole team. Then I told Giacomin, Eddie I've never seen anything as embarrassing as what happened last night. Now when those people throw that shit at you, you throw it right back at them and I'll be right beside you. Well guess what? The next game in Montreal, Giacomin was sensational. His whole career started from that moment on. That's what Eddie needed, as a confidence builder."

From that point on the Rangers turned their season around led by Giacomin. Eddie started 36 consecutive games from November 12 through February 5 and earned First Team All-Star honors, posting a 2.54 GAA with a league-leading nine shutouts. He also led the league in games (68), minutes played by a netminder (3,981) and wins (30). Eddie was in goal for every one of the Blueshirts' 30 victories and was selected as the team's MVP. He finished second to Chicago's Stan

Mikita in the voting for the Hart Trophy, which is given to the league's most valuable player.

And the Garden crowd never threw garbage at Eddie again as he became a fan favorite. During the next 10 seasons the words New York Rangers and Eddie Giacomin became synonymous as the skinny Italian netminder with the prematurely greying hair helped transform the Rangers from league doormats to legitimate Stanley Cup contenders. Giacomin earned the respect of the fans and franchise goaltender designation with his grit and determination which was evident even after he donned a mask for the first time in 1970–71.

Giacomin shared the Vezina Trophy with Gilles Villemure that season and was voted the team's MVP three times and won the Frank Boucher Trophy as the most popular Ranger. He played in six All-Star games and was selected as a First Team All-Star twice and Second Team All-Star three times.

But in the spring of 1975, the Rangers were ousted in the first round of the playoffs by the upstart New York Islanders, which proved to be the beginning of the end for Eddie and the reign of Emile Francis. That summer, John Davidson was acquired from St. Louis for Teddy Irvine, Bert Wilson, and Jerry Butler, and the following fall, on Halloween night, without warning, Eddie was put on waivers and claimed by the Detroit Red Wings.

Francis had been trying to make a deal for Eddie over the summer; however, at thirty-six with a bad knee and a $175,000 salary, he found no takers, so he had to put him on waivers. He explained that he wanted to develop the twenty-two-year-old Davidson as the next Rangers starter but knew he couldn't play him in the Garden where every goal he surrendered would have the fans clamoring for Giacomin. It wouldn't be fair to the young netminder.

"It was one of the toughest decisions I ever had to make," Francis recalled. "I liked Eddie Giacomin, but I had to put the interests of the New York Rangers ahead of my personal feelings."

Giacomin returned to the Garden two nights later dressed in the red road uniform of the Wings as the sellout crowd chanted "Eddie! Eddie!" throughout warmups and the national anthem as the Rangers became the visitors in their own building. The opening faceoff was delayed as Eddie wiped the tears away while at the other end of the ice, his former teammates tapped their sticks to the rhythm of the crowd. Eddie stopped 42 shots that night to beat the Rangers, 6–4, as the crowd booed every Rangers goal.

Giacomin held the team record for most shutouts (49) until surpassed in 2013–14 by Henrik Lundqvist. He also shares the team record for most assists in a game by a goaltender (two) with Mike Richter and John Vanbiesbrouck. He was the league leader in games and minutes played four times and led in wins and shutouts three times. He also led the league in games, minutes played, and victories in the 1972 playoffs as the Rangers reached the Stanley Cup Finals.

Giacomin played two more years with Detroit before retiring after the 1977–78 season. He was inducted into the Hockey Hall of Fame in 1987 and returned to the Rangers as a goaltending coach and special assignment scout when Phil Esposito took over the operation. In March 1989, Giacomin had his number 1 jersey retired and raised to the rafters alongside Rod Gilbert's number 7.

"There's no doubt in my mind, the best memory of my career was November 2, 1975," Giacomin recalled. "I don't think any athlete has been treated that way. Every other athlete has had a planned evening, but this was not planned. And I think it happened because, since I spent ten years with the Rangers, I also spent ten years with their fans. Everything I went through, they went through. Every goal, every win or loss, every fight. They went through it with me. And I think the feeling was 'how could you do that to one of us?' And I firmly believe that because of what the New York fans did for me that night I made the Hall of Fame. Because there are certain criteria for making the Hall of Fame. You have to have records, but most have been on Stanley Cup winners, I wasn't. I had something rare. I was so popular because of the New York fans. And I said it then and I'll say it now, the New York fans who I enjoyed playing for so much, put me in the Hall of Fame."

Regular Season

Season	Team	GP	W	L	T	GA	GAA	SO	MIN	G	A	PTS	PIM
1965–66	NYR	36	8	20	6	125	3.69	0	2033	0	0	0	10
1966–67	NYR	68	30	27	11	173	2.61	9	3976	0	0	0	8
1967–68	NYR	66	36	20	10	160	2.44	8	3933	0	0	0	4
1968–69	NYR	70	38	23	7	175	2.56	7	4109	0	0	0	2
1969–70	NYR	70	35	21	14	163	2.36	6	4141	0	2	2	2
1970–71	NYR	45	27	10	7	95	2.16	8	2638	0	0	0	4
1971–72	NYR	44	24	10	9	115	2.71	1	2549	0	3	3	4
1972–73	NYR	43	26	11	6	125	2.91	4	2576	0	2	2	6
1973–74	NYR	56	30	15	10	168	3.07	5	3281	0	1	1	4
1974–75	NYR	37	13	12	8	120	3.49	1	2065	0	0	0	20
1975–76	NYR	4	0	3	1	19	4.75	0	240	0	0	0	0
1975–76	DET	29	12	14	3	100	3.46	2	1736	0	0	0	0
1976–77	DET	33	8	18	3	107	3.59	3	1790	0	1	1	4
1977–78	DET	9	3	5	1	27	3.14	0	515	0	0	0	0
NYR Totals	-	539	267	172	89	1438	2.74	49	31,541	0	8	8	64
Career	-	609	290	209	96	1672	2.82	54	35,582	0	9	9	68

Playoffs

Season	Team	GP	W	L	T	GA	GAA	SO	MIN	G	A	PTS	PIM
1966–67	NYR	4	0	4	-	14	3.43	0	245	0	0	0	0
1967–68	NYR	6	2	4	-	18	3.02	0	358	0	0	0	0
1968–69	NYR	3	0	3	-	10	3.35	0	179	0	0	0	5
1969–70	NYR	5	2	3	-	19	4.15	0	275	0	0	0	0
1970–71	NYR	12	7	5	-	28	2.22	0	757	0	0	0	2
1971–72	NYR	10	6	4	-	27	2.72	0	596	0	0	0	2
1972–73	NYR	10	5	4	-	23	2.57	1	537	0	0	0	4
1973–74	NYR	13	7	6	-	37	2.83	0	785	0	0	0	6
1974–75	NYR	2	0	2	-	4	2.82	0	85	0	0	0	4
Career	NYR	65	29	35	-	180	2.83	1	3817	0	0	0	23

Cesare Maniago
Born: January 13, 1939 in Trail, British Columbia
6-3, 195lb
Caught: Left
Rangers Debut: January 8, 1966 vs. Chicago Black Hawks
Uniform #30
Seasons with Rangers: 2, 1965–66 to 1966–67

When Emile Francis acquired Ed Giacomin from the Providence Reds of the AHL on May 18, 1965, the plan was for the young goaltender to be worked into the lineup slowly, backing up Jacques Plante and becoming familiar with the league.

Plante, however, perhaps reading the handwriting on the wall, had other plans. He called Francis in early June, telling him that he was going to retire, citing health issues and his desire to spend more time with his family. Plante then told Francis that he planned to make the announcement to the press in two days, giving the Rangers GM just 48 hours to swing a deal for an experienced netminder before the rest of the GM's in the league knew that he was dealing from a disadvantage.

Rebuffed by Maple Leafs GM Punch Imlach when he tried to trade for veterans Johnny Bower or Terry Sawchuk, Francis then turned to Montreal where he struck a deal with GM Sam Pollock acquiring goaltender Cesare Maniago along with forward Garry Peters for Noel Price, Earl Ingarfield, Gordon Labossiere, Dave McComb, and cash on June 8, 1965. (Ingarfield was reacquired by the Rangers the following day when Montreal left him unprotected in the intra-league draft.)

Maniago, twenty-six, had played junior hockey for St. Michaels of the OHA. He had seen action in 21 NHL games with Toronto and Montreal and came into the season with a 2.90 GAA. At 6-foot-3 and 195 pounds, the lanky native of Trail, British Columbia, was the tallest goaltender in the league at that time. Maniago had spent the previous season with Minneapolis of the Central Hockey League where he was named to the All-Star team with an impressive 2.75 GAA and a league-leading six shutouts.

Cesare split the 1965–66 season between Baltimore of the AHL and the Rangers where he posted a 9–14–4 record in 28 games with two shutouts and a 3.50 GAA. Ed Giacomin posted an equally disappointing 8–20–6 record in 35 games with a 3.68 GAA.

Cesare lost his bid for the starter's role to Giacomin early in the 1966–67 season and was selected by Minnesota in the expansion draft that summer. He spent nine seasons with the North Stars, was later traded to Vancouver in 1976, and retired after the 1977–78 season.

Maniago was a good goaltender but had the misfortune of playing for some weak defensive teams. He also was on the wrong end of three historic NHL events. In 1961 while with Toronto he surrendered "Boom Boom" Geoffrion's 50th goal of the season, which made Boomer only the second player to score 50 goals in a season. Bobby Hull scored his 51st goal of the season against Maniago and the Rangers in 1966, which marked the first time a player scored more than 50 goals in a single season. He was also in goal for Vancouver when Stan Mikita scored his 500th career goal in 1977.

Regular Season

Season	Team	GP	W	L	T	GA	GAA	SO	MIN	G	A	PTS	PIM
1960–61	TOR	7	4	2	1	17	2.43	0	419	0	0	0	2
1962–63	MTL	14	5	5	4	42	3.07	0	820	0	0	0	2
1965–66	NYR	28	9	14	4	94	3.50	2	1611	0	2	2	2
1966–67	NYR	6	0	1	1	14	3.84	0	219	0	0	0	0
1967–68	MNS	52	22	16	9	133	2.77	6	2877	0	0	0	12
1968–69	MNS	64	18	34	10	198	3.29	1	3599	0	0	0	12
1969–70	MNS	50	9	24	16	163	3.39	2	2886	0	0	0	0
1970–71	MNS	40	19	15	6	107	2.70	5	2378	0	1	1	2
1971–72	MNS	43	20	17	4	112	2.65	3	2535	0	0	0	4
1972–73	MNS	47	21	18	6	132	2.90	5	2732	0	0	0	2
1973–74	MNS	40	12	18	10	138	3.48	1	2377	0	0	0	2
1974–75	MNS	37	11	21	4	149	4.21	1	2126	0	0	0	2
1975–76	MNS	47	13	27	5	151	3.36	2	2699	0	0	0	11
1976–77	VAN	47	17	21	9	151	3.36	1	2694	0	1	1	0
1977–78	VAN	46	10	24	8	172	4.03	1	2563	0	0	0	18
NYR Totals	-	34	9	15	5	108	3.54	2	1830	0	2	2	2
Career	-	568	190	257	97	1773	3.27	30	32,544	0	4	4	71

Playoffs

Season	Team	GP	W	L	T	GA	GAA	SO	MIN	G	A	PTS	PIM
1960–61	TOR	2	1	1	-	6	2.49	0	145	0	0	0	0
1967–68	MNS	14	7	7	-	39	2.62	0	893	0	0	0	0
1969–70	MNS	3	1	2	-	6	2.00	1	180	0	0	0	0
1970–71	MNS	8	3	5	-	28	3.51	0	479	0	0	0	0
1971–72	MNS	4	1	3	-	12	3.04	0	236	0	0	0	0
1972–73	MNS	5	2	3	-	9	1.76	2	306	0	0	0	2
Career	-	36	15	21	-	100	2.68	3	2239	0	0	0	2

Don Simmons
Born: September 13, 1931 in Port Colborne, Ontario
Died: September 24, 2010
5-10, 150lb
Caught: Right
Rangers Debut: November 10, 1965 vs. Boston Bruins
Uniform #30
Seasons with Rangers: 3, 1965–66, 1967–68 to 1968–69
Stanley Cup: Toronto, 1961–62
All-Star Games: 1, 1963

Courtesy of Jay Moran

Don Simmons was just the kind of old pro that Emile Francis needed to back up Ed Giacomin and Cesare Maniago while he was deciding which of his younger goaltenders would be his number one guy.

Simmons began his junior career with the Galt Black Hawks of the OHA in 1948 and later moved to the St. Catharines Teepees. He turned pro in 1951–52 with the EHL's Springfield Indians, earning Second Team All-Star honors his first two seasons.

Nicknamed "Dippy Don" for his habit of dropping low to block shots, Simmons made his NHL debut in 1956–57 with the Boston Bruins, replacing Terry Sawchuk, who missed much of the season due to what was called "nervous exhaustion." He helped the Bruins reach the Stanley Cup finals that season and the next and notched a career-high 24 wins in 1958–59.

While with the Bruins, Simmons became the second netminder to wear a mask in the NHL after it was introduced by Jacques Plante in 1959.

He was traded to the Toronto Maple Leafs for Ed Chadwick in 1961 and became Johnny Bower's backup, which meant he spent most of the time playing for Leafs farm clubs in Rochester and Tulsa.

But in June 1965, Simmons was left unprotected and was grabbed by Francis in the interleague draft. He spent most of the next four seasons playing for Rangers farm clubs in Baltimore, Vancouver, and Buffalo. However, he did see action in 22 games with the Rangers, posting a 4–10–4 record with a 3.46 GAA.

Simmons was a good goaltender who just happened to be playing in the wrong era. "If expansion came 10 years earlier, we would probably know a lot more about Don Simmons," said hockey historian Bob Duff. "I think he was the greatest backup in the history of the NHL."

Don retired following the 1968–69 season and founded a successful sporting goods business specializing in goaltending equipment in Fort Erie, Ontario. He passed away on September 24, 2010, at the age of seventy-nine.

Regular Season

Season	Team	GP	W	L	T	GA	GAA	SO	MIN	G	A	PTS	PIM
1956–57	BOS	26	13	9	4	63	2.42	4	1560	0	0	0	0
1957–58	BOS	39	15	14	9	92	2.42	5	2284	0	0	0	0
1958–59	BOS	58	24	26	8	183	3.16	3	3479	0	0	0	4
1959–60	BOS	28	12	13	3	91	3.26	2	1676	0	0	0	4
1960–61	BOS	18	3	9	6	58	3.23	1	1077	0	0	0	6
1961–62	TOR	9	5	3	1	21	2.33	1	540	0	0	0	0
1962–63	TOR	28	15	8	5	69	2.47	1	1679	0	0	0	0
1963–64	TOR	21	9	10	1	63	3.18	3	1189	0	0	0	0
1965–66	NYR	12	1	7	1	40	4.36	0	551	0	0	0	0
1967–68	NYR	5	2	1	2	13	2.61	0	299	0	0	0	0
1968–69	NYR	5	1	2	1	8	2.34	0	205	0	0	0	0
NYR Totals	-	22	4	10	4	61	3.47	0	1055	0	0	0	0
Career	-	249	101	101	41	701	2.89	20	14,539	0	0	0	14

Playoffs

Season	Team	GP	W	L	T	GA	GAA	SO	MIN	G	A	PTS	PIM
1956–57	BOS	10	5	5	-	29	2.90	2	600	0	0	0	0
1957–58	BOS	11	6	5	-	25	2.24	1	671	0	0	0	0
1961–62	TOR	3	2	1	-	8	2.90	0	165	0	0	0	0
Career	-	24	13	11	-	62	2.59	3	1436	0	0	0	0

Terry Sawchuk
Born: December 28, 1929 in Winnipeg, Manitoba
Died: May 31, 1970
5-11, 195lb
Caught: Left
Rangers Debut: October 26, 1969 vs. Montreal Canadiens
Uniform #30
Seasons with Rangers 1, 1969–70
Calder Trophy: 1951 (with Detroit)
Stanley Cups: 4, Detroit, 1951–52, 1953–54, 1954–55), Toronto (1966–67)
Vezina Trophy: 1951–52, 1952–53, 1954–55 (with Detroit) and 1966–67 with Toronto (shared with Johnny Bower)
Hockey Hall of Fame: 1971
All-Star selections: 1950–51, 1951–52, 1952–53 (First Team); 1953–54, 1954–55, 1958–59, 1962–63 (Second Team)
All-Star Games: 11, 1950–56, 1959, 1963–64, 1968

Courtesy of Jay Moran

Terry Sawchuk was one of the greatest goaltenders in NHL history. During hockey's "golden era" of the six-team league, Terry's records stood above those of his netminding brethren that included Glenn Hall, Jacques Plante, Johnny Bower, and Gump Worsley.

Terry began his 21-season NHL career in 1949–50, appearing in seven games with the Detroit Red Wings as a twenty year old. The next season he replaced Harry Lumley as the Wings' regular netminder and won the Calder Trophy as the NHL's Rookie of the Year. He then went to Boston in 1955 and returned to Detroit two years later. In 1964, he moved to Toronto and was selected by Los Angeles in the 1967 expansion draft. He returned to Detroit for a third time in 1968 and finished his career as a New York Ranger. Along the way, Terry won four Vezina Trophies and four Stanley Cups. He led the league in games played six times, wins five times, shutouts three times, and ranks second on the NHL's all-time shutouts list with 103.

When Don Simmons announced his retirement following the 1968–69 season Emile Francis needed an experienced goaltender to back up Eddie Giacomin. He had Gilles Villemure in the minors but with Giacomin playing in the majority of the games, Francis didn't want Villemure languishing on the bench.

Sawchuk, then forty years old and winding down his career, seemed to be the perfect solution. So, on June 17, 1969, Francis swung a deal that sent winger Larry Jeffrey to Detroit for Sawchuk and minor leaguer Sandy Snow.

In training camp that fall, Francis was shocked at Sawchuk's physical condition. "When I first played against him, he weighed two hundred and twenty pounds, but when I picked him up in New York, he weighed one hundred seventy pounds. He had been sick and lost a lot of weight and had a lot of family problems. But he was a great goalkeeper. The first year he played with the Red Wings they won the playoffs in eight straight games and he had four shutouts. His goals-against average was 0.62."

Physical condition aside, Terry did not let Emile down. He played eight regular-season games, posting a 3–1–2 record with a 2.91 goals-against average. He also recorded the 103rd shutout of his storied career on February 1, 1970, in a 6–0 win over the Pittsburgh Penguins at Madison Square Garden. "I'm old and tired but I try my best," Sawchuk told reporters after the game. Some of his teammates good-naturedly kidded that the shutout might have been Sawchuk's last. Sadly, they were right. Ironically, Sawchuk's very first shutout also came in New York at the old Garden, in a 1–0 victory over the Rangers on January 15, 1950, shortly after making his NHL debut with Detroit.

Known as "Ukey" to his friends, due to his Ukrainian heritage, Sawchuk also made three appearances in the playoffs that season, totaling 80 minutes and posting a 4.50 GAA. His final appearance as a Ranger came on April 14 in Game Five of the quarterfinals against the Bruins in Boston. With the Rangers trailing in the third period, Francis wanted to slow the pace of the game and replaced Giacomin with Sawchuk. After allowing Terry the league-mandated warmup period, Giacomin returned to the net at the next faceoff. The Rangers ultimately lost the game, 3–2, and the series in six games.

Tragically, six weeks later Terry Sawchuk was dead.

Sawchuk and teammate Ron Stewart had rented a house in Atlantic Beach, Long Island, where most of the Rangers stayed during the season. The two were old friends, having previously won Stanley Cups and roomed together in Toronto. They had a lot in common. Both were divorced, liked to drink, and were known to become belligerent when drinking.

The trouble began on April 29, thirteen days after the Rangers were eliminated from the playoffs. Stewart and Sawchuk were drinking at the E & J Pub, a local hangout that the players frequented. The pair began to argue about whose responsibility it was to clean the house before returning the keys to the owner. Stewart also claimed that Sawchuk owed him some money for household expenses. They began pushing each other in the bar and were asked to leave. The argument continued outside the bar until the bartender told them to go home. They each drove separately back to the house at 58 Bay Street where they started arguing again on the lawn in front of two witnesses, Stewart's girlfriend, Rosemary Sasso, a registered nurse, and Ben Weiner, a friend of Sawchuk's. Sawchuk moved to grab Stewart but was pulled back by Weiner. The two men stumbled and fell on Stewart. It is not known whether Sawchuk fell on Stewart's knee or a barbeque grill, but he immediately doubled over in pain. Seeing that Terry was in distress, Sasso called Dr. Dennis Nicholson, who found Sawchuk pale, in shock, and with very low blood pressure.

Sawchuk was taken to Long Beach Hospital where tests revealed that he had suffered damage to his gall bladder and liver. He then underwent surgery to remove his gall bladder. A few days later he had another operation to repair his liver.

Terry was in the hospital for three weeks before the story was broken on May 22 by Gerry Eskenazi of the *New York Times*. There were rumors of a cover-up, but Terry didn't want anyone to know because his father was in a Detroit hospital recovering from an automobile accident and he didn't want him to worry about him.

Sawchuk took a turn for the worse on May 29 and was transferred to New York Hospital, which specialized in acute illnesses. Tests found internal bleeding and he once again underwent surgery to further repair his liver.

Following the surgery, Sawchuk regained consciousness briefly but died in his sleep from a blood clot on May 31.

"The whole Sawchuk affair was one of the toughest things I had ever faced in my whole life," recalled Emile Francis. "I was out scouting in Quebec and I had to go to the hospital. He underwent a five-hour operation that lasted until midnight and the doctor came out and said, 'You might as well go home because there's nothing you can do here. We'll call you if anything changes.' They called me at six in the morning to tell me he died."

"I'll never forget it was Memorial Day weekend in New York and I had to go to get his body from the morgue on Second Avenue. And honest to God, there were thirty people lying on the floor in bags like we carry hockey sticks in. The guy that took me down there, I could tell he'd been drinking, I could smell it. He said, 'Okay, which one is the body you came to claim?' I mean I could have nailed him right there. I looked over and I see Terry's head sticking out from one of the bags with a tag around his neck to identify him. God damn, that's where he ended up, on the floor in a morgue in New York City on Memorial Day weekend. And I said to myself, 'If this guy only knew that's the greatest goalkeeper ever.' I mean I was sick, believe me."

According to Francis, "Terry was one of the greatest, maybe even the greatest. But you just never know in real life. It was a tragedy that far transcended hockey."

Regular Season

Season	Team	GP	W	L	T	GA	GAA	SO	MIN	G	A	PTS	PIM
1949–50	DET	7	4	3	0	16	2.29	1	420	0	0	0	0
1950–51	DET	70	44	13	13	138	1.97	11	4200	0	0	0	2
1951–52	DET	70	44	14	12	133	1.90	12	4200	0	0	0	2
1952–53	DET	63	32	15	16	119	1.89	9	3780	0	0	0	7
1953–54	DET	67	35	19	13	129	1.93	12	4004	0	1	1	31
1954–55	DET	68	40	17	11	132	1.96	12	4040	0	1	1	10
1955–56	BOS	68	22	33	13	177	2.60	9	4078	0	0	0	20

Season	Team	GP	W	L	T	GA	GAA	SO	MIN	G	A	PTS	PIM
1956–57	BOS	34	18	10	6	81	2.38	2	2040	0	0	0	16
1957–58	DET	70	29	29	12	206	2.94	3	4198	0	0	0	31
1958–59	DET	67	23	36	8	207	3.09	5	4019	0	0	0	12
1959–60	DET	58	24	20	14	154	2.66	5	3476	0	0	0	22
1960–61	DET	37	11	17	8	112	3.13	2	2148	0	1	1	8
1961–62	DET	43	14	21	8	141	3.28	5	2580	0	0	0	12
1962–63	DET	48	21	16	7	117	2.54	3	2760	0	0	0	14
1963–64	DET	53	25	20	7	138	2.64	5	3139	0	0	0	0
1964–65	TOR	36	16	13	7	92	2.56	1	2160	0	2	2	24
1965–66	TOR	27	10	11	3	80	3.16	1	1519	0	1	1	12
1966–67	TOR	28	16	6	3	66	2.81	2	1409	0	0	0	2
1967–68	LAK	36	10	17	5	99	3.07	2	1934	0	0	0	0
1968–69	DET	13	4	5	3	28	2.63	0	640	0	0	0	0
1969–70	NYR	8	3	1	2	20	2.91	1	412	0	1	1	0
NYR Totals	-	8	3	1	2	20	2.91	1	412	0	1	1	0
Career	-	971	445	336	171	2385	2.50	103	57,156	0	7	7	225

Playoffs

Season	Team	GP	W	L	T	GA	GAA	SO	MIN	G	A	PTS	PIM
1950–51	DET	6	2	4	-	13	1.68	1	463	0	0	0	0
1951–52	DET	8	8	0	-	5	0.62	4	480	0	0	0	0
1952–53	DET	6	2	4	-	21	3.38	1	372	0	0	0	10
1953–54	DET	12	8	4	-	20	1.60	2	751	0	0	0	2
1954–55	DET	11	8	3	-	26	2.36	1	660	0	0	0	12
1957–58	DET	4	0	4	-	19	4.53	0	252	0	0	0	0
1959–60	DET	6	2	4	-	19	2.82	0	405	0	0	0	0
1960–61	DET	8	5	3	-	18	2.32	1	465	0	0	0	0
1962–63	DET	11	5	6	-	35	3.18	0	660	0	0	0	0
1963–64	DET	13	6	5	-	31	2.75	1	677	0	0	0	2
1964–65	TOR	1	0	1	-	3	3.00	0	60	0	0	0	0
1965–66	TOR	2	0	2	-	6	3.00	0	120	0	0	0	0
1966–67	TOR	10	6	4	-	25	2.66	0	563	0	0	0	0
1967–68	LAK	5	2	3	-	18	3.86	1	280	0	0	0	0
1969–70	NYR	3	0	1	-	6	4.51	0	80	0	0	0	0
NYR Totals	-	3	0	1	-	6	4.51	0	80	0	0	0	0
Career	-	106	54	48	-	265	2.53	12	6288	0	0	0	26

Fast Fact: Terry Sawchuk was ranked Number 1 in *The Hockey News*'s Top 100 Goalies of All-Time publication in 2018. He is one of nineteen goalies on their list who have worn the Rangers uniform at some point of their career. The other eighteen are: Jacques Plante (No. 4), Lorne Chabot (No. 20), Johnny Bower (No. 22), Henrik Lundqvist (No. 24), Gump Worsley (No. 25), Harry Lumley (No. 28), Ed Giacomin (No. 30), Chuck Rayner (No. 37), John Vanbiesbrouck (No. 42), Mike Richter (No. 43), Davey Kerr (No. 44), Al Rollins (No. 49), John Ross Roach (No. 50), Jim Henry (No. 79), Kirk McLean (No. 82), Cesare Maniago (No. 86), Guy Hebert (No. 94), Don Simmons (No. 99).

Peter McDuffe
Born: February 16, 1948 in Milton, Ontario
5-9, 180lb
Caught: Left
Rangers Debut: December 10, 1972 vs. New York Islanders
Uniform #31
Seasons with Rangers: 2, 1972–73 to 1973–74

Peter McDuffe came up through the Chicago organization playing for the St. Catharines Black Hawks and led the OHA with a 2.93 GAA in 1966–67. In June 1969 he was left unprotected by the Black Hawks and claimed by Phoenix of the Western Hockey League in the reverse draft. However, a few weeks later he was sent to the Rangers in exchange for goaltender Don Caley and winger Sandy Snow. Assigned to Omaha by the Rangers, he led the CHL with 26 victories and was named a Second Team All-Star. The next year he was a First Team All-Star and shared MVP honors with Andre Dupont, Gerry Ouellette, and Joe Zanussi.

In May 1971 he was traded to St. Louis for the Blues' first-round draft pick in the 1971 entry draft. The Rangers used that draft pick to select Steve Vickers but there was much more to the deal than met the eye.

"I was carrying three goalkeepers and I couldn't trade McDuffe anywhere," recalled Emile Francis. "I was looking to get a first-round draft pick for him and St. Louis was one of my favorite trading partners at that time. So they agreed to take McDuffe for their first-round draft choice but with one little consideration. They said, 'Whoever you take with that first-round draft pick, if at the end of next year we decide we don't want to keep McDuffe we can give him back to you for the guy you took with our draft choice."

"So I traded McDuffe to St. Louis and he played there all year," Francis continued, "and at the end of the season Sid Solomon's son, who was making all the deals with me said, 'Well, we had a deal with you and you took Steve Vickers with our draft choice.' We had Vickers playing in Omaha and he was playing great. He said, 'There's only one way we would consider not taking Vickers back. You've got a big, tough defenseman down in Omaha named Steve Durbano.' So when he said Durbano I thought, What the hell? So I said well I can't trade him. Christ if I trade him, they'll run me right out of New York. He's a big, tough guy, just what we're looking for. So he said would you give that some thought? So I said, yeah let me think about it and I'll get back to you tomorrow.

"So I called my manager in Omaha, Jake Milford, and I said, 'Jake, has St. Louis had anyone around scouting?' He said, 'Oh yeah they've been following us around for about a month. Yeah, they sent a scout down here and he goes behind our goal when we're at one end and moves down to the other end of the ice when we go down there.' So I said, well shit, he can't be looking at the goalkeeper because he's not going to the National Hockey League, so they were looking at Durbano.

So I went back to them the next day and said I've been thinking about your deal for me to trade Durbano. I'm going to need more than McDuffe. I need Curt Bennett and a cash outlay of 20 grand and Vickers. He said you've got it. I thought, holy shit I got Vickers back, Curt Bennett, 20 grand and McDuffe for Steve Durbano! So now the next season, the first time St. Louis comes into the Garden, Vickers has a hat trick. So I spent extra time with the press because I knew that Solomon was going to be waiting for me. I finally leave the press room and I hear 'Emile!' So I turn to my left and there's Sid Solomon Jr. the acting general manager and his dad who's a fine guy and he says, 'That Vickers is quite a hockey player isn't he?' So I said well we had a lucky night tonight. He's playing with two great players,

Tkaczuk and Fairbairn. So he says, 'Oh is that right?' So I got the hell out of there. But we had a deal and he could've gotten Vickers back from me but when he sprung Durbano on me I had to take a couple of steps back."

McDuffe appeared in only seven games over two seasons with the Rangers, posting a 4–2–1 record with a respectable 2.85 GAA. He was then claimed by Kansas City in the 1974 expansion draft and played in 36 games for the woeful Scouts. But he lost his job when Kansas City acquired Denis Herron from Pittsburgh so he was traded to the Detroit Red Wings. McDuffe spent most of his time with the Wings' AHL affiliate then appeared in 12 games with the WHA's Indianapolis Racers before retiring in 1978.

Regular Season

Season	Team	League	GP	W	L	T	GA	GAA	SO	MIN	G	A	PTS	PIM
1971–72	STL	NHL	10	0	6	0	29	3.69	0	471	0	0	0	0
1972–73	NYR	NHL	1	1	0	0	1	1.00	0	60	0	0	0	0
1973–74	NYR	NHL	6	3	2	1	18	3.18	0	340	0	0	0	0
1974–75	KCS	NHL	36	7	25	4	148	4.23	0	2098	0	1	1	0
1975–76	DET	NHL	4	0	3	1	22	5.53	0	239	0	0	0	2
1977–78	INR	WHA	12	-	-	-	39	4.34	0	539	0	0	0	0
NYR Totals	-	NHL	7	4	2	1	19	2.85	0	400	0	0	0	0
Career	-	NHL	57	11	36	6	218	4.08	0	3208	0	1	1	2
Career	-	WHA	12	-	-	-	39	4.34	0	539	0	0	0	0

Playoffs

Season	Team	League	GP	W	L	T	GA	GAA	SO	MIN	G	A	PTS	PIM
1971–72	STL	NHL	1	0	1	-	7	7.00	0	60	0	0	0	0
Career	STL	NHL	1	0	1	-	7	7.00	0	60	0	0	0	0

Curt Ridley
Born: September 24, 1951 in Minnedosa, Manitoba
6-0, 180lb
Caught: Left
Rangers Debut: December 19, 1974 at Boston Bruins
Uniform #35, 31
Seasons with Rangers 1, 1974–75

Courtesy of Jay Moran

Curt Ridley had the misfortune of trying to break into the NHL, first with the Bruins and then the Rangers, at a time when both teams were well-stocked in goal.

Curt began his hockey journey like most Canadian kids playing on outdoor rinks in frigid temperatures. "In Canada that's what we do in the winter," recalled Ridley. "My dad was in the armed forces, the Air Force and we always had the greatest recreational complexes. When I was very young though it was always outdoors. But that's just what we did, 20, 30 below on outside rinks. I never played goal until I was twelve. I played for the Province of Quebec in a Pee-Wee international tournament. I played defense and when we moved to Manitoba they started a Junior A team and I tried out as a defenseman because I had been playing out for many years but realized quite shortly that, 'ain't gonna make the club.' So I went and stood over by the goaltenders and became the number one goalie. I was just in the right place at the right time."

Ridley began his junior career with the Portage Terriers of the Manitoba Junior Hockey League in 1968–69, playing 68 games over two seasons and posting a 3.31 GAA as well as five shutouts. He also played five games for the Brandon Wheat Kings of the Western Hockey League in 1970–71, posting an impressive 2.81 GAA.

Curt was then selected by the Boston Bruins in the second round (28th overall) of the 1971 amateur draft. The only problem was that the Bruins already had Gerry Cheevers and Ed Johnston and the odds of unseating one of those veterans were slim.

"Don't forget they also had Ross Brooks and Dan Bouchard," Ridley added. "They had a few goaltenders in front of me and being just a kid with no experience I knew it was going to be a tough road. But the

Bruins organization treated me very well. My first pro training camp with Boston, believe it or not a lot of times at night we'd get three or four of the other guys together and play Monopoly. Now figure that out, okay? And my first roommate in training camp with Boston was Ace Bailey. I tell you it broke my heart on 9/11, broke my heart. Great guy, just a fantastic dude." [Garnet "Ace" Bailey and Bruin scout Mark Bavis were passengers on United Airlines Flight 175 when it crashed into the World Trade Center in New York during the September 11, 2001 attacks.]

Curt never got to play for Boston, tending goal for the Bruins' farm clubs in Oklahoma City and Dayton instead. But in June 1973 Ridley was claimed by the Rangers in the reverse draft and assigned to the Providence Reds of the AHL.

"When the Bruins left me unprotected and I was selected by the Rangers I got a call from Dennis Ball who was the chief scout and he called and said, 'Welcome to the Rangers,' I said, 'Oh okay,' I knew Giacomin and Villemure were there and I thought here we go again, except, instead of five goalies in front of me in a way I guess there were only two. So things were looking up. The Rangers treated me fantastic and I loved Providence. The coach in Providence at the time was a guy named Johnny Muckler. Great guy and he also coached me later on down the road with the Dallas Black Hawks. But Providence was a great town."

Ridley made his NHL debut with the Rangers on December 19, 1974, in Boston under less than ideal circumstances. The Rangers brought nine players up from Providence to fill in for regulars who were under the weather and Curt was one of them. Curt got the start that night and wound up sharing a Rangers record that still stands today, although not one that he cares to remember. He surrendered four goals in the first period and two more in the first 43 seconds of the second period. But wait, that wasn't the record! The Bruins scored a record five goals in two minutes and 55 seconds against Curt and Eddie Giacomin. First Boston's Bobby Schmautz scored at 19:13 of the first period. Then Ken Hodge scored 18 seconds into the second period followed by a goal by Phil Esposito 23 seconds later. Giacomin then came in to replace the beleaguered Ridley and promptly surrendered a goal to Don

Marcotte 15 seconds after that. Johnny Bucyk then scored at 2:08 to set the record.

"If I remember correctly and it's close to 40 years, I think the flu bug was going around. Because quite a few of the Rangers were out, and I think Villemure had the flu. It was a great experience but to this day I still have nightmares. What was the score 10-something? 11-something? The Cat pulled me after six and Giacomin went in and they pumped some by him so I didn't feel that bad."

The Bruins won the game, 11–3, outshooting the Rangers, 44–16. Was it fair to be thrown into that situation as a rookie playing his first NHL game? "Not under that situation. No, not really," said Ridley. "Being limited with the Rangers players, their star players being out and Boston had a full blown out squad. I think [Bobby] Orr scored two on me, Espo scored two on me and Greg Sheppard."

Emile Francis later spoke to reporters about starting the rookie. "We've been thinking about playing Ridley a long time. There was no better place to play him than just 45 minutes from Providence. It's important for a goalie to get used to a defense and he had four of his buddies from Providence with him. He was the Lone Ranger in the first period. I took him out like you would take a pitcher out in baseball. I told him he played real well." "Emile was like a father figure to everybody. He just said, 'Man it was a tough one. Keep your chin up and don't worry about it. Stuff happens,'" Curt recalled.

Curt got another start 10 days later and beat the Kansas City Scouts, 2–1, at the Garden. "He gave me another shot and I should have had a shutout. Should have! But I think it was Simon Nolet. He put one over, I think it was my right side high in the corner. I should have had it. That would have been great; it could have redeemed myself in my own mind."

On September 9, 1975, Ridley was dealt to the Atlanta Flames for forward Jerry Byers, But once again he was third on the depth chart, this time behind Dan Bouchard and Phil Myre. So Curt ended up playing in Tulsa of the Central Hockey League where he had a very good year and won the Terry Sawchuk Trophy for allowing the fewest goals in the league.

"I was fortunate enough to be playing in Tulsa and Orland

Kurtenbach was the coach. I would imagine that he had a lot to do with it. The players in front of me were just fantastic and the next thing I knew I was in Vancouver."

The next year Curt was sent to Vancouver for the Canucks' first-round pick in the 1976 amateur draft. While with the Canucks, Curt played two games against Russian teams, shutting out Spartak Moscow, 2–0, in 1978 and beating Dynamo Moscow, 6–2, in 1980.

"I enjoyed playing against the Russians in Vancouver, Curt proudly recalled. "We played against them twice and I'm very happy to say that we were undefeated."

While in the Vancouver organization, Curt spent a good part of the 1978–79 season with the Dallas Black Hawks, leading them to the Adams Cup as CHL champions. He also won the Max McNab Trophy as playoff MVP that year. He played 96 games over four seasons with the Canucks and was then sent to Toronto for cash in February of 1980.

"I got hurt and Jake Milford [Vancouver GM] sent me back down to Dallas. He said, 'You're going down for two weeks to get yourself back in shape.' I said, 'Okay, that's fine.' Two weeks went by and I called him and said, 'Jake, what's happening?' Both goaltenders in Vancouver were playing very well at the time. I can understand that. He said, 'You stay down there for another week.' A week later I called again, and he said, 'No, no, no you stay down there.' So I asked him if he minded if I made some phone calls and try to make a deal for myself to get out of Vancouver. He said, 'No not at all.' So I made some calls and was sold to Toronto. I really enjoyed myself in Toronto, one of the Original Six teams like the Rangers and Bruins. And as a kid I always wanted to play in Toronto. Didn't play there long but I met some great players. You know a lot of players didn't get along with Punch Imlach. Let me tell you, he was the cat's ass. He was just great to me. I have nothing but praise for him. Punch was like in the old Eddie Shore days, either get with the program or hit the road. But it was his butt on the line."

After two seasons with the Maple Leafs, Curt's career wound down in the Central Hockey League in 1982. "I didn't really retire. The season was over and no one contacted me and I didn't contact them so it was over. I just walked away from the game and they walked away from me. I moved back to Winnipeg and worked for MTS where I sold telephone systems and wireless communications. After that, being from Winnipeg the cold got to me and I moved to Dallas, Texas, where I had played before and I've lived here ever since. I go to the Stars games every now and then, but I don't like crowds anymore. Fortunately, my wife works for a guy by the name of Roger Staubach who has a suite and he'll sometimes put the tickets up for sale at a very reduced price and so we watch from a suite."

Ridley posted solid NHL numbers but due to circumstances he became a true journeyman goaltender, playing for 13 teams in six leagues in a 12-year career. But he has no regrets. "As a player I was average, maybe a little less. But I had my moments, I also had some bad moments. I didn't think I'd ever play in the NHL, so it was all a plus. I met great people on and off the ice. I met some great booster club people who were just fantastic. It was a great experience playing against Bobby Orr, [Phil] Esposito, [Marcel] Dionne, [Lanny] McDonald, I could go on and on, it was a kid's dream. I played against Gordie Howe for God's sake. It was a dream that had come true."

Regular Season

Season	Team	GP	W	L	T	GA	GAA	SO	MIN	G	A	PTS	PIM
1974–75	NYR	2	1	1	0	7	5.19	0	81	0	0	0	0
1975–76	VAN	9	6	0	2	19	2.28	1	500	0	0	0	0
1976–77	VAN	37	8	21	4	134	3.88	0	2070	0	0	0	4
1977–78	VAN	40	9	17	8	136	4.07	0	2007	0	1	1	9
1979–80	VAN	10	2	6	2	39	3.93	0	595	0	0	0	0
1979–80	TOR	3	0	1	0	8	4.38	0	109	0	0	0	2
1980–81	TOR	3	1	1	0	12	5.80	0	124	0	0	0	2
NYR Totals	-	2	1	1	0	7	5.19	0	81	0	0	0	0
Career	-	104	27	47	16	355	3.88	1	5486	0	1	1	17

Playoffs

Season	Team	GP	W	L	T	GA	GAA	SO	MIN	G	A	PTS	PIM
1975–76	VAN	2	0	2	-	8	4.03	0	119	0	0	0	0
Career	VAN	2	0	2	-	8	4.03	0	119	0	0	0	0

Dunc Wilson
Born: March 22, 1948 in Toronto, Ontario
5-11, 175lb
Caught: Left
Rangers Debut: March 7, 1975 at Kansas City Scouts
Uniform #1, 31
Seasons with Rangers 2, 1974–75 to 1975–76

Emile Francis picked up Dunc Wilson on waivers from Toronto in February 1975 as insurance in case either Ed Giacomin or Gilles Villemure, who were both in their mid-thirties, went down with injuries.

Wilson began his hockey career in the OHL playing for Oshawa, Niagara Falls, and Peterborough. He was claimed by Philadelphia from Boston, who held his rights in a special internal amateur draft in June 1968 and turned pro with the Quebec Aces of the AHL in 1968. He played one game for the Flyers during the 1969–70 season and was claimed by Vancouver in the 1970 expansion draft.

In Vancouver he shared the goaltending chores that first season with veterans Charlie Hodge and George Gardner, but took over the number one spot the next two seasons. He recorded the first shutout in Canucks history in a scoreless tie with Toronto and Bernie Parent in October 1971. It was also Wilson's first career shutout.

On May 29, 1973, Wilson was traded to Toronto for Larry McIntyre and Murray Heatley. He stayed with the Maple Leafs for two seasons, sharing the crease with Doug Favell and Eddie Johnston among others. He was then placed on waivers on February 15, 1975, and claimed by the Rangers. Wilson saw action in three games at the end of the 1974–75 season, but made 20 appearances the next season when John Ferguson took over the Blueshirts.

Wilson is at least partially responsible for Rangers radio broadcaster Sal Messina's nickname of "Red Light" which was bestowed upon him by play-by-play man Marv Albert.

"We were out in Oakland one time, the Rangers had played in Toronto and from there they were going to Oakland," Messina recalled. "Dunc Wilson was in goal and the fans were calling him 'Red Light.' After the game [Rangers beat writer] Hugh Delano put that in the

[New York] *Post*. Now every goalie has been called 'Red Light' at one time or another, even back when we played with chicken wire instead of glass. So Dunc says to Delano, 'You shouldn't put that in the papers, my wife will think I'm fooling around.' So then Delano finds out about the other meaning of 'Red Light' and we had a big laugh. So he tells that story to Marv in Oakland while we were having lunch. That night we go on the air and he says, 'This is Marv Albert with Sal "Red Light" Messina.' And from that day on whenever we went on the air that's what he called me. Nobody else called me that, not Kenny Albert, or Sam Rosen. Just Marv. But it stuck."

Wilson was subsequently traded to Pittsburgh in October 1976 for a fourth-round draft pick that the Rangers used to select Dave Silk in 1978. He stayed with the Penguins for two seasons before finishing up his career back in Vancouver in 1978–79.

Regular Season

Season	Team	GP	W	L	T	GA	GAA	SO	MIN	G	A	PTS	PIM
1969–70	PHI	1	0	1	0	3	3.02	0	60	0	0	0	0
1970–71	VAN	35	3	25	2	128	4.30	0	1784	0	0	0	18
1971–72	VAN	53	16	30	3	173	3.62	1	2864	0	0	0	15
1972–73	VAN	43	13	21	5	159	3.94	1	2418	0	1	1	6
1973–74	TOR	24	9	11	3	68	2.91	1	1403	0	0	0	6
1974–75	TOR	25	8	11	4	86	3.71	0	1391	0	0	0	6
1974–75	NYR	3	1	2	0	13	4.35	0	179	0	0	0	0
1975–76	NYR	20	5	9	3	76	4.24	0	1076	0	0	0	11
1976–77	PIT	45	18	19	7	129	2.95	5	2622	0	1	1	21
1977–78	PIT	21	5	11	3	95	4.84	0	1179	0	1	1	0
1978–79	VAN	17	2	10	2	58	4.17	0	834	0	1	1	0
NYR Totals	-	23	6	11	3	89	4.25	0	1255	0	0	0	11
Career	-	287	80	150	32	988	3.75	8	15,810	0	4	4	83

John Davidson—Franchise Goaltender
Born: February 27, 1953 in Ottawa, Ontario
6-3, 205lb
Caught: Left
Rangers Debut: October 10, 1975 at Atlanta Flames
Uniform #35, 00, 30
Seasons with Rangers: 8, 1975–76 to 1982–83

Courtesy of Ken Tash

John Arthur Davidson was the St. Louis Blues' first-round pick (fifth overall) in the 1973 amateur draft following four strong seasons with Calgary of the WCJHL which included being named league MVP in his final season in 1972–73. The son of a Canadian Mounted Policeman, Davidson went directly from juniors to the NHL and became one of the leading candidates for the NHL's Rookie of the Year award. Unfortunately, he was hampered by a knee injury late in the season and the award eventually went to Denis Potvin of the Islanders.

At 6-foot-3 and 200 pounds, the twenty-two-year-old Davidson took up a lot of net, yet he was also extremely agile for a big man. He showed great promise in his first two years in St. Louis, posting an overall 3.37 GAA in 79 games for the offensively minded Blues. But during the summer of 1975 the Blues had acquired Gilles Gratton, a young netminder playing for the Toronto Toros of the WHA and selected goaltender Ed Staniowski in the first round of the amateur draft, making Davidson expendable.

Davidson was dealt to the Rangers along with winger Bill Collins in exchange for three of the Rangers' toughest players, Jerry Butler, Ted Irvine, and Bert Wilson on June 18, 1975. With both Ed Giacomin and Gilles Villemure getting on in years, GM Emile Francis knew that he had to start thinking about replacing them and "JD" was the best young netminder in the league. Davidson soon inherited the starting job when both Giacomin and Villemure departed early in the 1975–76 season.

"When I got traded to the Rangers I was a little surprised," said Davidson. "Even though in my second-year pro I wasn't very good. But my junior coach in Calgary was a guy named Scotty Monroe and he was pretty close to Emile Francis. They knew each other from

Saskatchewan over the years. So I suspect that Emile reached out and got a scouting report on me. And then once I got to New York, I was pretty excited. New York, an Original Six team, that whole thing. But when you go anywhere in the NHL you have to fight for your job, that's just how it is. And obviously with Eddie and Gilles there, they were two established, terrific goaltenders, and I had to go battle. And I ended up having a pretty good camp and a real good start and the next thing I knew Gilles was moved to Chicago and Eddie was moved to Detroit so it opened up for me. The Rangers were becoming a very young team and I was part of that youth movement. But Eddie and Gilles were both exceptional guys to be around. And even though we were all in the same position they were guys that would do anything to help you when you needed it. They were both really good team people and that was something that when you get into pro hockey and you're young, and you don't know a lot about it, it teaches you a lesson that when it's your turn to move on that you help people and those two guys were really good that way."

Davidson was under a lot of pressure coming into New York, being asked to replace the legendary Eddie Giacomin who had long been a fan favorite.

But the Garden fans warmed up to the young goaltender. "The fans were always good to me. I know when Eddie came back and he got the win, that was a special time for him and it gave the fans a chance to show how much he meant to them, and rightly so. I talked to Eddie after that game and he was really supportive to me personally and I'll never forget that. My only regret is that I never stayed healthy enough over the years because I think I had more to offer, but the fans are great in New York. If you give it everything and you play well that's all they need. If you don't, they'll let you know.

That's the culture in New York and as an athlete you have to learn to deal with that and if you can do it, it makes you a better human being and a better athlete. And I think that's what I learned when I was there, even in the TV world. It was great. There's only one New York in the universe."

Davidson appeared in a career-high 56 games his first season in New York, posting a 22–28–5 record with three shutouts and a 3.97

GAA for a Ranger team that was transitioning from the leadership of Emile Francis to the John Ferguson era.

According to Davidson, "When Emile left and Fergy came in, I had been in St. Louis and we had been through a number of coaches and general managers and that was only over my first two years, so I had gotten used to changes. But it's always shocking. I remember when Emile left I went over to his house in Long Beach and wished him all the best. He's a hell of a team guy. I worked with Emile on the Hall of Fame selection committee for years. I have a lot of respect for that man. He did a lot of good things that no one knows about. And then when Fergy came in, he was very similar—competitive, team-oriented battlers. But those are things we as players live with and deal with. We have no control, but that was when they were turning the franchise over and getting younger players."

During his second year with the Blueshirts, GM John Ferguson redesigned the traditional Rangers uniform and "JD" changed his number from 35 to 00, becoming the first NHL goaltender to do so. Davidson always claimed that it was Phil Esposito's idea. Espo wanted to wear 77 because his familiar number 7 was already taken by Rod Gilbert and talked JD into wearing 00.

"In hindsight, what was I thinking? said Davidson. "But it was more for Espo. He came to me and asked me about it and I said I'll support you any way I can. Rod Gilbert wore number 7 in New York and he was a legend. Phil wore number 7 in Boston and he was a legend, so the 77 thing happened. He asked me to help him and I was young. so I said absolutely. It was interesting. I'd get quite a few catcalls on the road, but that's okay. We got over it and got through it. But my favorite number was 30. I always liked 30."

Davidson did indeed switch to the more familiar number 30 when Fred Shero took over the club in 1978 and brought back the Rangers' traditional uniforms.

The highlight of Davidson's playing career came during the 1979 playoffs when he led the Fred Shero-coached Blueshirts past the Kings, Flyers, and then played the series of his life in beating the heavily-favored Islanders four games to two to advance to the Stanley Cup Finals against Montreal. The Rangers won the first game of the series but unfortunately a knee injury that Davidson aggravated during the Islanders series began acting up and the Blueshirts were swept the next four games by the powerful Canadiens. Yet despite being hampered by a bad knee throughout the later rounds of the playoffs, Davidson still led all playoff netminders in games played (18) and was the only one to post a shutout. He also had a better goals-against average (2.28) and save percentage (.921) than Cup-winner Ken Dryden (2.50, .899).

It was an unforgettable time for Davidson and the Rangers. "We had a good team. We were young and Phil and Carol Vadnais and some of the older players led us along and when you get on a roll it's pretty good. For us to beat Los Angeles, beat the Flyers, beat the Islanders, they had some good players, some good teams. Then we ran into a team in Montreal that must have had a dozen future Hall of Famers [actually, 10]. And I think it should have been at least a six-game series, but it wasn't. The great memories are my teammates, the coaches and how a hockey team can turn on a gigantic city like New York. That city was behind us. I'd wake up in the morning, this was when I lived up in Westchester and there would be gifts on the doorstep from the fans. And then after it was over, they took us downtown to thank the fans and a pretty big crowd showed up. We didn't win it or a real big crowd would have shown up. But that was a team that was exciting, it had some personality, it had a little bit of everything. Our management staff did a great job. An example would be in the Philly series, we lost Game One and then we got a new player. They brought in Bobby Sheehan. I didn't even know who Bobby was and he was great for us. Then we lost Ulfie Nilsson in the Islander series which hurt us. But you think back to the trainers, the coaches, the management, all of us, it was a real team effort.

Freddie Shero was the coach and he and his support system, Mike Nykoluk and that, found a way to get us to do things. It was always a little bit different but that's okay, I respect that. I think if you're a player and you're worth your salt and you play for different people and different coaches in different cities you take the best of each of them and it gives you a chance to be better at what you do. Those are memories I'll never forget. I think that was one of the great hockey memories of New York City. Obviously the 1994 team was special, but that 1979 team, I still have people coming up to me and asking about that in my travels. I remember ABC wanted to televise the seventh game across the country with Howard Cosell if we got there but we didn't and that would have been even better for the game. But we had the support of the entire city, millions and millions of people. People who didn't watch hockey were watching. It was awesome. I had a good run, my knee acted up late in the playoffs and that hurt us, but I was part of a good team that had a lot of fun that just got on a roll. That was special. There's nothing better than getting on a playoff roll."

That roll continued into Game One of the finals against Montreal where the Blueshirts won, 4–1. Unfortunately, the Rangers' run of good fortune ended abruptly and they went on to lose the next four games as the Canadiens won the Stanley Cup.

"We had a lead in Game Two, then they changed goalies and got a fluke goal and Dryden got better," remembered Davidson. "And my knee wasn't helpful. If we would have pushed that to six games, it would have been at home and who knows? To look at their personnel and where they were in their careers, they were a great hockey club, and we played hard."

In 1978, Davidson became the inspiration for the title of Foreigner's hit song "Double Vision." Members of the band were watching a game between the Rangers and the Buffalo Sabres when Davidson took a puck in the mask and had to leave the game. Later, broadcasters Jim Gordon and Bill Chadwick began talking about how Davidson was suffering from double vision. The name stuck and the song rose to number two on the Billboard charts and became a gold record.

Chronic back problems as well as four knee operations (two on each knee) severely limited Davidson's playing time during the last three seasons of his career and he retired in 1983 at the age of thirty.

Following his retirement Davidson became an analyst on Rangers broadcasts in 1983. He then spent two seasons working for *Hockey Night in Canada* before returning to the Rangers booth in 1986 where he was paired with Sam Rosen for more than 20 years. He also worked nationally televised regular season, playoff and all-star games as well as the Olympics for ABC, ESPN, CBS, and NBC.

During his broadcasting career, "JD" became known for punctuating the action on the ice with a well-timed "Oh Baby!" to emphasize a surprising play.

"I don't know where that came from, it just started," said Davidson. "It was just a reaction, just having fun. You do the games and you know you've got people watching who are rabid fans and you want to connect with them and have fun. A lot of times, there are people in this industry who take it so seriously. You want to do your job, you want to tell a story, and teach people about players—how they play the game, what kind of people they are, where they're from and then you want to have fun with it, and that's one thing we did, we had fun. Joe Whelan was our producer for the majority of those years, Sam, Al Trautwig, was a brilliant broadcaster. We just had fun. We were like our own team. A hockey team has a coach and a GM and this and that, and a television team has a producer and a director, cameramen, they all fill a need. We'd go on the road and go out together. It was like staying in the game without having to play the game for all those years. And we were very proud of what we did. I think that our network was the best. We were very serious about it, but we enjoyed it. . . . I talk to Sam all the time. Kenny Albert, Red Light Messina, we had a lot of fun together."

The 1993–94 season was an important one for John's broadcasting career. He was an integral part of the MSG Network's Rangers broadcast team that was named winner of the prestigious CableACE award for Outstanding Live Event and the next year Davidson won the New York Emmy Award for Outstanding On-Camera Achievement. But JD also has fond memories of that Stanley Cup winning team and their fans.

"During the season in traveling around and doing games for other networks, I knew the Rangers were the best team in the league and I conveyed that to them. Yet it still was hard, the Devils series in particular, that was one of the all-time great playoff series. Then you think of the Vancouver series. In my estimation that should have been four straight, but next thing you know it's a seven-game series, and probably the biggest thing was the tension in the building late in the seventh game with the two icings, and the faceoff to the right of [Mike] Richter. And then they won and the whole place went nuts! And there's that photo of Mark [Messier] jumping in the air. There were a lot of great players on that team and they each did their part, but Mark brought a belief to that city when Neil [Smith] got him and there was something in Mark Messier that proved that he could fight the odds and help lead a team to win a championship for New York City. So you put that whole year together, see how they fought the battles and found ways to win. There were injuries late, Vancouver was a big, physical hockey club and the longer it went the tougher it was. Pat Quinn against Mike Keenan, that was a battle in itself. Then once it was over to this day I couldn't be more proud of the city of New York because when they won that championship everybody celebrated on the street and then they had more than a million people down at the "Canyon of Heroes" and there wasn't one arrest and I'll tell you I look at some places and people are arrested and they break windows and burn cars, My God! New York City, it was so special. There's so much support in New York for the Rangers, longtime ticket holders, people who work for the team, I thought they deserved to win because they were the better team. But nothing's easy. That's why we play. And they had to fight their way through it and when it was over, it was very gratifying for those guys, It was a great time, very special people—Mike Richter, Brian Leetch, Adam Graves, Stephane Matteau, all those guys, [Sergei] Zubov, Kevin Lowe, Steve Larmer was outstanding. That was a good team."

In 2009, Davidson was honored by the Hockey Hall of Fame with the Foster Hewitt Memorial Award for his contributions to broadcasting. Sam Rosen, his longtime Rangers broadcasting partner, joined him in the Hall seven years later.

Looking back at his broadcasting career, Davidson says, "When I look at that I had a chance to stay in the game and get involved with television, thankfully with both Madison Square Garden Network and Hockey Night in Canada, then back to the Garden. And they had the foresight to allow us to work for other networks for playoffs, or All-Star games or Olympics, and they were very open about that and they gave you a chance to go and do your thing. But that also means you're away a lot. You're working so when you have something like the Hall of Fame you have a chance to say thanks to a lot of people: all the producers and directors, executives, cameramen and you also have the chance to say thanks to your family because you miss birthdays and things along those lines. So to go and have a celebration for a few days in Toronto, and go through the process and then see your plaque, it's pretty good. And then to see some of the others, like Sam go in, that to me is outstanding."

Even though Davidson's Ranger career was relatively brief, his stellar play and longtime association with the Rangers and their fans has earned him franchise goaltender status.

Davidson left the Rangers in 2006 to become president of the St. Louis Blues. He then moved to the Columbus Blue Jackets in the same capacity in 2012 before returning to the Garden in May 2019 as president of the Rangers.

While he was away from New York, he fondly recalled the experience of being part of the Rangers family: "The 1979 playoff run and being a part of the 1994 team, broadcasting with Sam and the network were certainly highlights. And more than that, being a young, green guy and being somewhat startled by New York and being able to handle it, learn it and make lifelong friends, and have an understanding of what New York's about and have a great life there for twenty-eight years. That was a fabulous part of my life. I'd recommend it to anybody, I tell everybody, if you ever have a chance to play in New York, do it! It's the greatest experience in the world."

Regular Season

Season	Team	GP	W	L	T	GA	GAA	SO	MIN	G	A	PTS	PIM
1973–74	STL	39	13	19	7	118	3.08	0	2297	0	0	0	10
1974–75	STL	40	17	15	7	144	3.66	0	2358	0	2	2	8
1975–76	NYR	56	22	28	5	212	3.97	3	3200	0	2	2	8
1976–77	NYR	39	14	14	6	125	3.55	1	2115	0	0	0	6
1977–78	NYR	34	14	13	4	98	3.18	1	1846	0	0	0	10
1978–79	NYR	39	20	12	5	131	3.53	0	2227	0	0	0	12
1979–80	NYR	41	20	15	4	122	3.18	2	2299	0	2	2	2
1980–81	NYR	10	1	7	1	48	5.17	0	557	0	1	1	2
1981–82	NYR	1	1	0	0	1	1.00	0	60	0	0	0	2
1982–83	NYR	2	1	1	0	5	2.50	0	120	0	0	0	0
NYR Totals	-	222	93	90	25	742	3.58	7	12,424	0	5	5	42
Career	-	301	123	124	39	1004	3.53	7	17,079	0	7	7	60

Playoffs

Season	Team	GP	W	L	T	GA	GAA	SO	MIN	G	A	PTS	PIM
1974–75	STL	1	0	1	-	4	4.06	0	59	0	0	0	0
1977–78	NYR	2	1	1	-	7	3.46	0	122	0	0	0	0
1978–79	NYR	18	11	7	-	42	2.28	1	1104	0	0	0	6
1979–80	NYR	9	4	5	-	21	2.35	0	537	0	0	0	0
1981–82	NYR	1	0	0	-	3	5.43	0	33	0	0	0	0
NYR Totals	-	30	16	13	-	73	2.44	1	1796	0	0	0	6
Career	-	31	16	14	-	77	2.49	1	1855	0	0	0	6

Double-Zero: Former Ranger Martin Biron also wore number 00 for three games when he was first called up by the Buffalo Sabres during the 1995–96 season. In 1998, the NHL ruled that the number could no longer be used.

CHAPTER SEVEN

John Ferguson's Brief Reign

Following a long stretch of relative stability under Emile Francis, the Rangers proceeded to burn through four general managers and eight coaches in the next 13 seasons.

First up was John Bowie Ferguson, who was offered the Rangers' coaching job by Francis during the summer of 1975. Fergy had gained exposure while serving as assistant coach and assistant GM for Team Canada in 1972, impressing many with his upbeat attitude even when the Russians dominated early in the eight-game Summit Series. He turned Francis down, however, supposedly because he wanted to keep an eye on his investment in the Montreal professional lacrosse franchise. He had also been offered coaching positions by the Bruins, Blues, Kings, Canucks, and the Toronto Toros of the WHA but was holding out until offered a general manager's position, so he could have more control over his own destiny and bring in the kind of players he wanted.

That opportunity finally came in January 1976 when Francis was fired and Rangers President Bill Jennings reached out to the former Montreal Canadiens enforcer and offered him a four-year deal that would pay him $100,000 annually to become the Blueshirts' GM. Francis had offered him only a one-year contract to coach the team when the two had met during the previous summer.

Fergy took over as GM as well as coach of the Rangers on January 7, 1976, reassigning former coach Ron Stewart to the scouting department. At thirty-seven years of age he was the youngest GM in the league at the time and the first GM or coach in the Rangers' 50-year history who was hired from outside of the organization.

Once Ferguson got to see the Rangers up close he immediately pronounced them overpaid and out of shape. His goal was to restore the players' pride and self-respect. And although he made some solid contributions, he is remembered more for his mistakes rather than his successes.

Following a last-place finish in the Patrick Division in 1975–76, Fergy set out to rebuild the team. In May 1976, in his first trade, he sent twenty-three-year-old winger Rick Middleton to the Bruins for thirty-one-year-old Ken Hodge. It is still viewed by many as the worst trade in Rangers history. According to Ferguson, the trade was made for several reasons. First, Phil Esposito was nagging him to acquire his old Bruins line mate. Secondly, the Rangers needed size and Hodge was 6-foot-2, 210 pounds, and third, the Blueshirts needed scoring and Hodge had scored a lot of goals with Esposito as his centerman. Hodge also won two Stanley Cups with the Bruins, so he had the kind of experience Fergy wanted in the Rangers locker room. However, the party line at the time was that the trade was made to get Middleton away from the New York City nightlife and save his career, which led one beat reporter to wonder aloud, "I guess they don't have any bars in Boston?" The trade was a disaster for the Rangers. "Ricky McNifty" cleaned up his act and had a great career in Boston, scoring more than 400 goals and recording almost 900 points in 12 seasons with the Bruins. Hodge, on the other hand, scored only 23 goals in 96 games over two seasons. He retired at the end of the 1977–78 season but later played 37 games with the Binghamton Dusters of the AHL in 1979–80.

Ferguson redeemed himself to some extent a few months later by acquiring Staten Island native Nicholas Evlampios Fotiu, who was under contract with the New England Whalers of the WHA at the time. To gain Fotiu's release, Ferguson had to promise the Whalers that the Blueshirts would play a preseason game in Hartford the next year with the Whalers keeping all the gate receipts. It turned out to be money well spent as Nicky stood up for his teammates and led the Rangers with 174 penalty minutes. In addition, his charity work and pregame ritual of throwing pucks into the upper reaches of the Garden made him a fan favorite.

Attempting to change their image Fergy did the unthinkable, doing away with the Blueshirts' traditional uniforms. The new uniforms, designed by Edd Griles, featured the Rangers crest on the front and wide stripes down the shoulders and sleeves. The new uniforms were supposed to make the players look bigger.

Ferguson also tried to add scoring punch to the lineup by sending

Billy Fairbairn and Nick Beverley to Minnesota in exchange for Bill Goldsworthy. The thirty-two-year-old right wing, who had posted 30- and 40-goal seasons with Minnesota, managed only 10 goals and 12 assists in 61 games with the Rangers that season.

The changes in personnel and uniforms didn't bring the desired results as the Rangers once again finished in last place in the Patrick Division with a 29–37–14 record for 72 points, a slight improvement over their dismal 29–42–9 record of the previous year.

The Rangers had an extra first-round pick in the 1977 amateur draft, thanks to a deal Emile Francis made three years earlier when he sent Gene Carr to the Los Angeles Kings. Ferguson selected Lucien DeBlois at number eight with their own pick and Ron Duguay thirteenth. Both were solid picks, but at the time Mike Bossy was still on the board waiting to be selected by the Islanders at number fifteen. Then in the second round, Fergy selected Mike Keating at number twenty-six, but seven picks later the Isles grabbed John Tonelli, who certainly was Ferguson's type of player.

That fall Ferguson turned the coaching reins over to former Montreal teammate Jean-Guy Talbot, who is remembered more for the warm-up suit he wore behind the bench than for any coaching expertise he may have imparted on the young Rangers. Talbot enjoyed being with the players and telling stories about the glory days of the Canadiens. However, many players complained that he didn't communicate with them and never told them what they were doing wrong on the ice.

In November 1977 with the team playing at a sub .500 level and sinking fast, Fergy sent Goldsworthy and Hodge, both thirty-three-year old, highly paid right wingers to New Haven of the AHL. Then on Thanksgiving eve, he released longtime Ranger Rod Gilbert. The thirty-six-year old right winger had scored only twice in the Rangers' first 19 games and it was apparent that Rod's best days were behind him. Fergy also didn't care for Gilbert's attitude and didn't consider him to be a team player. He feared that Rod's lackadaisical demeanor would rub off on the younger players. Gilbert was also the leader of a clubhouse clique that was constantly at odds with Phil Esposito. Unfortunately, the ouster of Gilbert later proved to be Ferguson's undoing.

Later that season with the financially strapped Cleveland Barons on the verge of folding, Madison Square Garden president Alan Cohen gave Ferguson $1 million to buy the contracts of goaltender Gilles Meloche and forwards Dennis Maruk and Charlie Simmer. Unfortunately, the league froze the Barons' assets before Ferguson could make the deal. But then John discovered that Ulf Nilsson and Anders Hedberg of the WHA's Winnipeg Jets would be free agents at the end of the season. So he shifted gears and spent the money on the two Swedes instead of Meloche, Maruk, and Simmer.

The Blueshirts finished the season with a 30–37–13 record and qualified for the playoffs, losing in the first round to Buffalo in a three-game series. However, the Blueshirts had lowered their goals against by 30 and with the Swedes on their way, it seemed as though things were looking up for Ferguson and the Blueshirts.

Unfortunately for Ferguson, Sonny Werblin took over as Garden president early in 1978. Rod Gilbert quickly caught Werblin's ear and launched a campaign to replace Ferguson with either Fred Shero or Scotty Bowman. When it was determined that Bowman wasn't interested, Werblin started talking to Fred Shero's agent even though "Freddie the Fog" was still under contract with Philadelphia. Flyers owner Ed Snider got wind of Werblin's actions and filed tampering charges against the Rangers with the NHL. The irony of the episode was that the Flyers wanted to get rid of Shero anyway, but now they could at least get something of value from the Rangers for his services. In the end the Rangers wound up giving the Flyers a first-round draft pick and $200,000 for the right to hire Shero as coach and general manager.

Later that summer, the Garden laid down a sheet of ice for an elaborate press conference to introduce Nilsson and Hedberg to the media. Fred Shero was pictured on the ice with the duo but not a word was said about the fact that it was Ferguson who signed them.

Rule Changes:

1977–78: Teams requesting a stick measurement to be assessed a minor penalty in the event that the measured stick does not violate the rules.

Doug Soetaert
Born: April 21, 1955 in Edmonton, Alberta
6-0, 180lb
Caught: Left
Rangers Debut: December 19, 1975 vs. Atlanta Flames
Uniform #31, 33, 1
Seasons with Rangers: 7, 1975–76 to 1980–81 and 1986–87
Stanley Cup: Montreal, 1985–86

Courtesy of Ken Tash

Doug Soetaert began playing goal as a child in the basement of his family's home in Edmonton. He played his way up through the local ranks and at age sixteen, began his junior hockey career with the Edmonton Oil Kings of the WCJHL where he had the opportunity to practice with Hall of Famer Jacques Plante, who was then the Edmonton Oilers' informal goalie coach. In 1975, he backstopped Canada to a silver medal in the World Junior Championships and was selected by Emile Francis in the second round (30th overall) of the 1975 amateur draft.

When Doug reported to Rangers training camp that fall, he was the low man on the depth chart with Ed Giacomin, Gilles Villemure, John Davidson, and Dunc Wilson ahead of him so he began the season in Providence of the AHL. But then the Blueshirts underwent their monumental shakeup in October and Giacomin and Villemure were no longer with the team.

In early December Wilson was rushed to the hospital with appendicitis and Soetaert was recalled to back up Davidson. On December 19 with Wilson still recovering and Davidson and the Rangers losing, 7–1, to the Flames, coach Ron Stewart decided to see what the rookie could do and put him in for the last 15:35 of the third period. The Flames fired nine shots but Soetaert stopped them all except for one by Tom Lysiak. Doug made his first start on January 6 in St. Louis, playing well but losing, 5–2, in a game where his teammates committed 45 giveaways. It turned out to be Emile Francis's last game as GM and Stewart's last as coach. But Eddie Johnston, the Blues netminder that night, complimented Soetaert following the game saying, "He showed a lot of guts, he's going to be all right."

Doug saw action in only 43 more games with the Rangers over the next four seasons but in 1980–81 he played in 39 games as one of five goaltenders the Blueshirts used that season.

Soetaert was then traded to Winnipeg in September 1981 in exchange for the Jets' 1983 third-round draft pick (Vesa Salo). He saw regular action in Winnipeg for three seasons before being traded again, this time to Montreal for Marc Holden in October 1984. He remained with the Canadiens for two seasons as a backup to first Steve Penney and then Patrick Roy and won a Stanley Cup with the Habs in 1986. While with Montreal he had the best record of any backup goaltender in the NHL that season (11–6–2 with a 2.67 GAA and three shutouts). "Soapy" returned to the Rangers as a free agent in July 1986 and appeared in 13 games that season before hanging up his pads at the end of the year at the age of thirty-one.

Following retirement, Doug became an assistant coach in the Rangers farm system and later took over as head coach and executive vice president of the Kansas City Blades of the IHL, leading them to a Turner Cup victory in 1991–92. Soetaert then became vice president and general manager of the Everett Silvertips (WHL), guiding them to three U.S. Division titles, a Western Conference championship and a Scotty Munro Trophy for the league's best record. Soetaert also spent a season as president of the Omaha Ak-Sar-Ben Knights and assistant general manager of the Calgary Flames.

Soetaert later served as head scout for Red Bull Hockey, where he was responsible for scouting all of Europe's pro leagues, covering the American Hockey League, and evaluating all possible free agents. He has also scouted for Red Bull Munich (DEL), Salzburg (Austrian Hockey League), and the Phoenix Coyotes in 2013–14.

Regular Season

Season	Team	GP	W	L	T	GA	GAA	SO	MIN	G	A	PTS	PIM
1975–76	NYR	8	2	2	0	24	5.29	0	272	0	1	1	0
1976–77	NYR	12	3	4	1	28	2.95	1	569	0	0	0	0
1977–78	NYR	6	2	2	2	20	3.34	0	360	0	0	0	0
1978–79	NYR	17	5	7	3	57	3.81	0	898	0	0	0	4
1979–80	NYR	8	5	2	0	33	4.57	0	434	0	0	0	0
1980–81	NYR	39	16	16	7	152	3.94	0	2317	0	0	0	2

Season	Team	GP	W	L	T	GA	GAA	SO	MIN	G	A	PTS	PIM
1981–82	WIN	39	13	14	8	155	4.32	2	2155	0	2	2	14
1982–83	WIN	44	19	19	6	174	4.12	0	2531	0	1	1	10
1983–84	WIN	47	18	15	7	181	4.29	0	2531	0	3	3	14
1984–85	MTL	28	14	9	4	91	3.41	0	1600	0	0	0	4
1985–86	MTL	23	11	7	2	56	2.77	3	1213	0	0	0	6
1986–87	NYR	13	2	7	2	58	5.17	0	673	0	0	0	14
NYR Totals	-	103	35	40	15	372	4.04	1	5523	0	1	1	20
Career	-	284	110	104	42	1029	3.97	6	15,553	0	7	7	68

Playoffs

Season	Team	GP	W	L	T	GA	GAA	SO	MIN	G	A	PTS	PIM
1981–82	WIN	2	1	1	-	8	4.00	0	120	0	0	0	0
1982–83	WIN	1	0	0	-	0	0.00	0	20	0	0	0	0
1983–84	WIN	1	0	1	-	5	15.00	0	20	0	0	0	0
1984–85	MTL	1	0	0	-	1	3.00	0	20	0	0	0	0
Career	-	5	1	2	-	14	4.67	0	180	0	0	0	0

Gilles Gratton
Born: July 28, 1952 in LaSalle, Quebec
5-11, 160lb
Caught: Left
Rangers Debut: October 6, 1976 vs. Minnesota North Stars
Uniform #33
Seasons with Rangers; 1 (1976–77)

Gilles Gratton was one of the most colorful characters to ever tend goal for the New York Rangers. Unfortunately, "Gratoony the Loony" was known more for his eccentric behavior, claims of past lives, and lion goaltender's mask than stopping pucks.

After three seasons with the Oshawa Generals of the OHA, Gratton was selected by the Buffalo Sabres in the fifth round (68th overall) in the 1972 amateur draft. That same year he was also selected by Edmonton in the WHA general player draft and eventually signed with the Ottawa Nationals, who had acquired his rights from Edmonton.

"Buffalo offered me $5,000 to sign and $8,000 for my first year and $10,000 my second," recalled Gratton. "Ottawa offered me $20,000 to sign and $25,000 for each of the next two years. So I had no choice."

Gratton stayed with the Ottawa Nationals/Toronto Toros franchise for three seasons. After his NHL rights were traded to St. Louis by Buffalo for cash in July 1975, he signed with the Blues. Ironically the addition of Gratton to the Blues' depth chart as well as the signing of their first-round draft pick, goaltender Ed Staniowski, made John Davidson expendable which led to his trade to the Rangers.

After playing only six games for the Blues, Gratton walked out on the team, claiming that he wanted to return to Toronto of the WHA. The Blues put him on the voluntary retired list but refused to place him on waivers, blocking his attempt to re-sign with the Toros. He sat out the remainder of the season and was signed by Rangers GM John Ferguson that summer. It was Fergy's first signing and probably his most memorable.

According to Gratton, "When my agent called to tell me that the Rangers wanted to sign me I really didn't want to play hockey anymore. Coming to New York was a mistake, I was out of shape, I hadn't played in a year and I didn't really want to play anymore. But I figured that John Davidson would play most of the games, so I thought, well I'll go and sit on the bench, get into shape slowly and get my money because I wanted to travel and go to India. But JD got hurt right away and I had to play. That year was hell for me. I smoked pot every day when I was there."

Gratton, the younger brother of the late Norm Gratton, a former Blueshirt, won his first start as a Ranger, a 6–5 opening night decision over Minnesota and appeared in a total of 41 of the Rangers' 80 games that season. He may have played in a few more if he didn't sometimes feign an illness or tell Ferguson that his planets were not aligned properly to get out of playing. But the real reason he refused to play was that he just didn't want to. In fact, he used to do a little dance when Ferguson would enter the Rangers locker room and toss John Davidson a puck before a game, meaning that JD would be playing that night and not Gratton. He also had a run-in with Rangers captain Phil Esposito which ultimately led to the end of his Rangers career.

"I had a situation with Phil Esposito, a bit of a conflict and I was told a few days later that I wouldn't be playing again. At that time Esposito was kind of king of the locker room. So I was told by Rod Gilbert, who I lived with, that there had been a meeting and that I was not going to play anymore. That was around January, I guess, and after that Fergy asked me to play a few times so I told him that my planets weren't aligned. But that wasn't true. I was just playing with his head. I just thought that since they told me I wasn't going to play, I wasn't going to play. So I told him that my planets were not aligned or I had an injury from a past life. But it wasn't true," said Gratton.

Gratton was the first Ranger goaltender to wear a birdcage-style mask. However, about midway through the season, he adopted his trademark lion mask, which he insists was inspired by pictures of tigers he saw while leafing through a copy of *National Geographic* magazine. Gilles took his idea to Toronto-based mask maker Greg Harrison, who turned the concept into a reality. Gratton surprised everyone when he unveiled the mask right before the opening faceoff of a game against the St. Louis Blues at the Garden on January 30, 1977. He kept the new mask in a box in his locker and wore his cage mask during warmups. He then hid the new mask under his arm during the playing of the national anthem and donned it for the first time right before the opening face-off.

"The crowd went oooohhh! The players and referees came down to see it. It was cool. It may have been the best $300 I ever spent," Gratton recalled.

Gratton believed that in a past life he had been a Spanish count who enjoyed throwing rocks at commoners and stoned people to death in Biblical times and that being a goaltender was his punishment for his past deeds. He also thought that his recurring abdominal pains were a result of being stabbed during the Spanish Inquisition. "It's kind of strange but I had memories when I was a kid and then later on I did past life regressions. I've been a twelfth century sailor, a fourteenth century Indian 'hobo,' a seventeenth century Spanish landowner, an eighteenth century Spanish priest and a nineteenth century British surgeon among other things."

Gratton, a free spirit, was known for "streaking" after practice and doing handstands in the shower. He is also an accomplished musician although he never had any lessons.

Prior to his final game with the Rangers, Gratton was slated to back up John Davidson and gave his suspender to a fan in the stands. When called on to play later in the game he was forced to stuff his jersey into his pants to help keep them up.

Gratton started the 1977–78 season with the Rangers' AHL club in New Haven, but his heart wasn't in it and his contract was eventually bought out. He then left for an ashram in India, leaving behind all his goaltending equipment including his famous mask. "I should have taken my mask because I would have gotten a lot of money for it today," he said. "I heard that the mask is in Boston, some collector has it. I now work for Classic Auctions and my boss tracked it down to a guy in Florida who paid me $5,000 for it with a promise of $5,000 more. But I never heard from him again. Then I heard that he sold it to someone in the Boston area."

Unfortunately, Gratton still feels the effects of the many concussions he suffered during his playing days, more than four decades ago. "I had a lot of concussions. I remember six, but I must have had more. Because in those days you got hit in the head, you threw up and were dizzy for three days but you kept playing. But we didn't know about concussions. When I was with the Toros of the WHA I got knocked out and the trainer came out and waved the smelling salts under my nose and I put the mask back on and kept playing. After the game I threw up. That was a concussion but we didn't know at the time. I've had headaches from the time I was twenty years old to about fifty. I had about three or four headaches a week. But over the last ten years it's been maybe one or two a week. But sometimes I get up and lose my balance and have to lay down. The headaches are not so bad, but now it's the dizziness. It's like everything is spinning around."

Gratton spent most of the 1980s and '90s in ashrams in India and the Catskills. He also worked as a photographer and is currently a consultant for Classic Auctions. He also wrote an autobiography with Greg Oliver titled *Gratoony the Looney*.

Gilles Gratton was a talented goaltender, but he lacked the desire to succeed. He has freely admitted that he really didn't like to play hockey and was only in it for the money which he used to finance his quest for spiritual enlightenment by meditating, going to ashrams and practicing yoga. "Meditating with the Monks in Tibet was something I always wanted to do as a kid. It was a dream of mine. I wasn't looking to run away but I couldn't wait to have enough money to travel. For me hockey was a way to gather up enough money to travel, to fulfill my real dreams."

Regular Season

Season	Team	League	GP	W	L	T	GA	GAA	SO	MIN	G	A	PTS	PIM
1972–73	OTN	WHA	51	25	22	3	187	3.71	0	3021	0	1	1	10
1973–74	TRT	WHA	57	26	24	3	188	3.52	2	3200	0	4	4	28
1974–75	TRT	WHA	53	30	20	1	185	3.85	2	2881	0	4	4	8
1975–76	STL	NHL	6	2	0	2	11	2.49	0	265	0	0	0	2
1976–77	NYR	NHL	41	11	18	7	143	4.23	0	2030	0	0	0	13
NYR Totals	-	NHL	41	11	18	7	143	4.23	0	2030	0	0	0	13
Career	-	NHL	47	13	18	9	154	4.03	0	2295	0	0	0	15
Career	-	WHA	161	-	-	-	560	3.69	4	9102	0	9	9	46

Playoffs

Season	Team	League	GP	W	L	T	GA	GAA	SO	MIN	G	A	PTS	PIM
1972–73	OTN	WHA	2	-	-	-	7	4.88	0	86	0	0	0	0
1973–74	TRT	WHA	10	-	-	-	25	2.78	1	539	0	0	0	5
1974–75	TRT	WHA	1	-	-	-	5	8.33	0	36	0	0	0	0
Career	-	WHA	13	-	-	-	37	3.36	1	661	0	0	0	5

Dave Tataryn
Born: July 17, 1950 in Sudbury, Ontario
5-9, 160lb
Caught: Left
Rangers Debut: March 9, 1977 vs. Minnesota North Stars
Uniform #25
Seasons with Rangers: 1, 1977–78

Dave Tataryn was one of four goaltenders used by John Ferguson during the 1976–77 season.

The Sudbury, Ontario, native began his career with the Niagara Falls Flyers of the OHA, leading them to the Memorial Cup championship in 1968. He was selected by the St. Louis Blues in the eighth round, (104th overall) in the 1970 amateur draft but decided to go the college route and enrolled at the University of Toronto, leading them to the University Cup as the top collegiate team in Canada.

He then played the next three seasons for Laurentian University where he earned a degree in health and physical education. After graduation he joined the Toronto Toros of the WHA in 1975–76 on a part-time basis, earning $100 a game if he was the backup and $200 if he played.

"I had a five-game tryout and was picked as a star in four of the games," Tataryn once told a reporter. "The biggest thrill of my life came in a game against Winnipeg. I stoned them all night before Bobby Hull scored the winning goal. Afterwards, he sent an autographed hockey stick over to me. That felt as good as getting my paycheck at the end of the week." In 23 games with the Toros that season Dave posted a 7–12–1 record.

Tataryn signed a three-year deal with the Toros but used an escape clause when the team moved to Birmingham, Alabama. He then bounced around the minors until signed by John Ferguson as a free agent in January 1977.

Tataryn appeared in two games for the Rangers, posting a 1–1–0 record with a bloated 7.50 GAA.

Following the 1976–77 season Tataryn returned to Canada and senior hockey, winning the Allen Cup in 1981 with the Petrolia Squires and another in 1983 with the Cambridge Terriers. In addition, he worked as a teacher and a farrier as well as opening his own goaltending school. He also served as goaltending coach for the University of Waterloo and the London Knights.

Regular Season

Season	Team	League	GP	W	L	T	GA	GAA	SO	MIN	G	A	PTS	PIM
1975–76	TRT	WHA	23	7	12	1	100	4.76	0	1261	0	0	0	2
1976–77	NYR	NHL	2	1	1	0	10	7.50	0	80	0	0	0	0
Career	NYR	NHL	2	1	1	0	10	7.50	0	80	0	0	0	0
Career	TRT	WHA	23	7	12	1	100	4.76	0	1261	0	0	0	2

Wayne Thomas
Born: October 9, 1947 in Ottawa, Ontario
6-2, 195lb
Caught: Left
Rangers Debut: October 15, 1977 at Montreal Canadiens
Uniform #1
Seasons with Rangers: 4, 1977–78 to 1980–81)
All-Star Games: 1, 1976

Courtesy of Ken Tash

Wayne Thomas played for the University of Wisconsin where he majored in Physical Education and was a WCHA Second Team All-Star in 1970. While still in college and property of the Maple Leafs, his rights were traded to the Kings with Brian Murphy and Gary Croteau for Grant Moore and Lou Devault in September 1968. The Kings later sent him to Montreal with Leon Rochefort and Gregg Boddy for Jack Norris, Larry Mickey, and Lucien Grenier in May 1970.

Thomas turned pro in 1970–71 and spent the next three seasons in the Montreal farm system. He was third on the Canadiens' depth chart behind Ken Dryden and Michel Plasse but made his NHL debut on January 14, 1973, shutting out the Vancouver Canucks, 3–0, becoming only the tenth netminder in league history to post a shutout in their first NHL game. The Canadiens won the Stanley Cup that season but Thomas did not see any playoff action. The next season Thomas played in 42 games for the Habs when Dryden left the team to study law.

In June 1975 Wayne was traded again, this time to Toronto for the Leafs' first-round pick in the 1976 amateur draft. He appeared in 64 games with Toronto in 1975–76 and made the All-Star team. However, he struggled the next season and was supplanted by young Mike Palmateer and played in only 33 games.

Thomas was placed on waivers at the beginning of the 1977–78 season and claimed by the Rangers just two days before the start of the season.

Due to lingering injuries to John Davidson, Thomas became the Blueshirts' number one goaltender, seeing action in 41 games. His playing time slowly decreased over the next three seasons as the Rangers' goaltending situation remained unsettled and he retired at the end of the 1980–81 season. He then spent four years as an assistant coach for the Blueshirts.

He then served as an assistant coach with Chicago and St. Louis and was head coach of Salt Lake City of the IHL, taking the Golden Eagles to the Turner Cup Championship in 1985–86. He also coached the Peoria Rivermen for two seasons. Thomas then joined the San Jose Sharks organization in 1993 and remained with them in various front office capacities until he retired in 2015.

Regular Season

Season	Team	GP	W	L	T	GA	GAA	SO	MIN	G	A	PTS	PIM
1972–73	MTL	10	8	1	0	23	2.37	1	583	0	1	1	2
1973–74	MTL	42	23	12	5	111	2.77	1	2406	0	2	2	6
1975–76	TOR	64	28	24	12	196	3.20	2	3679	0	0	0	18
1976–77	TOR	33	10	13	6	116	3.87	1	1799	0	1	1	4
1977–78	NYR	41	12	20	7	141	3.60	4	2349	0	1	1	9
1978–79	NYR	31	15	10	3	101	3.64	1	1666	0	0	0	0
1979–80	NYR	12	4	7	0	44	3.98	0	664	0	0	0	0
1980–81	NYR	10	3	6	1	34	3.42	0	597	0	2	2	2
NYR Totals	-	94	34	43	11	320	3.64	5	5276	0	3	3	11
Career	-	243	103	93	34	766	3.34	10	13,743	0	7	7	41

Playoffs

Season	Team	GP	W	L	T	GA	GAA	SO	MIN	G	A	PTS	PIM
1975–76	TOR	10	5	5	-	34	3.48	1	587	0	0	0	0
1976–77	TOR	4	1	2	-	12	3.58	0	201	0	0	0	0
1977–78	NYR	1	0	1	-	4	4.00	0	60	0	0	0	0
NYR Totals	-	1	0	1	-	4	4.00	0	60	0	0	0	0
Career	-	15	6	8	-	50	3.54	1	848	0	0	0	0

Hardy Astrom
Born: March 29, 1951 in Skelleftea, Sweden
6-0, 170lb
Caught: Left
Rangers Debut: February 25, 1978 at Montreal Canadiens
Uniform #31
Seasons with Rangers: 1, 1977–78

Long before Henrik Lundqvist was born, Hardy Astrom was the Rangers' first Swedish goaltender. He was scouted by GM John Ferguson at the 1977 World Championships in Vienna where he helped his country earn a silver medal.

Astrom was signed as a free agent in March 1977 and made his NHL debut on the evening of February 25, 1978, at the Montreal Forum as the 20–29–11 Rangers faced off against the 42–7–7 Canadiens, who were riding a 28-game unbeaten streak. The Blueshirts had not beaten the Canadiens in the Forum in six years, but on this night Astrom made 29 saves as the Rangers skated away with a 6–3 victory.

Ferguson had told reporters a few days earlier that he had a surprise in store for the Montreal game. With Wayne Thomas nursing a sore wrist and John Davidson's knees and back in need of a rest, the Rangers recalled Astrom from their New Haven (AHL) farm club where he had posted an impressive 15–5–2 record with a 2.78 GAA.

Astrom had been the Swedish National team's number one netminder and had faced the Soviet Union and Czechoslovakia in the Olympics so he was apparently unfazed by the pressure. "It was my first game in the NHL but I had played big games before with Sweden. I had beaten the Russians in Moscow and the Czechs in Prague," Hardy told the press. "I thought I had a good chance of beating the Canadiens in Montreal."

That would turn out to be the highlight of Astrom's Ranger career. He played a total of four games for the Blueshirts, going 2–2–0 with a 3.50 GAA.

Astrom was not happy with the way he was treated in the NHL and returned to play for Skelleftea of the Swedish league. In July 1979 his NHL rights were dealt to the Colorado Rockies for Bill Lochead. He appeared in 79 games over two seasons with the Rockies, posting a 15–42–12 record with a 3.76 GAA for coach Don Cherry's defensively challenged Rockies. He spent some time with Oklahoma City in the CHL before returning to Sweden and retiring following the 1985–86 season.

Regular Season

Season	Team	GP	W	L	T	GA	GAA	SO	MIN	G	A	PTS	PIM
1977–78	NYR	4	2	2	0	14	3.50	0	240	0	0	0	0
1979–80	CLR	49	9	27	6	161	3.77	0	2566	0	0	0	6
1980–81	CLR	30	6	15	6	103	3.77	0	1639	0	1	1	2
NYR Totals	-	4	2	2	0	14	3.50	0	240	0	0	0	0
Career	-	83	17	44	12	278	3.75	0	4445	0	1	1	8

CHAPTER EIGHT

Freddie the Fog Finally Gets His Chance

After being bypassed many times by Emile Francis, Fred Shero finally got a chance to coach the Rangers when he replaced John Ferguson as GM and coach in June of 1978.

Shero was cerebral. He always claimed to be the first Ranger to hold a New York City library card which he obtained while playing in 145 games as a defenseman with the Blueshirts from 1947 to 1950. He was a thinker, a student with many interests—philosophy, boxing, Shakespeare, and architecture among them—but hockey most of all. Following his retirement as a player in 1958, Shero coached for six seasons in the Rangers' minor-league system, leading his teams to four first-place finishes and two league championships. Yet he was bypassed three times when Emile Francis made changes behind the Rangers bench. Shero had a well-known drinking problem and Francis didn't want any part of it. So, in 1971, when Flyers GM Keith Allen was looking to replace coach Vic Stasiuk, he was given permission to speak to Shero and he jumped at the opportunity to move up to the NHL.

"Freddie the Fog" turned the Flyers into the Broad Street Bullies and won two Stanley Cups in the City of Brotherly Love. But by 1978 he had worn out his welcome and the Flyers were not sad to see him go to the Rangers, especially when the NHL found the Blueshirts guilty of tampering and forced them to give the Flyers a first-round draft pick and $200,000 for the right to hire Shero as coach and general manager.

Shero took over the Rangers in 1978–79 and got off to a great start by bringing back their traditional uniforms and taking them to the Stanley Cup Finals that spring. That team featured Ulf Nilsson, Anders Hedberg, Phil Esposito, Ron Greschner, and Don Murdoch, and finished in third place in the Patrick Division. They then plowed through the Kings, Flyers, and Islanders thanks to the spectacular goaltending of John Davidson and some timely goals by speedy Bobby Sheehan, who was called up from the minors during the Flyers series. But after they won the opening game of the Finals against Montreal, captain Phil Esposito suggested that Shero take the team out of town, away from the distractions of Montreal so they could focus on the series. He refused and legend has it that a group of Blueshirts went out on the town and they proceeded to lose the next four games.

Another key factor in the series loss to Montreal was that the Blueshirts were pushed around handily by the Montreal defense, especially Larry Robinson. The Rangers didn't have anyone to counter the Canadiens' size. So in November 1979 in a deal largely credited to Garden boss Sonny Werblin and Colorado Rockies owner Arthur Imperatore, the Rangers sent Pat Hickey, Lucien DeBlois, Mike McEwen, and Dean Turner to the Rockies for hulking defenseman Barry Beck.

Despite the run to the finals, Shero found himself on thin ice from the beginning of the 1979–80 season due to a number of administrative mistakes. He had brought in his longtime buddy Mickey Keating to be the de facto general manager because Freddie had no taste for the paperwork which was a requirement of the position.

Keating, however, was simply not qualified for the job and was not respected by Rangers players, the press, and team officials throughout the league. Among the Shero-Keating duo's chief blunders was their failure to book a training camp site for the fall of 1979, forcing the team to scramble to find a site in Richmond, Virginia. Shero later traded troubled winger Don Murdoch to the Oilers for checking forward Cam Connor. The problem was that not only did Shero think he was getting defenseman Colin Campbell in return, but he never told Werblin about the deal and Murdoch was one of Sonny's favorite players. Shero and Keating also had a deal in place to send Phil Esposito to the Black Hawks for Jim Harrison but when the Chicago center failed a required physical due to a bad back the deal was squashed.

Shero also began delegating more of his day-to-day coaching duties to his assistant, Mike Nykoluk, preferring to stay in his office while Nykoluk ran practices. However, Nykoluk was not known as a disciplinarian and many of the players took advantage of him, often showing up late for practice or not at all.

After a second-round ouster from the playoffs in 1980, Sonny Werblin warned Shero to get more involved and to cut down on his drinking. Werblin also brought in Craig Patrick as director of hockey operations to keep an eye on him. Patrick played for eight seasons in the NHL and had served as assistant general manager and assistant coach of the gold medal-winning 1980 US Olympic team. He was also a member of the Rangers royal family, being the grandson of Lester Patrick, son of Lynn, and nephew of Muzz, all of whom played for and coached the Blueshirts.

Patrick wound up taking over as GM and coach in November 1980 when the Rangers got off to a 4–13–3 start and Shero was fired despite having two years remaining on his five-year contract.

Steve Baker
Born: May 6, 1957 in Boston, Massachusetts
6-3, 200lb
Caught: Left
Rangers Debut: November 28, 1979 vs. Minnesota North Stars
Uniform #35
Seasons with Rangers: 4, 1979–80 to 1982–83

Courtesy of Steve Baker

Steve Baker seemed destined to be the Rangers' goaltender of the future after going undefeated in nine of the first ten starts in his NHL career. Destiny had other plans, however, as Steve's career was derailed by a devastating groin injury from which he never fully recovered.

Baker grew up in the Boston area and was primarily interested in baseball until the Bruins began winning Stanley Cups and dominating the league. With that, more rinks began popping up and the youngster's interest shifted towards hockey.

According to Baker, "I was quite an accomplished catcher and I had two older brothers who frankly needed a target. They were playing hockey at that time and I got elected. I used to put on a lot of the catcher's gear and stand in front of the garage doors while my brothers shot pucks at me. When we told people how to find our house all we had to do was tell them to look for the garage doors with the holes in them—that was the Baker home. I started skating when I was about five or six and really started getting into organized youth hockey at about eight. I decided that I wanted to pursue a professional career probably when I was a junior or senior in high school."

Baker then went on to play at Union College in Schenectady, New York, under the tutelage of Ned Harkness, who was in the process of starting a hockey program at the school.

Steve compiled an impressive 27–5–1 record with a 3.28 GAA in three seasons with the Skating Dutchmen. However, in Steve's junior year, Harkness resigned abruptly over allegations that he had violated NCAA recruiting rules and, in a show of solidarity with their coach, the entire varsity squad refused to play the remainder of their schedule. Steve finished that season with the Toledo Goaldiggers of the IHL.

In 1977, Steve was drafted by both the Rangers (third round, 44th overall) and the Birmingham Bulls (fifth round, 40th overall) of the WHA.

"The Bulls drafted me in the fifth round the same year I was drafted by the Rangers in the third round," remembered Baker. "Bill Jennings was president of the Rangers and his daughter Priscilla was a freshman at Union College when I arrived on campus in the fall of 1975. I think maybe Mr. Jennings was getting some reports from Priscilla because she knew a lot about hockey, having been around it her whole life. But I believe that Birmingham ended up selling my rights to the New England Whalers because the Bulls had signed Pat Riggin. So they brought Pat in pretty much from juniors. He was a pretty good goaltender and he had a nice career, but it made me kind of expendable. Actually, my first pro training camp was with the New England Whalers when they had the likes of Gordie Howe, Mark and Marty Howe, Davey Keon, Johnny "Pie" McKenzie, Gordie Roberts, Jack McIlhargey, any number of great guys and talents.

"I remember Gordie taking myself and another former Union College guy, Pete Crawford [Marc's brother], to his Connecticut home for lunch. I remember his wife, Colleen, made us grilled cheese and tomato sandwiches. We had a little tomato soup and he walked us around his home. He had an indoor pool and he showed us his Stanley Cups and Avco Cup trophies on his mantle. It was just an experience that I'll never forget. It just shows the kind of guy he was that he did that kind of stuff."

Baker made his Rangers debut at the age of twenty-two on November 28, 1979, a 4–4 tie with Minnesota at the Garden. He then went on to lose only one of his next nine starts. "I had a good start. I had a good training camp. I had gotten married that summer and came to camp in good shape, mentally healthy and ready to go. That was Freddie Shero's second year. We had camp down in Richmond, Virginia. I remember Danny Summers, the chief scout telling me, 'Steve, we know what you've done here, just go down to New Haven, play well and you're gonna get your shot.' Ultimately it came a little unexpectedly. I mean I had gone down and I was playing very well. I think my record was 8–1 or something like that and the Rangers were struggling a little bit and the call came down and as luck would have it I wasn't feeling well. I had a pretty bad head cold and a little bit of a fever but when you get that phone call, man you start to feel good in a hurry. My wife is Italian, so she started feeding me the homemade chicken soup and it kind of cleared me up a little bit and I took the ride down to Rye for practice. I remember that next day, you know sometimes when you're not feeling well sometimes you just don't have the legs out there and so I felt a little leg heavy. But the night of the game I was as excited as could be. I knew that most of my family was flying in from Boston on the shuttle and whatever tickets I could get I gave to them. Beyond that I think they just got scalpers out front.

"I do remember that Minnesota scored late, we were up 4–3. It was kind of a fluke goal. I think the puck got thrown from down low to up high on the point and a guy let a slap shot go through a lot of traffic. But the puck was coming at me end-over-end and wound up hitting somebody and bounced another way. Next thing you know it hit somebody else and jumped over my shoulder and into the net. So it was kind of a fluke but at least I got out with a point back in those days.

"We left that night to go to Buffalo to play the Sabres the next night, so you had Gilbert Perreault and the French Connection line coming at you. And I think we ended up losing, 2–1, on a power play goal late in the game. But then in my third game I got my first NHL win, a 2–0 shutout with 38 saves in St. Louis. That was pretty exciting. I started out great but then of course JD [John Davidson] had been the number one guy and took them to the finals the year before. So everybody was kind of waiting on him to get his health back and he worked hard doing that and when he came back he kind of took on more of a superior role in terms of the amount of game time and so forth and I was spotted a little bit more. But it was a great experience and I wouldn't have given it up for the world."

With five goaltenders on the Rangers' roster at the beginning of the 1980–81 season, Steve started the year in New Haven. But ultimately when given the opportunity he helped lead the Blueshirts to the semifinals of the Stanley Cup playoffs.

"That was another thrill of a lifetime. We still had a lot of goaltenders under contract and I was still the young guy coming up. I was on a 'two way' contract at that time so it was just a business decision. The club showcased some of the other goaltenders pursuing a potential trade. So I went down and was there for a while and then they ended up bringing me back up. Craig Patrick had taken over as the coach and GM and he came in and said, 'Bakes you're going to be the guy. You're going to carry the load here for the rest of the year.' He gave me the opportunity to play pretty much every game.

"JD had gone down with injuries by then, I think Wayne Thomas had moved into a coaching role and Dougie Soetaert was sent down. So they brought Stevie Weeks up to back me up and he got into one game. I think it was the last game of the season and he played great against the Islanders but I played all the other games down the stretch.

"I remember we finished in 14th place out of 21 teams and 16 teams made the playoffs. So we just squeezed in and we eliminated the number five team, the Kings with the Triple Crown Line, Marcel Dionne, Charlie Simmer, and Dave Taylor. And certainly pushing past St. Louis, the number two team overall, in a six-game series was a thrill. Mike Liut was an excellent goaltender out of Bowling Green and they had Bernie Federko and Wayne Babych and they were a really good hockey club. I think they lost out on the Presidents' Trophy in the last game of the season to the Islanders.

So there we were, the 14th-place team standing in the semifinals against the Islanders, who were the defending Stanley Cup champions.

And they were in the midst of their second of four Stanley Cups. They were an absolute machine. Physically I wasn't in great shape at that time. I was having some back spasm issues. I wish that I could have played a little bit better, but it is what it is. A lot of teams got beat by the Islanders four-love. We got a lot further than a lot of people anticipated that we were going to get."

At 6-foot-3 and 200 pounds, Steve was big for a goaltender at that time but he considered his size as well as his agility and glove hand to be his biggest assets. "Because I played a lot of baseball I thought I had a great glove hand," Steve recalled. I used to call my glove hand my bread-and-butter. Because you can control the play with your glove hand. If you decide to put the puck back in play you can do that or you can cover it up and stop play. I felt I had very good quickness and agility for a good-sized guy. It's not unusual today because they want most of today's goalers six feet and up. They're all big bodies, big men and very athletic and quick. I think I fit that mold back then maybe a little ahead of my time. With the quickness and the ability to go up and down off the knees and play that butterfly style, use my feet, drop the paddle and find pucks through traffic.

I remember JD always saying to me 'up and out' even in practice he used to say if you're struggling a little bit and that puck is starting to look like a BB coming at you as opposed to a softball just move out a little further and the pucks are going to start hitting you."

Unfortunately, Steve was plagued by injuries throughout his career, the most serious was a torn groin that happened on October 31,1981, at the Boston Garden.

"That's the biggest regret I have about my career," says Steve. Honestly I made the mistake of trying to play with a slightly pulled groin, not a smart move for any athlete but certainly not a goaltender. That year [coach] Herb Brooks decided that he wanted to go play in a tournament over in Sweden, so I had a go to Sweden and then back to the US. And Herbie had some different ideas about the way he wanted the team to play and we really struggled in the beginning of the year. We had half the guys playing that up-and-down your lane hockey style and we had half the guys trying to play Herbie's bob-and-weave possession game and intrinsically what happens is when things start to go bad you go back to what you know and so even less guys were doing what Herbie wanted us to do. It took us half a year for that team to figure out that system. But when they did they really turned it on. Remember we had the 'Smurfs' and we really did well in the playoffs.

"But we struggled at the beginning of the year. I got off to a bad start and the team got off to a terrible start. I remember playing against Gretzky's Oilers on a Wednesday night if memory serves me correctly and my groin was bothering me a little bit before the game, but I played the game. I think we lost, 5–3, and after the game my groin was tightening up pretty good. The next day we had a practice and I took it really easy and got heat packs on it to keep it warm. We shuttled into Boston and it was Halloween night and I think it was halfway through the second period and young Tom Fergus came in and let a wrist shot go to my right side and I did a split kick and all I know is it felt like I had a horse tied to my left leg and my right leg was tied to a wall, like they were pulling me apart. And my groin exploded, just literally exploded. Worst pain I ever had in my life.

"Back then we had a doctor on call for the team. Your trainers weren't medical guys; they'd sharpen skates and make sure your gear was okay. It wasn't like it is today, but of course we weren't making the kind of money these kids are today. But they put me on the injured reserve list and basically said 'tell us when you're ready to play again.' I'll tell you, it was a tough, arduous task to rehabilitate a torn groin. I pushed myself and I came back too early. They sent me down to Springfield to get some games in but I was still having that nightmarish mindset that if I kicked this way this thing was going to rip on me again. I gave it my best. I don't know if maybe I got blackballed 'This guy's got a severe injury,' whether that kept me from being able to find my way back into the league again?"

Steve won a Calder Cup with the AHL's Maine Mariners in 1984 and then retired at the age of twenty-seven, finishing his Rangers career with a 20–20–11 record in 57 games with three shutouts and a 3.70 GAA. In 14 playoff games, Baker posted a 7–7 record with a 4.00 GAA.

Not surprisingly, Steve's iconic Empire State Building mask is still a favorite with fans more than thirty years after his retirement. "That was a Greg Harrison mask out of Toronto and I can't claim any credit other than wanting it in Ranger red, white, and blue. But he was the one who came up with the concept of the Empire State Building in the front of the face with the star at the top and a star on each cheek. I remember when they had the Olympics in Calgary the NHL wanted to put on an exposition of all the NHL masks and Greg called me up and asked if he could loan them the mask. The league loved the exhibit so much that they said they'd like to do one in the Hall of Fame. So Greg said do you mind if we send it up to the Hall of Fame, and I said no, not at all. People can enjoy it and someday maybe my family can get up there and enjoy it and say, 'hey dad played a little bit!'"

Steve returned to Union College to complete his education, earning a BA in Economics. He then spent twenty-five years as an executive in the broadcast and regional sports network industry. He currently resides in Texas where he is an advisor and broker of precious metals. Steve was also inducted into the Union College Hall of Fame in 2007.

Although Steve's Rangers career was relatively brief, he still has many fond memories of his time in New York.

"Playing on the Garden's big stage provided one of my life's greatest moments. It was an honor and privilege to wear Ranger Blue and play in front of the league's best fans. They were very kind to me. I will always be grateful for this world class experience."

Regular Season

Season	Team	GP	W	L	T	GA	GAA	SO	MIN	G	A	PTS	PIM
1979–80	NYR	27	9	8	6	79	3.41	1	1389	0	0	0	2
1980–81	NYR	21	10	6	5	73	3.49	2	1256	0	0	0	5
1981–82	NYR	6	1	5	0	33	6.03	0	328	0	0	0	0
1982–83	NYR	3	0	1	0	5	2.98	0	101	0	0	0	0
Career	NYR	57	20	20	11	190	3.71	3	3074	0	0	0	7

Playoffs

Season	Team	GP	W	L	T	GA	GAA	SO	MIN	G	A	PTS	PIM
1980–81	NYR	14	7	7	-	55	4.01	0	824	0	0	0	4
Career	NYR	14	7	7	-	55	4.01	0	824	0	0	0	4

CHAPTER NINE

Another Patrick Takes the Helm

Following Fred Shero's dismissal in November 1980, Craig Patrick took over as general manager and stepped behind the bench as coach on an interim basis, becoming the fourth member of the Rangers royal family to take charge of the club. His father, Lynn, was a former coach of the Blueshirts while his grandfather Lester and Uncle Muzz both served as general manager and coach. All three of his predecessors played for the Rangers while Craig saw NHL action with the California Golden Seals, Kansas City Scouts, St. Louis Blues, and Washington Capitals.

Patrick originally planned to hire Herb Brooks, the coach of the 1980 gold medal-winning United States Olympic team, under whom Patrick had served as an assistant. Brooks, however, was already under contract to coach in Europe. But Patrick was able to quickly turn the team around and the Blueshirts finished in fourth place and had a surprising playoff run thanks to the strong goaltending of Steve Baker, beating Los Angeles and St. Louis in the first two rounds before getting swept by the Islanders in the semifinals.

Brooks arrived for the 1981–82 season and brought with him a new European style of play. He also recruited diminutive center Mark Pavelich who had been an integral part of the 1980 USA Olympic team. The transition from dump-and-chase to cycling and puck possession wasn't easy and the Blueshirts faltered until midseason when they finally felt comfortable with Herbie's new system.

By January the "Smurfs," as the smallish Rangers were nicknamed, began putting some winning streaks together, culminating with a nine-game unbeaten streak in March. They finished in second place with 92 points earning Brooks Coach of the Year honors from *The Sporting News*. But after beating Philadelphia in the opening round they were once again ousted by the Islanders.

The Blueshirts dropped to fourth place with 80 points the next season and once again beat the Flyers in the opening round of the Stanley Cup playoffs before losing to the Islanders. They rebounded with a 93-point, fourth-place finish the next season but for the fourth consecutive year were eliminated from the playoffs by the Islanders, this time in the opening round as former Olympian Ken Morrow beat Glen Hanlon with a slap shot from the point in overtime in the decisive Game Five.

Brooks reached the 100-win plateau faster than any previous Rangers coach, but all was not well beneath the surface. He was not comfortable being a subordinate to Patrick, who had been his assistant at the Olympics, and he wanted more input into personnel moves. Brooks tried to force the issue during the summer by offering to resign, an idea that was rejected by Patrick. The two men also had vastly different personalities. Brooks was intense and ambitious, while Patrick was quiet and laid back.

But in January 1985 with the Rangers in danger of missing the playoffs with a dismal 15–22–8 record, Patrick dismissed Brooks and stepped back behind the bench. He didn't do much better than his predecessor, but the Rangers did make the playoffs only to be swept in the first round by the Flyers.

The next season, Patrick hired Ted Sator as his coach. Sator had coached in Europe and spent a year as an assistant under Mike Keenan in Philadelphia. He stressed a defensive game but the Blueshirts struggled for most of the season before catching fire in the playoffs, defeating the Flyers and Capitals before losing to the Canadiens in the conference finals.

Sator and his assistants, Jack Birch and Reg Higgs, rubbed a lot of players the wrong way, however. Mark Pavelich quit the team in March and Barry Beck demanded a trade during the offseason.

Patrick's contract was not renewed that summer even though the Rangers posted an overall 204–196–60 record during his tenure and had made the playoffs each year. Although Patrick had made some excellent draft selection over the years (Brian Leetch, Darren Turcotte, James Patrick, John Vanbiesbrouck, Jan Erixon, Mike Richter, Ulf Dahlin, Tomas Sandstrom, and Tony Granato), Garden management felt the team was "moving sideways" and that Patrick was not aggressive enough at the previous season's trading deadline. Patrick later went on to become the GM of the Pittsburgh Penguins and built a team that would win the Stanley Cup in 1991 and 1992.

Rule Changes:

1981–82: If both of a team's listed goaltenders are incapacitated, the team can dress and play any eligible goaltender who is available.

1983–84: The NHL introduced a regular-season overtime period of five minutes. If neither team scored during the extra session each was awarded a point in the standing for the tie.

Steve Weeks
Born: June 30, 1958 in Scarborough, Ontario
5-11, 170lb
Caught: Left
Rangers Debut: April 2, 1981 at New York Islanders
Uniform #31
Seasons with Rangers: 4, 1980–81 to 1983–84

Steve Weeks spent four years playing for Northern Michigan University and was selected by Fred Shero in the 11th round of the 1978 amateur draft (176th overall). He turned pro in 1980–81, playing for the Rangers' farm team in New Haven and made his NHL debut on April 2, 1981, in a 2–1 loss to the Islanders. Weeks also made a brief 14-minute appearance in the Blueshirts' 10–3 victory over the LA Kings in the third game of the preliminary round of the playoffs.

Steve began the next season as the Blueshirts' number one netminder due to lingering injuries to John Davidson and Steve Baker. However, in December 1981, in an effort to take some of the pressure off Weeks, GM Craig Patrick acquired Eddie Mio from Edmonton and the pair essentially split the goaltending duties down the stretch. Steve appeared in 49 of the team's 80 contests, posting a 23–16–9 record with one shutout and a 3.77 GAA. But it was Mio who got the call in the playoffs, playing in eight of the Rangers' 10 games against the Flyers and Islanders while Weeks made only four appearances.

Mio took over the starting role the next season and when the Rangers acquired Glen Hanlon in January 1983, Weeks was sent to Tulsa of the CHL. Following the season, Mio was traded to Detroit and Weeks rejoined the Rangers as Hanlon's backup.

In September 1984, Weeks was traded to Hartford for future considerations. He spent four seasons with the Whalers backing up first Greg Millen and then Mike Liut before moving on to the Vancouver Canucks. The well-traveled goaltender also played for the Islanders, Kings, and Senators before retiring in February 1993. Weeks then went on to become a goaltending coach for Hartford, Carolina, and Atlanta.

Regular Season

Season	Team	GP	W	L	T	GA	SA	SV	SV%	GAA	SO	MIN	G	A	PTS	PIM
1980–81	NYR	1	0	1	0	2	22	20	.909	2.04	0	59	0	0	0	0
1981–82	NYR	49	23	16	9	179	1357	1178	.868	3.77	1	2849	0	3	3	0
1982–83	NYR	18	9	5	3	68	491	423	.862	3.92	0	1040	0	2	2	0
1983–84	NYR	26	10	11	2	90	667	577	.865	3.98	0	1358	0	0	0	4
1984–85	HAR	24	10	12	2	92	726	634	.873	3.80	2	1454	0	0	0	0
1985–86	HAR	27	13	13	0	99	723	624	.863	3.85	1	1542	0	1	1	9
1986–87	HAR	25	12	8	2	78	615	537	.873	3.42	1	1367	0	0	0	0
1987–88	HAR	18	6	7	2	55	388	333	.858	3.60	0	918	0	0	0	2
1987–88	VAN	9	4	3	2	31	286	255	.892	3.38	0	550	0	0	0	0
1988–89	VAN	35	11	19	5	102	953	851	.893	2.98	0	2056	0	0	0	4
1989–90	VAN	21	4	11	4	79	623	544	.873	4.15	0	1142	0	0	0	0
1990–91	VAN	1	0	1	0	6	29	23	.793	6.11	0	59	0	0	0	0
1991–92	NYI	23	9	4	2	62	566	504	.890	3.61	0	1032	0	0	0	2
1991–92	LAK	7	1	3	0	17	136	119	.875	4.04	0	252	0	1	1	0
1992–93	OTT	7	0	5	0	30	144	114	.792	7.22	0	249	0	0	0	0
NYR Totals	-	94	42	33	14	339	667	577	.865	3.83	1	5306	0	5	5	4
Career	-	291	112	119	33	990	7707	6717	.872	3.73	5	15,927	0	7	7	21

Playoffs

Season	Team	GP	W	L	T	GA	SA	SV	SV%	GAA	SO	MIN	G	A	PTS	PIM
1980–81	NYR	1	0	0	-	1	10	9	.900	4.29	0	14	0	0	0	0
1981–82	NYR	4	1	2	-	9	63	54	8.57	4.27	0	127	0	0	0	5
1985–86	HAR	3	1	2	-	8	64	56	.875	2.86	0	168	0	0	0	0

Season	Team	GP	W	L	T	GA	SA	SV	SV%	GAA	SO	MIN	G	A	PTS	PIM
1986–87	HAR	1	0	0	-	1	22	21	.955	1.65	0	36	0	0	0	0
1988–89	VAN	3	1	1	-	8	79	71	.899	3.43	0	140	0	0	0	2
NYR Totals	-	5	1	2	-	10	73	63	.857	4.27	0	141	0	0	0	5
Career	-	12	3	5	-	27	165	148	.897	3.34	0	485	0	0	0	7

Fast Fact: Steve Weeks is one of nine goaltenders to have played for both the Rangers and the Islanders. The other eight are John Vanbiesbrouck, Glen Healy, Mike Dunham, Jamie McLennan, Steve Valiquette, Kevin Weekes, Chad Johnson, and Martin Biron.

John Vanbiesbrouck—Franchise Goaltender
Born: September 4, 1963 in Detroit, Michigan
5-8, 176lb
Caught: Left
Rangers Debut: December 5, 1981 at Colorado Rockies
Uniform #34
Seasons with Rangers: 11, 1981—82; 1983—84 to 1992-93
Vezina Trophy: 1985–86
All-Star selections: 1985–86 (First Team); 1993–94 (Second Team)
All-Star Games: 3, 1994, 1996–97

Courtesy of the New York Rangers

When John Vanbiesbrouck was sixteen years old, he was bypassed in the local Midget hockey league draft. Not one to let disappointment derail his dreams, the Detroit native tried out for the Sault Ste. Marie Greyhounds of the Ontario Hockey League. He made the team and won the F. W. "Dinty" Moore Trophy awarded annually to the rookie goaltender with the lowest goals-against average, all the while wearing glasses under his birdcage mask. That June he was selected by Rangers GM Craig Patrick in the fourth round, (72nd overall) in the 1981 entry draft.

"Beezer" made his NHL debut on the evening of December 5, 1981, when John Davidson and Steve Baker were sidelined with injuries. "They wouldn't put me in if they didn't think I had the ability," the self-assured eighteen year old told reporters before the game. "I'll shake for a while but I'll calm down after the first few shots. It's definitely gonna be a win." Beezer stood behind his words, beating the Colorado Rockies, 2–1, that night in Denver. (By the way, Beezer's backup that night was minor leaguer Rick Strack who was summoned from the Springfield Indians of the AHL.) Vanbiesbrouck was returned to the Greyhounds following the game and in 1982–83 led the OHL in games played and was second in wins (39) as the team posted the OHL's best record at 48–21–1.

Vanbiesbrouck turned pro in 1983 and spent most of the season with the Rangers' CHL team in Tulsa although he did make three appearances with the Blueshirts, going 2–1–0. He made the team coming out of training camp in 1984–85, splitting time with veteran Glen Hanlon.

At the beginning of the 1985–86 season, coach Ted Sator had so much confidence in Beezer that he sent Hanlon to Adirondack of the AHL. That season Vanbiesbrouck led the league with 31 wins, was a First Team All-Star, and was awarded the Vezina Trophy. He also backstopped the Rangers past Philadelphia and Washington in the playoffs before losing to Patrick Roy and the Canadiens in the conference finals.

Cocky, competitive, and opinionated, John sometimes rubbed his teammates the wrong way. He was often called "The Mouth" because he wasn't afraid to say whatever was on his mind, even as a rookie. He also wasn't shy about pointing out his teammates' mistakes as well as his own. But he got the job done on the ice. He had a quick glove hand and was an excellent positional goaltender.

Vanbiesbrouck missed the start of the 1987–88 season due to a broken jaw courtesy of training-camp slap shot from teammate Tomas Sandstrom. The following offseason he nearly lost the use of his left hand when the glass coffee table he was sitting on shattered. He required five hours of microsurgery to remove glass fragments from his wrist and repair lacerations to the ulnar nerve and three tendons. The initial diagnosis had Beezer out for six months but following a summer of extensive rehab, he was ready for opening night in October.

Vanbiesbrouck, who had shared the goaltending duties with Glen Hanlon and later Bob Froese, got a new partner in 1989–90, Mike

Richter. Beezer played the majority of the games that year but starting in 1990–91 the pair split the workload for the next three years. Nicknamed "VanRichterBrouck" the duo gave the Rangers their best goaltending combo since Ed Giacomin and Gilles Villemure in the 1970s. Coach Roger Neilson alternated them through the first 76 games of the 1991–92 season, setting a record that will probably never be broken, and the Rangers won the Presidents' Trophy with the league's best overall record.

Beezer was rumored to be part of deals that then-GM Phil Esposito was ready to make with Edmonton for first Mark Messier and later Wayne Gretzky. Then in June 1991, Vanbiesbrouck was rumored to be part of a package that GM Neil Smith offered to Quebec for center Eric Lindros whom the Nordiques had selected with the first overall pick in the 1991 amateur draft. The rest of the package reportedly going to Quebec was Tony Amonte, Doug Weight, Alex Kovalev, three first-round draft picks and $12 million. It turned out that Nordiques president Marcel Aubut had accepted deals for Lindros, who had previously stated that he would not play for Quebec, from both the Flyers and the Rangers. Independent arbitrator Lawrence Bertuzzi ultimately ruled that the Flyers had made their offer before the Rangers. Neil Smith claimed at the time that he was delayed in making the trade because then-Garden owners Paramount Communications was slow to get back to him with their approval.

The twenty-nine-year-old Vanbiesbrouck could sense that he was expendable. In 1993 when the NHL expanded again, the Rangers could only protect one goaltender and it was decided that they would bet the future of the franchise on Richter. So instead of losing Vanbiesbrouck for nothing in the draft, he was traded to Vancouver for future considerations (Doug Lidster). Vancouver also left him exposed in the draft so that they could protect their starting goaltender, Kirk McLean, so Beezer was selected by the Florida Panthers where he would once again play for Roger Neilson.

It was a tough time for Beezer. Not only did he have to deal with getting his family acclimated to a new city, but about two months earlier, his older brother Frank committed suicide. It was a devastating loss for Vanbiesbrouck, who looked up to his brother and learned many life lessons from him. "Frank never knew it, but he taught me more about goaltending just by me watching him than any words can possibly say," Vanbiesbrouck once told a reporter. "No one has ever helped me more become what I've become. I have no answers to this day what went wrong, if I even could've helped him. All I know is, my whole life—my whole perspective—changed after that day."

Beezer played for the Panthers for five seasons, becoming the face of the new franchise and taking them to the Stanley Cup Finals in 1996. He later played for three of the Rangers' fiercest rivals—the Flyers, Islanders, and Devils—before retiring in 2002.

During his 11-year Ranger career, Vanbiesbrouck won numerous team awards and set several franchise records. In 1984–85, he was the inaugural winner of the Rangers Fan Club Rookie of the Year award as well as the Rangers Good Guy award (given by the hockey writers). In 1985–86, he was chosen as the Rangers MVP, won the Players' Player Award and given the Frank Boucher Trophy (most popular), and the "Crumb Bum" Award (community service) in 1986–87. He was also the co-winner (with Kelly Kisio) of the Steven McDonald Extra Effort Award in 1989–90.

Beezer also holds the Rangers' team record for most career assists (25) and shares the record for most assists in a game (two) and season (five), as well as most career penalty minutes (212) by a goaltender. Vanbiesbrouck also competed in many international tournaments while with the Blueshirts including the World Junior Championships (1982 and 1983), World Championships (1985, 1987, 1989, and 1991), as well as the Canada Cup (1987 and 1991). Vanbiesbrouck also played for Team USA in the 1998 Winter Olympics. In addition, his 882 NHL games played and 374 victories are the most recorded by an American-born goaltender and he was inducted into the US Hockey Hall of Fame in 2007.

Following his retirement, Vanbiesbrouck served as coach and GM of the Sault Ste. Marie Greyhounds of the OHL. In 2003, John resigned after using a racial slur while talking about one of his own players, captain Trevor Daley. He then worked as an analyst and broadcaster for the Versus network and HDnet. He also covered the 2010 Winter Olympic games for Westwood One radio and later served as general manager and director of hockey operations for the Muskegon Lumberjacks of the USHL for five years. In May 2018, Beezer was named assistant executive director of hockey operations for USA Hockey.

John Vanbiesbrouck played for seven coaches under three GMs and helped get the Rangers into the playoffs seven times during his tenure on Broadway. He was the rock that each of those coaches counted on and built the team around and certainly deserves to be counted among the Rangers' franchise goaltenders.

Regular Season

Season	Team	GP	W	L	T	GA	SA	SV	SV%	GAA	SO	MIN	G	A	PTS	PIM
1981–82	NYR	1	1	0	0	1	-	-	-	1.00	0	60	0	0	0	0
1983–84	NYR	3	2	1	0	10	84	74	.881	3.35	0	179	0	0	0	2
1984–85	NYR	42	12	24	3	165	1359	1194	.879	4.21	1	2354	0	5	5	17
1985–86	NYR	61	31	21	5	184	1623	1439	.887	3.33	3	3320	0	3	3	16
1986–87	NYR	50	18	20	5	161	1364	1203	.882	3.64	0	2651	0	1	1	18
1987–88	NYR	56	27	22	7	187	1700	1513	.890	3.38	2	3315	0	5	5	46
1988–89	NYR	56	28	21	4	197	1662	1465	.882	3.69	0	3207	0	5	5	30
1989–90	NYR	47	19	19	7	154	1361	1207	.887	3.38	1	2734	0	2	2	24
1990–91	NYR	40	15	18	6	126	1154	1028	.891	3.35	3	2257	0	3	3	18
1991–92	NYR	45	27	13	3	120	1331	1211	.910	2.85	2	2526	0	3	3	23
1992–93	NYR	48	20	18	7	152	1525	1373	.900	3.31	4	2757	0	1	1	18
1993–94	FLA	57	21	25	11	145	1912	1767	.924	2.53	1	3440	0	0	0	38
1994–95	FLA	37	14	15	4	86	1000	914	.914	2.47	4	2087	0	1	1	6
1995–96	FLA	57	26	20	7	142	1473	1331	.904	2.68	2	3178	0	2	2	10
1996–97	FLA	57	27	19	10	128	1582	1454	.919	2.29	2	3347	0	2	2	8
1997–98	FLA	60	18	29	11	165	1638	1473	.899	2.87	4	3451	0	3	3	6
1998–99	PHI	62	27	18	15	135	1380	1245	.902	2.19	6	3712	0	1	1	12
1999–00	PHI	50	25	15	9	108	1143	1035	.906	2.20	3	2950	0	1	1	6
2000–01	NYI	44	10	25	5	120	1177	1057	.898	3.04	1	2390	0	0	0	8
2000–01	NJD	4	4	0	0	6	93	87	.935	1.50	1	240	0	0	0	0
2001–02	NJD	5	2	3	0	10	117	107	.915	2.00	0	300	0	0	0	4
NYR Totals	-	449	200	177	47	1457	13193	11736	.890	3.45	16	25,380	0	28	28	212
Career	-	882	374	346	119	2502	24708	22206	.899	2.98	40	50,475	0	38	38	310

Playoffs

Season	Tm	GP	W	L	T	GA	SA	SV	SV%	GAA	SO	MIN	G	A	PTS	PIM
1983–84	NYR	1	0	0	-	0	0	0	0	0.00	0	0	0	0	0	0
1984–85	NYR	1	0	0	-	0	12	12	1.000	0.00	0	19	0	0	0	0
1985–86	NYR	16	8	8	-	49	477	428	.897	3.28	1	897	0	2	2	2
1986–87	NYR	4	1	3	-	11	110	99	.900	3.39	1	195	0	0	0	2
1988–89	NYR	2	0	1	-	6	54	48	.891	3.36	0	107	0	0	0	0
1989–90	NYR	6	2	3	-	15	153	138	.902	3.02	0	298	0	0	0	4
1990–91	NYR	1	0	0	-	1	22	21	.955	1.16	0	52	0	0	0	0
1991–92	NYR	7	2	5	-	23	179	156	.872	3.75	0	368	0	0	0	2
1995–96	FLA	22	12	10	-	50	735	685	.932	2.25	1	1332	0	1	1	20
1996–97	FLA	5	1	4	-	13	184	171	.929	2.38	1	328	0	0	0	0
1998–99	PHI	6	2	4	-	9	146	137	.938	1.46	1	369	0	0	0	2
NYR Totals	-	38	13	20	-	105	1,007	902	.896	3.26	2	1936	0	2	2	10
Career	-	71	28	38	-	177	2072	1895	.915	2.68	5	3965	0	3	3	32

Fast Fact: John Vanbiesbrouck is one of only four goaltenders to play for both the Rangers and New Jersey Devils. The others are Kirk McLean, Mike Dunham, and Kevin Weekes. Vanbiesbrouck and Dunham are the only two netminders to have played for the Rangers, Islanders, and Devils.

Eddie Mio
Born: January 31, 1954 in Windsor, Ontario
5-10, 180lb
Caught: Left
Rangers Debut: December 19, 1981 at Pittsburgh Penguins
Uniform #41
Seasons with Rangers: 2, 1981–82 to 1982–83

Eddie Mio made a name for himself at Colorado College from 1972 to 1976 where he had an outstanding career, earning First and Second Team All-Star berths as well as being named to the NCAA West First All-American team for two consecutive seasons.

In 1974, he was drafted by both the Chicago Black Hawks of the NHL and the Vancouver Blazers of the WHA. He wound up playing for neither club, however, spending a couple of seasons in the minors with Tidewater, Erie, and Hampton before getting a break with the Indianapolis Racers of the WHA.

Mio only played 22 games over two seasons with the Racers but became good friends with a young player named Wayne Gretzky. They became such good buddies that Eddie was Wayne's best man at his July 1988 wedding to actress Janet Jones. In March 1978, Mio was traded with "The Great One" and Peter Driscoll to the Edmonton Oilers for cash and future considerations.

Nelson Skalbania, the owner of the Racers, was forced to make the deal due to financial difficulties. He actually had two deals for Gretzky on the table, one with the Winnipeg Jets and the other with the Edmonton Oilers. Both deals also involved Mio and Peter Driscoll. The trio boarded a private jet and headed to western Canada, even though at the time of departure they didn't know where the plane was going to land, Edmonton or Winnipeg.

The pilots, being as confused as the passengers, wanted to know who was paying for the flight. Gretzky had the big contract but was too young to have a credit card. Mio and Driscoll were broke. So Eddie pulled out his Visa card with a $300 limit, and signed for a $10,000 trip on a Learjet.

Somewhere in midair, the pilot was told that they were to land in Edmonton and Eddie was eventually reimbursed by Peter Pocklington and the Oilers.

Mio spent almost three seasons in Edmonton as the Oilers were merged into the NHL. But after playing 43 games for Edmonton in 1981–82 Mio found himself squeezed out of the crease by Grant Fuhr and Andy Moog and was dealt to the Rangers for Lance Nethery on December 11, 1981.

Eddie made his Ranger debut in a 3–3 tie with Pittsburgh on December 19. He shared the workload with Steve Weeks and appeared in 24 more of the Rangers' remaining 48 games that season, posting a 13–6–5 record with a 3.56 GAA. He also started eight of the Rangers' ten playoff games against the Flyers and Islanders going 4–3 with a 3.79 GAA.

The next season Mio saw action in 41 games during the regular season and once again shouldered the load in the playoffs, starting eight of the Rangers' nine matches against Philadelphia and the Islanders.

During the 1982–83 season the Rangers had acquired Glen Hanlon from Vancouver and had young John Vanbiesbrouck coming up through the system so Mio was deemed expendable. In June GM Craig Patrick packaged Mio in a deal with Ron Duguay and Eddie Johnstone and sent them to the Red Wings for Willie Huber, Mike Blaisdel, and Mark Osborne.

Mio played three more years with the Red Wings and retired at the end of the 1985–86 season.

Regular Season

Season	Team	League	GP	W	L	T	GA	SA	SV	SV%	GAA	SO	MIN	G	A	PTS	PIM
1977–78	INR	WHA	17	6	8	0	64	470	406	.864	4.27	0	900	0	0	0	0
1978–79	INR	WHA	5	2	2	1	13	153	140	.915	3.22	1	242	0	0	0	2
1978–79	EDO	WHA	22	7	10	0	71	482	411	.853	3.99	1	1068	0	1	1	2
1979–80	EDM	NHL	34	9	13	5	120	907	787	.868	4.22	1	1706	0	1	1	4
1980–81	EDM	NHL	43	16	15	9	155	1165	1010	.867	3.90	0	2387	0	5	5	6
1981–82	NYR	NHL	25	13	6	5	89	777	688	.885	3.56	0	1499	0	0	0	4
1982–83	NYR	NHL	41	16	18	6	136	1156	1020	.882	3.46	2	2362	0	3	3	8
1983–84	DET	NHL	24	7	11	3	95	674	579	.859	4.42	1	1289	0	1	1	6
1984–85	DET	NHL	7	1	3	2	27	172	145	.843	4.32	0	375	0	0	0	2
1985–86	DET	NHL	18	2	7	0	83	452	369	.816	6.33	0	787	0	1	1	17
NYR Totals	-	NHL	66	29	24	11	225	1933	1708	.884	3.50	2	3861	0	3	3	12
Career	-	NHL	192	64	73	30	705	5303	4598	.867	4.07	4	10,405	0	11	11	47
Career	-	WHA	44	15	20	1	148	1105	957	.866	4.02	2	2210	0	1	1	4

Playoffs

Season	Team	League	GP	W	L	T	GA	SA	SV	SV%	GAA	SO	MIN	G	A	PTS	PIM
1978–79	EDO	WHA	3	-	-	-	6	-	-	-	4.00	0	90	0	0	0	0
1981–82	NYR	NHL	8	4	3	-	28	223	195	.874	3.79	0	442	0	0	0	0
1982–83	NYR	NHL	8	5	3	-	32	297	265	.892	4.00	0	478	0	0	0	0
1983–84	DET	NHL	1	0	1	-	3	24	21	.875	2.86	0	63	0	0	0	0
NYR Totals	-	NHL	16	9	6	-	60	520	460	.885	3.92	0	920	0	0	0	0
Career	-	NHL	17	9	7	-	63	24	21	.884	3.85	0	983	0	0	0	0
Career	-	WHA	3			-	6	-	-	-	4.00	0	90	0	0	0	0

Glen Hanlon
Born: February 20, 1957 in Brandon, Manitoba
6-0, 185lb
Caught: Right
Rangers Debut: January 9, 1983 vs. New Jersey Devils
Uniform #1
Seasons with Rangers: 4, 1982–83 to 1985–86

Following a stellar junior career with the hometown Brandon Wheat Kings, Glen Hanlon was selected by the Vancouver Canucks in the third round (40th overall) in the 1977 amateur draft. He spent four seasons with the Canucks where the fans considered him to be "The Franchise" until he was hampered by injuries to his back and knees and lost his starting job to Richard Brodeur. He was dealt to the St. Louis Blues in March 1982 for Rick Heinz, Tony Currie, Jim Nill, and the Blues' fourth-round pick in the 1982 entry draft.

In St. Louis, Glen backed up incumbent Mike Liut and appeared in only 16 games over two seasons. He was eventually traded to the Rangers by Blues GM Emile Francis along with Vaclav "Big Ned" Nedomansky for defenseman Andre Dore in January 1983.

Upon his arrival in New York, Hanlon split the rest of the season with Eddie Mio. But by the next season Mio had been traded to Detroit and Glen became the starter, playing in 50 games and posting a decent 28–14–4 record. Hanlon split the goaltending duties with young John Vanbiesbrouck the next season and by 1985–86 Beezer had emerged as the starter and Hanlon, along with two draft picks, were sent to Detroit that summer for Kelly Kisio, Lane Lambert, Jim Leavins, and Detroit's fifth-round pick in one of Phil Esposito's first deals as Rangers general manager.

Hanlon played five more seasons with the Red Wings and retired in 1991. He became the goaltending coach for the Canucks in 1992 and moved up to become the coach of the AHL's Portland Pirates in 1999. He was then named assistant coach of the Washington Capitals in 2002 and eventually replaced head coach Bruce Cassidy midway through the 2003–04 season. In May 2016, Hanlon was named GM of the WHL's Vancouver Giants.

Regular Season

Season	Team	GP	W	L	T	GA	SA	SV	SV%	GAA	SO	MIN	G	A	PTS	PIM
1977–78	VAN	4	1	2	1	9	94	85	.904	2.70	0	198	0	0	0	2
1978–79	VAN	31	12	13	5	94	921	827	.898	3.10	3	1819	0	1	1	28
1979–80	VAN	57	17	29	10	193	1644	1451	.883	3.48	0	3331	0	1	1	43
1980–81	VAN	17	5	8	0	59	411	352	.856	4.44	1	797	0	1	1	10
1981–82	VAN	28	8	14	5	106	768	662	.862	3.96	1	1604	0	0	0	22
1981–82	STL	2	0	1	0	8	41	33	.805	6.33	0	76	0	0	0	0
1982–83	STL	14	3	8	1	50	412	362	.879	4.47	0	671	0	0	0	0
1982–83	NYR	21	9	10	1	67	634	567	.894	3.45	0	1176	0	0	0	2
1983–84	NYR	50	28	14	4	166	1515	1349	.890	3.52	1	2828	0	2	2	30
1984–85	NYR	44	14	20	7	175	1444	1269	.879	4.19	0	2506	0	0	0	4
1985–86	NYR	23	5	12	1	65	608	543	.893	3.35	0	1164	0	1	1	4
1986–87	DET	36	11	16	5	104	974	870	.893	3.20	1	1953	0	0	0	20
1987–88	DET	47	22	17	5	141	1292	1151	.891	3.23	4	2617	0	1	1	30
1988–89	DET	39	13	14	8	124	1052	928	.882	3.56	1	2092	0	1	1	12
1989–90	DET	45	15	18	5	154	1156	1002	.867	4.03	1	2290	0	3	3	24
1990–91	DET	19	4	6	3	46	438	392	.895	3.20	0	862	0	0	0	4
NYR Totals	-	138	56	56	13	473	4201	3728	.887	3.70	1	7665	0	3	3	40
Career	-	477	167	202	61	1561	13,404	11,843	.884	3.61	13	25,975	0	11	11	237

Playoffs

Season	Team	GP	W	L	T	GA	SA	SV	SV%	GAA	SO	MIN	G	A	PTS	PIM
1979–80	VAN	2	0	0	-	3	27	24	.889	3.00	0	60	0	0	0	0
1981–82	STL	3	0	2	-	9	58	49	.845	4.97	0	109	0	0	0	0
1982–83	NYR	1	0	1	-	5	47	42	.894	5.00	0	60	0	0	0	12
1983–84	NYR	5	2	3	-	13	166	153	.922	2.53	1	308	0	0	0	6
1984–85	NYR	3	0	3	-	14	98	84	.857	5.02	0	167	0	0	0	0
1985–86	NYR	3	0	0	-	6	32	26	.813	4.89	0	74	0	0	0	0
1986–87	DET	8	5	2	-	13	227	214	.943	1.68	2	464	0	0	0	2
1987–88	DET	8	4	3	-	22	170	148	.871	3.07	1	431	0	0	0	6
1988–89	DET	2	0	1	-	7	47	40	.851	5.35	0	78	0	0	0	0
NYR Totals	-	12	2	7	-	38	343	305	.889	3.74	1	609	0	0	0	18
Career	-	35	11	15	-	92	872	780	.894	3.15	4	1751	0	0	0	26

Ron Scott
Born: July 21, 1960 in Guelph, Ontario
5-8, 155lb
Caught: Left
Rangers Debut: February 2, 1984 at Calgary Flames
Uniform #35, 31
Seasons with Rangers: 4, 1983–84, 1985–86 to 1987–88

Ron Scott signed with the Rangers as an undrafted free agent in May 1983 following a junior career with the Cornwall Royals of the QMJHL and three seasons with the Michigan State University Spartans. While at Michigan State, Scott was named *The Hockey News* College Player of the Year in 1981–82 and earned NCAA All-American honors twice.

With John Vanbiesbrouck, Glen Hanlon, and later Bob Froese manning the crease in New York, Scott spent most of his Rangers career playing for their minor-league affiliates in Tulsa, New Haven, and Denver. He did manage to appear in 16 NHL games over four seasons, posting a 3–7–4 record with a 3.85 GAA.

Scott signed with the Kings as a free agent in January 1990 and saw action in 12 regular-season games and one playoff contest.

The next season he found himself as their third-string goaltender, this time behind Kelly Hrudey and Daniel Berthiaume. He spent 1990–91 with New Haven of the AHL and retired at the end of the season.

Regular Season

Season	Team	GP	W	L	T	GA	SA	SV	SV%	GAA	SO	MIN	G	A	PTS	PIM
1983–84	NYR	9	2	3	3	29	253	224	.885	3.60	0	483	0	0	0	0
1985–86	NYR	4	0	3	0	11	56	45	.804	4.24	0	156	0	0	0	0
1986–87	NYR	1	0	0	1	5	35	30	.857	4.62	0	65	0	0	0	0
1987–88	NYR	2	1	1	0	6	41	35	.854	4.01	0	90	0	0	0	0
1989–90	LAK	12	5	6	0	40	319	279	.875	3.67	0	654	0	0	0	2
NYR Totals	-	16	3	7	4	51	385	334	.868	3.86	0	794	0	0	0	0
Career	-	28	8	13	4	91	704	613	.871	3.77	0	1448	0	0	0	2

Playoffs

Season	Team	GP	W	L	T	GA	SA	SV	SV%	GAA	SO	MIN	G	A	PTS	PIM
1989–90	LAK	1	0	0	-	4	10	6	.600	7.45	0	32	0	0	0	0
Career	LAK	1	0	0	-	4	10	6	.600	7.45	0	32	0	0	0	0

Terry Kleisinger
Born: October 10, 1960, in Regina, Saskatchewan
6-0 190lb
Caught: Right
Rangers Debut: October 12, 1985, at Hartford Whalers
Uniform #44
Seasons with Rangers: 1, 1985–86

Terry Kleisinger was signed by Craig Patrick as an undrafted free agent on October 8, 1985. He played his college hockey at the University of Wisconsin under legendary coach "Badger" Bob Johnson where he appeared in 80 games, posting a 47–30–2 record with nine shutouts and a 3.32 GAA in four seasons.

Kleisinger missed the entire 1984–85 season due to a case of mononucleosis. The following fall he reported to Ranger training camp and made enough of an impression on new coach Ted Sator in preseason that veteran goaltender Glen Hanlon began the season in the AHL while Terry stayed with the Rangers as John Vanbiesbrouck's backup. Sator was determined to make his mark with his new team as he also dispatched high-scoring Pierre Larouche to Hershey and fan favorite Nick Fotiu to New Haven.

But Kleisinger was not an NHL-caliber netminder. He made his Rangers debut on October 12 in an 8–2 loss at Hartford and played in three more games over the next few weeks, posting an 0–2–0 record and a 4.40 GAA. Hanlon and later Larouche were recalled and Kleisinger was sent to the minors in early November. Kleisinger retired during the 1986–87 season.

Regular Season

Season	Team	GP	W	L	T	GA	SA	SV	SV%	GAA	SO	MIN	G	A	PTS	PIM
1985–86	NYR	4	0	2	0	14	109	95	.872	4.42	0	190	0	0	0	2
Career	NYR	4	0	2	0	14	109	95	.872	4.42	0	190	0	0	0	0

CHAPTER TEN

Espo's Chaotic Era

Phil Esposito's tenure as Rangers general manager was one of the most chaotic chapters in team history. Unlike most of his predecessors in the GM's seat, Esposito inherited a pretty solid team. They were primarily a young squad that had qualified for the playoffs six consecutive years under Craig Patrick and made it to the conference finals the previous season. Patrick was a patient planner but Garden management didn't think he was aggressive enough to take the team to the next level, so they brought in Esposito who had been critiquing Patrick and the Blueshirts from the comfort of the broadcast booth where he was a color analyst alongside play-by-play man Sam Rosen.

If Craig Patrick wasn't aggressive enough for the Garden's taste, they would not have that problem with Espo. "Trader Phil" took over the Blueshirts on July 14, 1986, and made more than fifty player moves during his three seasons as general manager. Some were good, some bad, and a few were downright ugly. Esposito will always be remembered for trading promising young forwards Mike Ridley and Kelly Miller along with Bobby Crawford to the Washington Capitals for Bobby Carpenter and a 1989 second-round pick and then three months later sending Carpenter and defenseman Tom Laidlaw to the Kings for thirty-five-year-old Marcel Dionne, Jeff Crossman, and a 1989 third-round pick. Dionne found the going much tougher in the tight-checking Patrick Division compared to the wide-open Smythe Division but managed to score 42 goals in his three-year, 118-game Ranger career. Meanwhile, Ridley notched 218 goals in his eight seasons with the Caps before moving on to Vancouver and Toronto and Miller spent the next 13 seasons with the Caps, accumulating 162 goals and 246 points.

Espo also lured former Montreal Canadiens legend Guy Lafleur out of retirement. The thirty-seven-year-old right winger scored 18 goals with 27 assists in 1988–89 and brought a degree of dignity and leadership into the Blueshirts locker room.

But it was the moves that he was not allowed to make that defined his stint in the Rangers front office. Espo claimed that he had a deal in place to acquire Mark Messier from Edmonton in 1986 when Oilers owner Peter Pocklington started to have financial difficulties. The deal would have sent John Vanbiesbrouck, Tomas Sandstrom, Kelly Kisio, a draft pick, and cash to the Oilers for the future Hall of Famer. But Jack Diller and Richard Evans, who ran the Garden for Paramount, shot him down.

Then in 1988, Espo was said to have another trade in place that would have sent Vanbiesbrouck, Sandstrom, Kisio, and $15 million to the Oilers for Wayne Gretzky but once again Diller and Evans refused to make the deal.

Espo always claimed that Paramount, who owned the Garden at the time, was more concerned about the Knicks than the Rangers. If they could have gotten Michael Jordan from the Chicago Bulls for $15 million, they would have jumped at the chance. But as far as the Rangers were concerned, they had a full house, a sellout every night. Gretzky wasn't going to put any more people in the seats. All they cared about was the bottom line and didn't give a damn about winning the Stanley Cup.

Espo went through three coaches in his three seasons at the helm. He inherited Ted Sator from Craig Patrick and kept him behind the bench to start the 1986–87 season. But after a 5–10–4 start Esposito fired Sator and hired Tom Webster to coach the team. That plan fizzled out after only 18 games when Webster developed an inner ear problem which made it impossible for him to fly and travel with the team. Espo and assistant coaches Wayne Cashman and Ed Giacomin took over the bench duties and the Rangers finished in fourth place with a 34–38–8 record and lost to the Flyers in the opening round of the playoffs.

In 1987–88, fiery Michel Bergeron was hired as coach. And just as they had done nine years earlier when they overpaid for the right to sign Fred Shero, the Rangers once again got fleeced. Bergeron was still under contract with the Quebec Nordiques and the Rangers had to send a first-round draft pick (Quebec selected Daniel Dore) and $100,000 to the Nordiques for permission to sign "Le Petit Tigre." But as was later revealed, Quebec GM Martin Madden was happy to make the deal since he was barely on speaking terms with Bergeron and was glad to be rid of him.

The Rangers finished in fifth place in Bergeron's first year behind the bench but showed great improvement for most of the next season, spending more than two months in first place. However, the Blueshirts suffered a 9–19 slide beginning in February, falling to third place in the standings and losing their home-ice playoff advantage.

By then, Bergeron had once again worn out his welcome. On April 1, 1989, with only two games remaining in the regular season, Esposito fired Bergeron and named himself coach through the following season.

Esposito accused Bergeron of insubordination. There had been rumors of a power struggle between the two men and Bergeron showed no loyalty or respect for Esposito. He refused to take Espo's calls while on the road or scout the Rangers minor-league team in Denver. He was also known to call opposing coaches and GMs and initiated trade talks behind Espo's back. Bergeron pushed for trades that ultimately made Esposito look bad, such as sending the productive Walt Poddubny to Quebec in a deal for the oft-injured Normand Rochefort. He also refused to play Marcel Dionne and demanded that the future Hall of Famer be sent down to Denver.

The rift deepened in December when the coach made a very public demand for a contract extension after MSG renewed Espo's contract for another season. Espo refused to discuss it saying, "He has a contract, I expect him to honor it."

Bergeron was also very hard on younger players that were called up from Denver, ridiculing their rookie mistakes and saying, "I don't teach, I coach." Darren Turcotte and Mark Janssens were shuttled in and out of the lineup while other youngsters simply let it be known that they would rather not be recalled than be embarrassed by Bergeron. Only Tony Granato and Brian Leetch got a fair shot at cracking the lineup, but only because their talent was far too obvious to ignore.

Esposito had decided to fire Bergeron after the season was over but ran out of patience as the team neared the playoffs. The final straw came following a 4–3 loss in Detroit on March 29 when Bergeron called his players "chickens" in the press. Espo called the coach and suggested that he apologize to the players, but Bergeron refused. Esposito then asked Garden VP Jack Diller if he had his support to make the move. When Diller said yes, Bergeron was a goner.

Esposito's move behind the bench was anything but successful. The Blueshirts lost the last two games of the season and were ousted from the opening round of the playoffs by the Penguins in a four-game sweep. By the final game Espo was so desperate that he started a rookie by the name of Mike Richter in goal. It was Richter's first NHL game and he played well in the 4–3 loss but the Rangers were just overmatched by Mario Lemieux and the Penguins.

Esposito was given a vote of confidence by Garden brass following the playoffs, but a few weeks later VP Jack Diller changed his mind and fired Phil on May 24, saying, "It is our belief that new hockey leadership is necessary at this time to achieve the goals we have set for the franchise."

So once again the Rangers organization was in disarray. With Esposito gone and a new GM yet to be hired, there was no one to run the entry draft in June. It was left to Joe Bucchino, Espo's assistant and former stick boy, to make the selections and he didn't do too badly, picking Steven Rice and Rob Zamuner among others.

Ironically, Bergeron was rehired by Quebec two weeks after he was fired by the Rangers. This came as no surprise to Esposito or anyone else in the Rangers organization who knew that Bergeron had kept in constant contact with the Nordiques the entire time he was in New York. He lasted one year in Quebec, posting a woeful 12–61–7 record before being let go at the end of the season.

Bob Froese
Born: June 30, 1958 in St. Catharines, Ontario
5-11, 176lb
Caught: Left
Rangers Debut: December 23, 1986 vs. New Jersey Devils
Uniform #33
Seasons with Rangers: 4, 1986–87 to 1989–90
William Jennings Trophy: 1985–86 (with Philadelphia, shared with Darren Jensen)
All-Star selections: 1985–86 (Second Team)
All-Star Games: 1, 1986

Public Domain

Bob Froese began his hockey journey on the frozen ponds and rinks of St. Catharines, Ontario, where he followed in his father's footsteps and became a goaltender.

"It's funny, when I was a kid I would put catalogs on my legs for pads and stuff like that but the funniest thing that I thought was pretty ingenious, I went downstairs to drain my mother's bleach bottle which was white to make a mask. So I made little cut outs and thought it was great. I had strings tied around it to hold it on, but I didn't wear it too long before I was ready to pass out. I didn't realize I was asphyxiating myself from the smell of the bleach. You learn fast or die young," he said.

Bob played his junior hockey with the hometown St. Catharines Black Hawks and moved with the team when they became the Niagara Falls Flyers of the OHA. He was selected by the St. Louis Blues in the 10th round (160th overall) in the 1978 amateur draft.

After one season in the Blues' minor-league system Bob was signed as a free agent by Philadelphia in 1981 and made his NHL debut at the age of twenty-four with the Flyers in January 1983. He recorded his first NHL shutout in only his third game, ironically against the Rangers. As Pelle Lindbergh's backup, Froese posted a 17–4–3 record with an impressive 2.52 GAA. Lindbergh struggled the following season and Froese assumed the starter's role, appearing in 12 more games than Lindbergh. However, in 1985–86, Flyers management tabbed the Swede as their goaltender of the future and Froese was once again relegated to a backup role and often incurred the wrath of coach Mike Keenan.

"I've always had great relationships with any coach or any teammate I ever played with," he said. "Mike Keenan was the one guy that I didn't have a great relationship with and I can understand it now, in fact it's only been in the last year and a half that someone explained it to me and it makes perfect sense. I just wish I would've known about it sooner. But the difference between Lindbergh and I is that he was a quarter horse and I was a Clydesdale. I wasn't supersensitive or temperamental; there are a lot of goaltenders who are but that's part of their psyche, who they are. But what was explained to me is that I played better if I had good competition; the better the competition I had, the better I played. Pelle was not like that. Pelle needed to be number one and he didn't do well, didn't flourish amid competition. And Mike Keenan recognized that, and so Mike's plan was to put me down and to treat me in a way that Pelle could recognize that he was number one. I just wish Mike would've let me in on the plan, it would've been a little bit easier for me to deal with. But it was ingenious because it worked. Mike had a lot of idiosyncrasies like a lot of people do but he was a great motivator. Sometimes he didn't know when to take his finger off the button, but he could get teams to work hard, but sometimes only for a short period of time. I think fear is a short-term motivator but the desire to please your coach is a long-term motivator."

On November 10, 1985, Lindbergh died from injuries suffered when he lost control of his customized Porsche and crashed into a wall. The goaltender's alcohol-related death had a profound impact on Bob and many of his teammates.

"It was a life-changing event for me and I think a lot of us made a promise or vow, I know a lot of guys said that day that they wouldn't drink anymore. That wasn't a big thing in my life although I haven't touched a drop of alcohol since that day. It was life-changing as far as what I do now. I've been a pastor for twenty-one years with the same church outside of Buffalo but that day I surrendered my life to the Lord because I was afraid to die. Because I understood from growing up that when you die there are only two places; you either go to heaven or hell."

Froese was then thrust back into the starting role and led the NHL with five shutouts and shared the William Jennings Trophy with teammate Darren Jensen. However, after the Flyers were beaten by the Rangers in the division semifinals in 1986, Keenan was unhappy with his goaltending situation and Froese lost his starting role to Ron Hextall. Bob asked for a trade around Halloween of that year and was finally dealt to the Rangers for defenseman Kjell Samuelsson and a 1989 second-round draft pick (Patrik Juhlin) on December 18, 1986.

According to Froese, "I was surprised that I was traded to the Rangers because they had John Vanbiesbrouck, and he and I were numbers one and two the previous year for the end-of-season All-Star selections. But I really appreciated Phil Esposito. I thought he was a wonderful guy to play for. I really looked up to him in a lot of ways. I thought he had a handle on what being a 'team' meant and that was apparently because of the way the old Boston Bruins were. I know a lot of players appreciated him and I still hold him in high regard, not only because he was a great athlete and a great leader, but he was really a person who cared about other people."

"When I got there, Beezer was the guy and he had done well. And goalies are naturally competitive and any goalie who says they're not is lying—there is only one net. But it actually worked out because Beazer played the majority of the home games and I played the majority of the road games. So that's the way it worked out at that point. I was just happy to be in a place where I felt I was wanted, and Phil had done well by me as far as the way he treated me and financially and so I was happy to be there."

Bob's first start as a Ranger came unexpectedly on December 23, 1986, five days after being acquired from Philly. John Vanbiesbrouck was scheduled to start the game but shortly before warmups it was discovered that his arm and chest protector had been left at the Rangers practice site in Rye Playland in Westchester, so Froese got the call. "I thought it was a joke," Froese told reporters. "It was about a minute before we went out for warmups and I was just chatting with Ron Greschner when someone came by and said some of Johnny's pads were up in Rye and that I'd be starting."

The Rangers beat the Devils that night, 8–5. "Yeah it was a real goaltender's duel," 'Frosty' said wryly. "But the most important thing is to get the W. It's like I told the guys after the game, if you get me eight goals every night, it's going to be easy."

In a November 1987 game against the Islanders, Bob was briefly credited with a goal when Billy Smith dashed to the bench on a delayed Ranger penalty and an errant pass by Brent Sutter flew past point man Gerald Diduck and into the Islanders' empty net. At the time official scorer Ed Hertenstein deemed that Froese was the last Ranger to touch the puck and was therefore credited with the goal. "I was just happy that the goal counted because it was a game we wound up winning, 3–1, Froese said. "But after the game I was in the locker room and I saw it on the tape and I said, 'that's not my goal.' And I remember [Islanders GM] Bill Torrey and Billy Smith came out and said that I wanted the goal. I couldn't have cared less! So all along I was saying I don't want it and Espo was telling me to keep my mouth shut because it was good for public relations. It was interesting but one of my closest friends on the team, David Shaw, finally got credit for the goal. I told him that he owed me because he had a bonus clause for goals."

Because of his easygoing manner Bob was well-liked by teammates and fans as well as the media and was given the Rangers Good Guy Award in 1987–88.

Bob suffered a shoulder injury early in the 1989–90 season and after appearing in only 15 games, retired at the end of the campaign. He then transitioned easily into a coaching role, mentoring a young Mike Richter.

"Mike and I became close friends and that's why I eventually became the goalie coach. I left when Mike Keenan came in and I went to Don Maloney who was just a wonderful guy and I worked for him on the Island. But Mike was a phenomenal athlete and just a great goaltender. But as good a goaltender as he was, I found him to be an even better person. There's a picture that I have of me with my arms around Mike and John and part of my role was to make sure that the competition didn't have a negative effect on Mike in regards to dealing with a veteran like John and to, in some way, protect Mike and I understood my role. I still think that Mike Richter was one of the best specimens as a goalie, he did things I only wish I could do but he was a super teammate, one of the pleasures in my life is to have known and played with a guy like that," said Froese.

Bob Froese provided the Rangers with consistent goaltending for four seasons. In 98 games with New York, Bob compiled a 36–43–8 record with one shutout and a 3.63 GAA. In six playoff appearances with the Blueshirts, he went 1–3 with a 4.56 GAA.

Bob made another transition more than two decades ago when he became a pastor. He earned a Bachelor of Science degree in religion from Liberty University, then a master's degree in religion at Liberty's Baptist Theological Seminary and finally a PhD from Trinity Theological Seminary. He has served as senior pastor at Faith Fellowship Church in Clarence, New York, for more than twenty years.

As Froese tells it, "The senior elder in our church asked me if I would consider joining the pastoral staff and I thought he was nuts. I had a wonderful position working with the goaltenders and the young players and I really enjoyed it. But the more I prayed about it the more the Lord began leading me towards being a pastor. And it's not something I looked forward to because I always joke about it, I'm not complaining but in hockey as a goalie they shoot at you from the front but sometimes as a pastor they shoot at you from the back. But it's been twenty-one years and I've been able to get my schooling and I eventually earned my PhD and I worked at it with the same energy and the same diligence as I did in my hockey career. And there isn't a day that goes by that I'm not thankful that the Lord led me to this decision."

Regular Season

Season	Team	GP	W	L	T	GA	SA	SV	SV%	GAA	SO	MIN	G	A	PTS	PIM
1982–83	PHI	25	17	4	2	59	569	510	.896	2.52	4	1405	0	2	2	2
1983–84	PHI	48	28	13	7	150	1324	1174	.887	3.15	2	2855	0	2	2	10
1984–85	PHI	17	13	2	0	37	427	390	.913	2.39	1	927	0	1	1	2
1985–86	PHI	51	31	10	3	116	1270	1154	.909	2.55	5	2724	0	1	1	8
1986–87	PHI	3	3	0	0	8	88	80	.909	2.67	0	180	0	0	0	0
1986–87	NYR	28	14	11	0	92	784	692	.883	3.76	0	1469	0	2	2	0
1987–88	NYR	25	8	11	3	85	697	612	.878	3.54	0	1440	0	1	1	6
1988–89	NYR	30	9	14	4	102	787	685	.870	3.78	1	1621	0	1	1	6
1989–90	NYR	15	5	7	1	45	354	309	.873	3.33	0	812	0	0	0	0
NYR Totals	-	98	36	43	8	324	2622	2298	.876	3.64	1	5342	0	4	4	12
Career	-	242	128	72	20	694	6300	5606	.890	3.10	13	13,433	0	10	10	34

Playoffs

Season	Team	GP	W	L	T	GA	SA	SV	SV%	GAA	SO	MIN	G	A	PTS	PIM
1983–84	PHI	3	0	2	-	11	77	66	.857	4.29	0	154	0	0	0	0
1984–85	PHI	4	0	1	-	11	71	60	.845	4.52	0	146	0	0	0	2
1985–86	PHI	5	2	3	-	15	125	110	.880	3.07	0	293	0	1	1	0
1986–87	NYR	4	1	1	-	10	96	86	.896	3.64	0	165	0	0	0	7
1988–89	NYR	2	0	2	-	8	51	43	.843	6.67	0	72	0	1	1	0
NYR Totals	-	6	1	3	-	18	147	129	.877	4.57	0	237	0	1	1	7
Career	-	18	3	9	-	55	418	363	.868	4.00	0	825	0	2	2	9

Mike Richter—Franchise Goaltender
Born: September 22, 1966 in Abington, Pennsylvania
5-11, 185lb
Caught: Left
Rangers Debut: April 9, 1989 vs. Pittsburgh Penguins (playoffs)
Uniform #35
Seasons with Rangers: 15, 1988–90 (playoffs) to 2002–03
Stanley Cup: Rangers, 1993–94
All-Star Games: 1992, 1994, 2000

Courtesy of the New York Rangers

Mike Richter's Rangers career cannot be judged solely by statistics alone. In 14 seasons on Broadway he never led the league in goals-against average, save percentage, or shutouts. He had a losing record in eight of those seasons and even led the league in losses during a dismal 1999–2000 season. But Richter had a career year in 1993–94 and was one of the main reasons the Rangers were able to end their fifty-four-year Stanley Cup drought that spring.

Richter grew up playing hockey on the streets of Abington, Pennsylvania, a suburb of Philadelphia, and first gained the attention of scouts when he later starred at Germantown Academy and then Northwood Prep in Lake Placid, New York.

Rangers GM Craig Patrick selected Richter in the second round, (28th overall) in the 1985 entry draft following his graduation from high school. He went on to play for the University of Wisconsin but left after his sophomore year to join the United States national team. He appeared in the 1987 World Championships in addition to starting four games for the United States at the 1988 Calgary Winter Olympics.

Following the Olympics, Richter joined the Rangers' IHL team in Denver and made his NHL debut on April 9, 1989, when Phil Esposito called him up from the minors to start the fourth game of the division SemiFinals against the Pittsburgh Penguins. The Blueshirts had lost the first three games of the series by a combined 15–8 score and Espo was looking for anything to give his team a spark against the Mario Lemieux-led Penguins. Richter played well, making 30 saves, but lost, 4–3.

The Rangers had a new general manager, Neil Smith, and a new coach in Roger Neilson in 1989–90. Mike was the first winner of the Lars-Erik Sjoberg Award as the team's best rookie in training camp and he appeared in 23 games that season, posting a 12–5–5 record with a 3.00 GAA.

Over the next three seasons, Mike and John Vanbiesbrouck gave the Rangers their most effective goaltending duo since the days of Ed Giacomin and Gilles Villemure. The pair were nicknamed "VanRichterBrouck" and led the Blueshirts to a second-place finish in 1990–91. The following year, coach Roger Neilson alternated his two goaltenders through the first 76 games of the season, setting a record that will probably never be broken, and the Rangers won the Presidents' Trophy as the team with the league's best overall record. Both goaltenders stumbled in the playoffs, however.

After beating New Jersey in a seven-game series, the Rangers faced the defending Stanley Cup champion Pittsburgh Penguins. The Blueshirts were leading the series, two games to one, and were trying to hold on to a 4–2 lead in the fourth game when Ron Francis put a 65-foot slap shot past Richter about midway through the third period. It was Francis's second goal of the game and it had a deflating effect on the Rangers. Bob Errey scored to send the game into overtime where Francis completed his hat trick with the game-winner. The Rangers never recovered and lost the final two games of the series as the Penguins went on to win their second consecutive Stanley Cup.

Richter experienced a subpar season in 1992–93 as the Rangers went through some turmoil and missed the playoffs. There was also an expansion draft coming in June and the pressure was on Neil Smith to decide whether he was going to protect Vanbiesbrouck, who was twenty-nine years old, or Richter, who was three years younger. Smith decided to protect Richter and sent Beezer to Vancouver for defenseman Doug Lidster.

Richter proved to be the correct choice as Mike thrived on the additional work and had an exceptional season in 1993–94, leading the league in victories (42–12–6, with five shutouts and a 2.57 GAA), including a franchise-record 20-game unbeaten streak (17–0–3). He also received the MVP Award at the 1994 All-Star game at Madison Square Garden. In that game, Richter faced Vancouver's Pavel Bure on a penalty shot, stopping the "Russian Rocket" as he deked to the stick side.

The Rangers won the Presidents' trophy again that season and led by Mike's superior goaltending plowed through the Islanders (4–0), Capitals (4–1), and Devils (4–3) on their way to the Stanley Cup Finals against the Vancouver Canucks.

In the fourth game of the series with the Blueshirts up two games to one, but down by a goal in the second period, Richter once again faced Bure on a penalty shot. Bure tried the same fake and once again Richter prevailed, enabling the Blueshirts to come back and win the game, 4–2, and go on to win the tense seven-game battle for the Stanley Cup.

As an example of how close the series was, the Rangers scored a total of 21 goals against the Canucks (including one empty-netter), while Richter held Vancouver to 19 goals. In 23 playoff games that spring, Mike posted a 16–7 record with four shutouts and a 2.07 GAA.

In 1996, Mike represented the United States at the World Cup and was selected as the tournament's most valuable player. Richter also appeared in the 1998 and 2002 Olympics, earning a silver medal in Salt Lake City in 2002.

Among Richter's assets were his focus, agility, and ability to play his angles extremely well. He was also a fitness fanatic who kept himself in top shape. Unfortunately, injuries hampered Mike beginning in 2000 when he tore the anterior cruciate ligament in his left knee at the All-Star Skills competition. The injury required reconstructive surgery. After months of grueling rehab work Richter returned from the injury only to tear the ACL in his other knee five months later. Then Mike suffered a fractured skull and concussion in March 2002 when he was struck on the side of the head by a slapshot from Chris Tamer of the Atlanta Thrashers. Richter returned at the beginning of the 2002–03 season but was inadvertently kneed in the head by Oiler Todd Marchant on November 5. He tried to return from the injury, but the risk was too great and he retired before the start of the 2003–04 season. Mike then became only the third Ranger to have his number retired as his No. 35 jersey was raised to the rafters of the Garden in February 2004.

Richter never played for any other NHL team but the Rangers, but in June 1998, when he was a free agent, he was claimed by the Nashville Predators in the expansion draft and then re-signed by the Blueshirts less than a month later. Then in June 2002 right before he was set to become a free agent, his rights were sent to Edmonton for a fourth-round draft pick. Once again, he was re-signed by the Rangers a few days later.

At the time of his retirement, the Rangers seventh "franchise goaltender" held many career team regular season and playoff records, but has since been surpassed by Henrik Lundqvist. He still holds the team record for most saves in a single game (59 at Vancouver on January 31, 1991) and most wins in a playoff year (16 in 1994). He also shares the team record for assists by a goaltender in a single game (two) with Ed Giacomin and John Vanbiesbrouck and the Blueshirts record of four shutouts in a single playoff year with Davey Kerr.

Mike also appeared in three All-Star games and was the MVP of the 1994 midseason exhibition. In addition, he was selected as the Rangers MVP twice (1999–2000, 2001–02) and won the Players' Player Award (1990–91, 1999–2000). He was given the Frank Boucher Trophy as the most popular Ranger four times (1990–91, 1998–99, 1999–2000, 2001–2002). He also won the team's "Crumb Bum" Award for community service (1996–97), the Rangers Good Guy Award (1990–91) and the Rangers Fan Club Rookie of the Year (1989–90).

After retiring, Mike earned a degree in Ethics, Politics and Economics with a concentration in Environmental Policy from Yale University and is currently the president of Brightcore Energy and remains active in Ranger alumni and charity events.

Regular Season

Season	Team	GP	W	L	T	GA	SA	SV	SV%	GAA	SO	MIN	G	A	PTS	PIM
1989–90	NYR	23	12	5	5	66	686	620	.904	3.00	0	1320	0	3	3	0
1990–91	NYR	45	21	13	7	135	1392	1257	.903	3.12	0	2596	0	1	1	4
1991–92	NYR	41	23	12	2	119	1205	1086	.901	3.11	3	2298	0	0	0	6
1992–93	NYR	38	13	19	3	134	1180	1046	.886	3.82	1	2105	0	5	5	2
1993–94	NYR	68	42	12	6	159	1758	1599	.910	2.57	5	3710	0	0	0	2
1994–95	NYR	35	14	17	2	97	884	787	.890	2.92	2	1993	0	0	0	2
1995–96	NYR	41	24	13	3	107	1221	1114	.912	2.68	3	2396	0	1	1	4
1996–97	NYR	61	33	22	6	161	1945	1784	.917	2.69	4	3598	0	0	0	4
1997–98	NYR	72	21	31	15	184	1888	1704	.903	2.66	0	4143	0	1	1	2
1998–99	NYR	68	27	30	8	170	1898	1728	.910	2.63	4	3878	0	0	0	0
1999–00	NYR	61	22	31	8	173	1815	1642	.905	2.87	0	3622	0	0	0	4
2000–01	NYR	45	20	21	3	144	1343	1199	.893	3.28	0	2635	0	0	0	0
2001–02	NYR	55	24	26	4	157	1675	1518	.906	2.95	2	3195	0	0	0	4
2002–03	NYR	13	5	6	1	34	329	295	.897	2.94	0	694	0	0	0	0
Career	NYR	666	301	258	73	1840	19,219	17,379	.904	2.89	24	38,183	0	11	11	3

Playoffs

Season	Team	GP	W	L	T	GA	SA	SV	SV%	GAA	SO	MIN	G	A	PTS	PIM
1988–89	NYR	1	0	1	-	4	30	26	.867	4.12	0	58	0	0	0	0
1989–90	NYR	6	3	2	-	19	181	162	.895	3.45	0	330	0	0	0	0
1990–91	NYR	6	2	4	-	14	182	168	.923	2.69	1	313	0	0	0	0
1991–92	NYR	7	4	2	-	24	226	202	.894	3.50	1	412	0	0	0	0
1993–94	NYR	23	16	7	-	49	623	574	.921	2.07	4	1417	0	0	0	2
1994–95	NYR	7	2	5	-	23	189	166	.878	3.60	0	384	0	0	0	0
1995–96	NYR	11	5	6	-	36	308	272	.883	3.27	0	661	0	0	0	0
1996–97	NYR	15	9	6	-	33	488	455	.932	2.11	3	939	0	1	1	0
Career	NYR	76	41	33	-	202	2227	2025	.909	2.68	9	4514	0	1	1	2

Mike Richter and the Candy Bars

by Patrick Hoffman

When it comes to being a hockey fan, there are many dreams that we all have.

We all want our teams to win the Stanley Cup. We want to be able to touch hockey's Holy Grail, and lastly, we all want to hang out with our favorite team and more importantly, our favorite player.

During the strike-shortened 1994–95 NHL season, I had the unbelievable opportunity to do the latter. It was then that I had my ultimate hockey fan experience: getting to spend time with my hockey idol Mike Richter of the New York Rangers.

Back then, I was a Pee-Wee goaltender. At the time, I had been a netminder for five years and had modeled my game after Richter.

While I knew how to cut down the angles, control my rebounds, and play the puck behind the net, there was one area of my game that I was inconsistent with. It was stopping breakaways, which leads me to the whole point of this story.

I did not learn how to stop a breakaway from the usual suspects. Was it from a goalie coach? No. Was it from summer hockey camps? No again.

I was stuck. I was looking for guidance from someone, somewhere.

That all changed on March 10, 1995. It was then that I learned how to stop a breakaway from Richter, who at the time, was one of the best goaltenders in one-on-one situations.

That day, my father and I—he then being the lawyer for former Rangers head coach and current NHL senior VP and director of hockey operations Colin Campbell—were going to travel with the Rangers to Montreal. The team was scheduled to take on the Canadiens the very next night at the Montreal Forum.

When we got to John F. Kennedy Airport in Queens, New York, I introduced myself to the players. I mingled, as any hockey-obsessed kid would, with the likes of Mark Messier, Adam Graves and Brian Leetch.

While that was all good and dandy, the real person I wanted to talk shop with was Richter. As such, I took a walk around the airport and was able to find him in a small magazine shop.

Star-crossed, I introduced myself to the lifelong Blueshirt and told him my problem when it came to stopping breakaways. I knew he was a nice guy, having met him before, so I was confident he would have some valuable tips, but what I didn't know was that he was going to explain it all for me.

Richter looked at a nearby shelf and grabbed two small 3 Musketeers bars, a Reese's Peanut Butter Cup, and a Snickers. At first, I assumed he was being courteous and buying me some candy, but then he took to the ground and started setting up the chocolates.

In the middle of the shop, Richter used the two 3 Musketeers bars as the net, the Reese's as the goaltender and the Snickers as the shooter. With each candy bar having assumed its respective role, Richter demonstrated what I needed to change.

He told me that my best bet was to do everything possible to stay with the shooter and let him make the first move. He continued by showing me how to play the correct angle and not start backing into my crease until the shooter was the perfect distance away.

Since that day, I have been a changed man when faced with an opponent on the break.

After always coming up on the losing end in penalty shot situations prior to Richter's lesson, I went 5-for-5 to close out the season. In later years, I continued to excel, winning breakaway competitions at the high school level and in men's leagues.

Looking back, it's safe to say I owe at least part of my ability as a goaltender to the best teacher I ever had.

Patrick Hoffman has covered the NHL for Sportsnet.ca, Kukla's Korner, Spector's Hockey, About.com, NHL Network Radio blog, TheHockeyNews.com, The Fourth Period, Stan Fischler's The Fischler Report, as well as several other outlets.

CHAPTER ELEVEN

Return to Glory

Neil Smith will always be remembered as the general manager who assembled the team that ended the Rangers' fifty-four-year Stanley Cup drought.

But it didn't happen overnight and it certainly wasn't easy. It took five seasons, three coaches, and several deals involving big name players to finally accomplish what many fans thought would never happen in their lifetime.

Smith had been a tall, skinny defenseman for Western Michigan University who became the first WMU player to be drafted by an NHL team, going to the Islanders in the 13th round of the 1974 amateur draft. After bouncing around the minors for a few years, he hung up his skates and joined the Islanders scouting department, working under Jim Devellano. When Devellano left to become GM of the Detroit Red Wings, Smith followed him and worked his way up to become director of scouting and GM of the Adirondack Red Wings of the AHL, a team that won two league championships with Smith in charge. Smith had been on the Garden's radar since his scouting days with the Islanders and when Scotty Bowman, Herb Brooks, and Bob Johnson all turned down the GM job following the dismissal of Phil Esposito, the Garden's executive vice president, Jack Diller, reached out to Neil, who jumped at the opportunity.

Smith's philosophy was to build through the draft which was a vast departure from the usual Rangers mantra of "Win Now!" But slowly he prevailed. He also reorganized the scouting department, replacing some of Espo's cronies and adding European scout Christer Rockstrom.

Smith wisely hired Roger Neilson to coach the team he inherited from Phil Esposito which included a mix of veterans and some good young players with raw talent such as Brian Leetch, Darren Turcotte,

Ulf Dahlen, and Mark Janssens. Neilson had seven seasons of NHL coaching experience and had taken the Canucks to the Stanley Cup Finals in 1982. He also had a reputation as a teacher and pioneer in the use of videotape and was a stabilizing influence on the younger players, a stark contrast from the chaos of the Esposito-Bergeron debacle.

The Rangers got off to a fast 8–1–3 start in 1989–90 but began slipping by midseason. Smith then pulled off his first big deal as GM, sending Tomas Sandstrom and Tony Granato to the Los Angeles Kings for high-scoring center Bernie Nicholls. Smith was active again at the trading deadline, sending Ulf Dahlen and a fourth-round draft pick to Minnesota for speedy Mike Gartner.

The Blueshirts finished the regular season in first place in the Patrick Division with a 36–31–13 record. They beat the Islanders in the division semifinals but fell to the Washington Capitals in the second round of the playoffs. Nevertheless, it was quite a rebound season for the Blueshirts and a solid building block for the future.

That summer Smith drafted defenseman Michael Stewart in the first round. Stewart never played a game for the Rangers but Smith did better in subsequent rounds, selecting Doug Weight, Sergei Zubov, and Sergei Nemchinov.

The Rangers finished with the same 36–31–13 record the following season, good enough for second place. Once again they were ousted from the playoffs by the Caps, this time in the opening round.

During the summer of 1991, Smith selected Alexei Kovalev in the first round of the draft, making him the first Russian ever selected in the opening round. He also signed Adam Graves as a free agent away from the Edmonton Oilers. Neil had previously scouted and selected Graves for Detroit in the second round of the 1986 entry draft. The twenty-three-year-old left winger wasn't known as a big scorer but was tough and would stand up for his teammates. Graves was a Type 1 Free Agent and under the rules at the time, Smith had to surrender a player of equal value to Edmonton, Troy Mallette.

"Big Deal Neil" then had the opportunity to make the most important trade of his tenure and acquired Mark Messier, one of the greatest leaders the NHL has ever known. As they had in 1988 when they ran into financial trouble and had to deal Wayne Gretzky to Los Angeles, the Edmonton Oilers needed cash and were willing to trade off their assets. Messier was acquired on October 4, 1991, for Bernie Nicholls, Steven Rice, and Louie DeBrusk. As part of the deal, David Shaw was later sent to Edmonton for Jeff Beukeboom.

Smith was subjected to criticism for making the Messier deal. Many felt that Mark already had a lot of hockey mileage on his thirty-one-year-old body and that his best years were behind him. Messier silenced the critics by leading the Rangers in scoring (35–72–107) as the Blueshirts finished with the best overall record in the NHL. But once again they fell short in the playoffs.

They got past the New Jersey Devils, winning a seventh game in the playoffs for the first time in franchise history and then faced the defending Stanley Cup Champion Pittsburgh Penguins. The Blueshirts were leading the series two games to one and held a 4–2 lead in the fourth game when the roof fell in. About midway through the third period, Ron Francis put a 65-foot slap shot past Mike Richter. It was Francis's second goal of the game and it had a deflating effect on the Rangers. Bob Errey scored to send the game into overtime, where Francis scored his third goal of the game to win it for the Penguins. The Rangers never recovered and lost the final two games of the series, as Pittsburgh went on to win their second consecutive Stanley Cup under the leadership of former Rangers general manager Craig Patrick.

The 1992–93 season was marred by inner turmoil between the captain and the coach. Messier was not a fan of Neilson's defensive style of play and wasn't shy about airing his feelings. As Neilson once said, "Mark didn't always like the way I coached and I didn't always like the way he played." Messier's production fell to 25–66–91, a 16-point drop-off from the previous season and the Rangers faltered. Neilson was fired in January and replaced by assistant coach Ron Smith on an interim basis. He could do little to revive the team and the Rangers finished out of the playoffs, leading Neil Smith to bring in Mike Keenan as coach.

"Iron Mike" Keenan had previously taken the Flyers to the Stanley Cup Finals in 1985 and 1987, losing both times to the Edmonton Oilers.

After the Flyers were eliminated in the first round of the 1988 playoffs, he was fired but quickly resurfaced with the Blackhawks as both coach and GM. He took them to the finals in 1992, losing to Pittsburgh and he abruptly quit during the following season.

Under Keenan, the Rangers dominated the league once again, finishing with the best record in the NHL. Urged by Keenan to beef up his team for the playoffs, Smith made a number of deals at the trading deadline, acquiring Steve Larmer, Stephane Matteau, Brian Noonan, Glenn Anderson, Nick Kypreos, and Craig MacTavish at the cost of Tony Amonte, Mike Gartner, Todd Marchant, James Patrick, and Darren Turcotte. After the dust had settled, the Rangers wound up with seven former Edmonton players in the lineup, earning them the nickname "Oilers East."

They breezed through the first two rounds of the playoffs against the Islanders and Washington Capitals. Messier then backed up his "guarantee" for a win in the sixth game and Stephane Matteau scored his famous double-overtime goal in the seventh to squeak past the Devils in the conference finals. They then managed to survive a grueling seven-game series against the Vancouver Canucks to win their first Stanley Cup in fifty-four years.

Unfortunately, that turned out to be the apex of Smith's career as an NHL general manager.

Mike Keenan was guilty of the same kind of duplicitous behavior that Michel Bergeron had exhibited while working for Phil Esposito a few years earlier. It was discovered that during the Stanley Cup Finals he was negotiating with the Detroit Red Wings to take over as GM and coach. He then abruptly declared himself a "free agent" on July 15, 1994, when he claimed that the Rangers had "materially breached" his contract with the team by not paying his bonus on time. He then met with the Red Wings on July 16, apparently didn't like their offer, and wound up signing a five-year deal with the St. Louis Blues the next day. The Rangers subsequently demanded an investigation by NHL commissioner Gary Bettman, who allowed Keenan to join the Blues as coach and general manager. However, as compensation for Keenan's leaving with four years remaining on his Ranger contract, Bettman approved the Blues' trade of Petr Nedved to the Rangers for

Esa Tikkanen and Doug Lidster. Nedved was thought to be a future star at the time.

Bettman ordered the Rangers to pay Keenan a $608,000 bonus and for Keenan in turn to repay the team $400,000 of it. He then suspended Keenan from performing any coaching or general manager duties for the Blues for sixty days and fined him $100,000 for "conduct detrimental to the league." Bettman also found the Blues and Detroit Red Wings guilty of tampering and fined them $250,000 and $25,000 respectively.

Colin Campbell was named Rangers coach, but the 1994–95 season was delayed and shortened due to a lockout by the owners. When play resumed, the Rangers finally got to raise their Stanley Cup banner to the rafters at Madison Square Garden in January 1995. They finished in fourth place and lost to the Flyers in the second round.

What followed was a series of ill-advised trades and free agent signings. In a last-ditch effort to recapture some of the Oilers magic, Smith signed Wayne Gretzky as a free agent in 1996. With "The Great One" once again teamed with Messier, the Rangers made it to the conference finals but lost to the Flyers.

That was the last time the Blueshirts made the playoffs with Smith in charge. Campbell was replaced midway through the 1997–98 season by John Muckler who had previously coached the Oilers to a Stanley Cup victory. Muckler had also served as GM for the Buffalo Sabres, so he likely also had his sights set on Smith's job. The pair spent most of the next two seasons disagreeing about the readiness of Manny Malhotra, Smith's 1998 first-round draft pick. Smith wanted to keep him with the Rangers while Muckler gave the youngster little ice time. In 2000, Smith asked his MSG bosses for permission to fire Muckler. His request was denied, and they were both dismissed at the end of the season.

Smith then went on to work as an analyst for various networks, including ESPN, TSN, Versus, and NHL Network. In June 2006, Smith was named general manager of the New York Islanders, thus becoming the only person in NHL history to serve as general manager with both New York teams.

However, Islanders owner Charles Wang had created a management structure in which decisions were to be made by a group of advisors rather than by the general manager alone. Within a month of hiring Smith, Wang changed his mind and fired him, claiming that he didn't believe that Neil could work within those constraints. Smith later owned and coached the Johnstown Chiefs and Greenville Road Warriors of the ECHL and continues to work as a broadcaster.

Rule Changes:

1991–92: Video replays were employed to assist referees in goal/no goal determinations. The goal crease was changed to a semi-circle and increased in size. Penalties were added for crease infringement and unnecessary contact with the goaltender. Goals were disallowed if the puck entered the net while a player of the attacking team was standing on the goal crease line, was in the goal crease, or placed his stick in the goal crease.

1998–99: The league instituted a two-referee system with each team to play 20 regular-season games with two referees and a pair of linesmen. Also, the goal lines, blue lines, defensive zone faceoff circles and markings all moved two feet closer to center, creating 13 feet of room behind the nets and cutting the neutral zone from 58 to 54 feet. The goal crease was altered so that it extended only one foot beyond each goal post (eight feet across in total) and has straight sides for the first 4'6". Only the top of the crease remained rounded.

1999–2000: Each team to play 25 home and 25 road games using the two-referee system. Crease rule revised to implement a "no harm, no foul, no video review" standard. An attacking player's position, whether inside or outside the crease, does not in itself, determine whether a goal should be allowed or disallowed. The on-ice judgment of the referee(s)—instead of video review—will determine whether a goal is good or not.

In addition, regular season games tied at the end of three periods will result in each team being awarded one point in the standings. As before, there will be a five-minute sudden death overtime when the score is tied after three periods, but each team will play four on four, with four skaters and a goaltender. In the event that penalties dictate that one team has a two-man advantage, the penalized team plays with three skaters, while the team with the two-man advantage adds a fifth skater. A team scoring in overtime will receive one additional point in the standings.

Corey Hirsch
Born: July 1, 1972 in Medicine Hat, Alberta
5-10, 175lb
Caught: Left
Rangers Debut: January 19, 1993 at Detroit Red Wings
Uniform #31
Seasons with Rangers: 1, 1992–93

Corey Hirsch was selected by Neil Smith in the eighth round (168th overall) in the 1991 entry draft following three outstanding seasons with the Kamloops Blazers of the WHL. Hirsch then capped off his junior career in 1992 by being named the Canadian Major Junior Goaltender of the Year and top netminder in that season's Memorial Cup tournament.

He spent most of the 1992–93 season with the Binghamton Rangers and led the AHL with 35 wins and a 2.79 GAA. For his efforts he earned a spot on the All-Star team, the Dudley "Red" Garrett Memorial Trophy for AHL Rookie of the Year, and shared the Harry Holmes Memorial Trophy, awarded annually to the goaltenders of the AHL team with the lowest goals against average, with teammate Boris Rousson.

The red-haired native of Medicine Hat, Alberta, also made his NHL debut with the Rangers that season, appearing in four games and posting a 1–2–1 record with a 3.75 GAA.

The next season Hirsch played 45 games with the Canadian National Team and was also a member of Canada's Olympic Team. At the 1994 Olympics in Lillehammer, Norway, Corey won a silver medal after losing in a shootout to Sweden in the gold medal game. The shootout-winning goal by Peter Forsberg was memorialized on a Swedish postage stamp, featuring the image of a generic goalie because Hirsch refused to allow his likeness to be used.

He was traded to the Vancouver Canucks in April 1995 for Nathan Lafayette and spent the next four years in the Canucks organization.

Hirsch later signed with Nashville as a free agent in 1999 and also saw action with Anaheim, Washington, and Dallas. He then spent two seasons playing in Europe and became a goaltending consultant for Hockey Canada and the 2007 and 2008 national teams. He then served as goaltending coach for Toronto and St. Louis.

In 2017, Hirsch revealed that he suffered from a debilitating form of obsessive-compulsive disorder and often contemplated suicide. He has since received psychiatric help for his problem and is a TV analyst for Sportsnet.

Regular Season

Season	Team	GP	W	L	T	GA	SA	SV	SV%	GAA	SO	MIN	G	A	PTS	PIM
1992–93	NYR	4	1	2	1	14	116	102	.879	3.75	0	224	0	0	0	0
1995–96	VAN	41	17	14	6	114	1173	1059	.903	2.93	1	2338	0	2	2	2
1996–97	VAN	39	12	20	4	116	1090	974	.894	3.27	2	2127	0	1	1	6
1997–98	VAN	1	0	0	0	5	34	29	.853	6.05	0	50	0	0	0	0
1998–99	VAN	20	3	8	3	48	435	387	.890	3.13	1	919	0	0	0	0
2000–01	WSH	1	1	0	0	0	8	8	1.000	0.00	0	20	0	0	0	0
2002–03	DAL	2	0	1	0	4	39	35	.897	2.46	0	97	0	0	0	0
NYR Totals	-	4	1	2	1	14	116	102	.879	3.75	0	224	0	0	0	0
Career	-	108	34	45	14	301	2895	2594	.896	3.13	4	5775	0	3	0	0

Playoffs

Season	Team	GP	W	L	T	GA	SA	SV	SV%	GAA	SO	MIN	G	A	PTS	PIM
1995–96	VAN	6	2	3	-	21	166	145	.873	3.73	0	338	0	0	0	2
Career	VAN	6	2	3	-	21	166	145	.873	3.73	0	338	0	0	0	2

Glenn Healy
Born: August 23, 1962 in Pickering, Ontario
5-9, 190lb
Caught: Left
Rangers Debut: October 7, 1993 vs. Tampa Bay Lightning
Uniform #30
Seasons with Rangers: 4, 1993–94 to 1996–97
Stanley Cup: Rangers, 1993–94

Courtesy of the New York Rangers

John Vanbiesbrouck and Mike Richter formed a pretty solid goaltending duo for the Rangers beginning in 1989–90. But when expansion came along in 1993 (in which the Anaheim Mighty Ducks and Florida Panthers joined the league) the Rangers could only protect one of them and chose Richter, trading Beezer to Vancouver for Doug Lidster.

Needing a veteran to back up Richter, Neil Smith acquired Glenn Healy from the Tampa Bay Lightning in June 1993. Healy had played four years of college hockey with Western Michigan University and signed with the LA Kings as a free agent following graduation in 1985. He notched his first NHL win at Madison Square Garden in October 1987 and played a total of 87 games for the Kings over three seasons. He signed with the Islanders in 1989 and led them to the conference finals in 1992–93, appearing in all 18 playoff games that season and placing fourth among playoff netminders with nine victories and a 3.19 GAA.

But then, in the same expansion draft that cost the Rangers Vanbiesbrouck, Healy was left unprotected and selected by the Anaheim Mighty Ducks. The next day Healy was then claimed by Tampa Bay in Phase II of the expansion draft in which Tampa Bay, Ottawa, and San Jose were allowed to select players from the rosters of the Panthers and Mighty Ducks.

But Glenn's whirlwind tour of NHL teams wasn't quite over yet. He was then sent to the Rangers in return for Tampa Bay's third-round pick in the 1993 entry draft which the Blueshirts had acquired in an earlier deal.

Healy slid nicely into the backup role behind young Mike Richter. He was reliable and well-liked by his teammates, fans, and the media, who presented him with their Good Guy Award in 1995–96. He also shared the Rangers Fan Club's Ceil Seidel Award for Dedication with Adam Graves in 1995–96 and fulfilled every hockey player's life-long dream by getting his name on the Stanley Cup in 1994.

In August 1997 Healy signed with the Toronto Maple Leafs and retired at the end of the 2000–01 season. He then worked as an analyst for *Hockey Night in Canada* and TSN. In 2008 he left the broadcasting booth to take a position with the NHL Players' Association. He subsequently left the NHLPA and returned to broadcasting. He is currently the director of the NHL Alumni Association.

Healy is a bagpipe aficionado and returned to New York City with a pipe band on the first anniversary of the attacks on 9/11 to play in Carnegie Hall. "That was probably one of the most moving experiences I've had," Healy told Sean Fitz-Gerald, of Canada's *National Post*. "We played the very last song of the night. They shut down the house lights, and we had a cop come out for each piper. Cops took our pipes.

No one could see what was going on. We all put Rangers sweaters on. The house lights came on, the pipe band is standing with Rangers sweaters on, and we played 'New York, New York.' And Brian Leetch, who was at the concert, said to me, 'it was the first time we've had a standing ovation since we won the Cup.'"

Regular Season

Season	Team	GP	W	L	T	GA	SA	SV	SV%	GAA	SO	MIN	G	A	PTS	PIM
1985–86	LAK	1	0	0	0	6	35	29	.829	7.12	0	51	0	0	0	0
1987–88	LAK	34	12	18	1	135	1005	870	.866	4.34	1	1865	0	2	2	6
1988–89	LAK	48	25	19	2	192	1502	1310	.872	4.27	0	2699	0	1	1	28
1989–90	NYI	39	12	19	6	128	1204	1076	.894	3.49	2	2197	0	1	1	7
1990–91	NYI	53	18	24	9	166	1557	1391	.893	3.32	0	2999	0	2	2	14
1991–92	NYI	37	14	16	4	124	1045	921	.881	3.80	1	1960	0	1	1	18
1992–93	NYI	47	22	20	2	146	1316	1170	.889	3.30	1	2655	0	2	2	2
1993–94	NYR	29	10	12	2	69	567	498	.878	3.03	2	1368	0	2	2	2
1994–95	NYR	17	8	6	1	35	377	342	.907	2.36	1	888	0	2	2	2
1995–96	NYR	44	17	14	11	124	1237	1113	.900	2.90	2	2564	0	1	1	8
1996–97	NYR	23	5	12	4	59	632	573	.907	2.61	1	1357	0	0	0	4
1997–98	TOR	21	4	10	2	53	453	400	.883	2.98	0	1068	0	0	0	0
1998–99	TOR	9	6	3	0	27	257	230	.895	2.97	0	546	0	0	0	0
1999–00	TOR	20	9	10	0	59	527	468	.888	3.04	2	1164	0	1	1	2
2000–01	TOR	15	4	7	3	38	331	293	.885	2.62	0	871	0	0	0	0
NYR Totals	-	113	40	44	18	287	2813	2526	.898	2.79	6	6177	0	5	5	16
Career	-	437	166	190	47	1361	12,045	10,684	.887	3.37	13	24,252	0	15	15	93

Playoffs

Season	Team	GP	W	L	T	GA	SA	SV	SV%	GAA	SO	MIN	G	A	PTS	PIM
1987–88	LAK	4	1	3	-	20	127	107	.843	5.04	0	238	0	0	0	4
1988–89	LAK	3	0	1	-	6	59	53	.898	3.72	0	97	0	0	0	2
1989–90	NYI	4	1	2	-	9	79	70	.886	3.25	0	166	0	1	1	0
1992–93	NYI	18	9	8	-	59	524	465	.887	3.19	0	1109	0	3	3	0
1993–94	NYR	2	0	0	-	1	17	16	.941	0.89	0	68	0	0	0	0
1994–95	NYR	5	2	1	-	13	93	80	.860	3.39	0	230	0	0	0	0
1998–99	TOR	1	0	0	-	0	5	5	1.000	0.00	0	20	0	0	0	0
NYR Totals	-	7	2	1		14	110	96	.876	2.82	0	298	0	0	0	0
Career	-	37	13	15		108	905	797	.881	3.36	0	1928	0	4	4	6

Jamie Ram
Born: January 18, 1971 in Scarborough, Ontario
5-11, 175lb
Caught: Left
Rangers Debut: February 3, 1996 at Colorado Avalanche
Uniform #34
Seasons with Rangers: 1, 1995–96

Courtesy of the New York Rangers

Jamie Ram was selected by Neil Smith in the 10th round (213th overall) of the 1991 entry draft after only one year at Michigan Tech. He played three more seasons with the Huskies, earning First Team All-Star honors in his senior year.

He was assigned to the Binghamton Rangers in 1994–95 and brought up on February 3, 1996, to back up Glenn Healy in a game against the Avalanche in Colorado. The Rangers were having a bad night and coach Colin Campbell pulled Healy at the 13:55 mark of the second period after surrendering seven goals. Ram played the rest of the game and did not allow a goal.

He was returned to Binghamton shortly thereafter and did not play in the NHL again.

Ram signed as a free agent with the San Jose Sharks in 1997 and moved to the Anaheim Mighty Ducks organization the next season.

Ram also played in Japan, Finland, Sweden, and Russia and retired at the end of the 2003–04 season.

Regular Season

Season	Team	GP	W	L	T	GA	SA	SV	SV%	GAA	SO	MIN	G	A	PTS	PIM
1995–96	NYR	1	0	0	0	0	9	9	1.000	0.00	0	27	0	0	0	0
Career	NYR	1	0	0	0	0	9	9	1.000	0.00	0	27	0	0	0	0

Jason Muzzatti
Born: February 3, 1970 in Toronto, Ontario
6-2, 210lb
Caught: Left
Rangers Debut: October 9, 1997 at Calgary Flames
Uniform #31
Seasons with Rangers: 1, 1997–98

Jason Muzzatti was acquired by Neil Smith from the Carolina Hurricanes for a fourth-round draft pick to back up Mike Richter after Glenn Healy signed as a free agent with the Toronto Maple Leafs in the summer of 1997.

Muzzatti had been the starting goaltender for Michigan State, earning CCHA Second Team All-Star honors in 1988 and a CCHA First Team All-Star and a NCAA West Second Team All-American berth in 1990. He was the first-round pick (21st overall) of the Calgary Flames in the 1988 NHL entry draft.

Muzzatti made his NHL debut with the Flames during the 1993–94 season and was claimed on waivers by the Hartford Whalers at the beginning of the 1995–96 campaign. He spent most of his time in Hartford backing up Sean Burke and was traded to the Rangers shortly after the Whalers moved to North Carolina.

While in New York, Muzzatti lost his backup role to Dan Cloutier and finished up with a 0–3–2 record in six appearances with a 3.26 GAA. He was traded to San Jose in exchange for Rich Brennan on March 24, 1998. He missed most of the following season due to heart surgery. In 1998, Muzzatti moved to Europe and finished his career playing for teams in Germany, Finland, and Italy.

Regular Season

Season	Team	GP	W	L	T	GA	SA	SV	SV%	GAA	SO	MIN	G	A	PTS	PIM
1993–94	CGY	1	0	1	0	8	35	27	.771	8.00	0	60	0	0	0	0
1994–95	CGY	1	0	0	0	0	8	8	1.000	0.00	0	10	0	0	0	0
1995–96	HAR	22	4	8	3	49	551	502	.911	2.90	1	1013	0	0	0	33
1996–97	HAR	31	9	13	5	91	815	724	.888	3.43	0	1591	0	1	1	18
1997–98	NYR	6	0	3	2	17	156	139	.891	3.26	0	313	0	0	0	10

Season	Team	GP	W	L	T	GA	SA	SV	SV%	GAA	SO	MIN	G	A	PTS	PIM
1997–98	SJS	1	0	0	0	2	13	11	.846	4.49	0	27	0	0	0	0
NYR Totals	-	6	0	3	2	17	156	139	.891	3.26	0	313	0	0	0	10
Career	-	62	13	25	10	167	1578	1411	.894	3.32	1	3014	0	1	1	61

Dan Cloutier
Born: April 22, 1976 in Mont Laurier, Quebec
6-1, 195lb
Caught: Left
Rangers Debut: January 3, 1998 at Washington Capitals
Uniform #34, 39
Seasons with Rangers: 2, 1997–98 to 1998–99

Courtesy of the New York Rangers

Dan Cloutier became the first goaltender ever selected by the Rangers in the opening round when he was taken by Neil Smith with the 25th overall pick in the 1994 entry draft.

Cloutier's pedigree was sound, having played for the Memorial Cup-winning Sault Ste. Marie Greyhounds in 1993. He also appeared in three games for Team Canada's gold medal-winning squad at the 1995 World Junior Championships as well as backstopping the Guelph Storm to the 1996 Memorial Cup finals.

With Mike Richter firmly ensconced as the Blueshirt's number one netminder, Cloutier spent most of his Rangers career in Binghamton and Hartford of the AHL. He appeared in only 34 games over two seasons with the Rangers, posting a 10–13–4 record with a 2.62 GAA.

Cloutier is probably best remembered by Rangers fans for a wild fight he had with Islanders goaltender Tommy Salo in the third period of a late-season game between the two rivals on April 4, 1998. The Islanders had just scored to take a 3–0 lead and coach Mike Milbury called a timeout which incensed the Rangers, who felt he was rubbing it in. At the next faceoff, Milbury and Rangers coach John Muckler both sent out their tough guys and mayhem ensued as each of the five skaters paired up and started swinging. Each was a pretty even matchup except for P. J. Stock and Mariusz Czerkawski, with Stock clearly getting the better of the Islander. When it became apparent that none of the Islanders could break free to help their teammate, Salo raced up ice to intercede. Cloutier followed suit and wound up pummeling the Islanders goaler with at least fifteen unanswered punches. Once he had finished with Salo, Cloutier skated to the Islanders bench and challenged them to come out and fight him. There were no volunteers.

"Dan was a feisty guy," said Jeff Beukeboom in Gil Martin's book, *Ice Wars*. "He was a pretty good goalie but he was feisty. That was part of his game. He was competitive. It was just in the heat of the moment but afterwards it was hilarious. Everyone got a good chuckle out of it."

Cloutier was eventually traded to Tampa Bay with Niklas Sundstrom and the Rangers' first- and third-round picks in the 2000 draft for Chicago's first round pick (which was previously acquired by Tampa Bay) in the 1999 draft. Neil Smith used that pick to select Pavel Brendl, who was labeled a can't miss prospect. Unfortunately, Brendl came to training camp overweight and under-motivated and never played a game for the Rangers.

Cloutier later spent five seasons with the Vancouver Canucks before winding up his NHL career with the Los Angeles Kings in 2007–08.

Regular Season

Season	Team	GP	W	L	T	GA	SA	SV	SV%	GAA	SO	MIN	G	A	PTS	PIM
1997–98	NYR	12	4	5	1	23	248	225	.907	2.50	0	551	0	0	0	19
1998–99	NYR	22	6	8	3	49	570	521	.914	2.68	0	1097	0	0	0	2
1999–00	TBL	52	9	30	3	145	1258	1113	.885	3.44	0	2492	0	0	0	29
2000–01	TBL	24	3	13	3	59	541	482	.891	3.52	1	1005	0	0	0	4
2000–01	VAN	16	4	6	5	37	348	311	.894	2.43	0	914	0	0	0	0
2001–02	VAN	62	31	22	5	142	1440	1298	.901	2.43	7	3502	0	0	0	20
2002–03	VAN	57	33	16	7	136	1477	1341	.908	2.42	2	3376	0	3	3	24
2003–04	VAN	60	33	21	6	134	1554	1420	.914	2.27	5	3539	0	1	1	22
2005–06	VAN	13	8	3	1	36	334	298	.892	3.11	0	681	0	0	0	4
2006–07	LAK	24	6	14	2	85	608	523	.860	3.98	0	1281	0	1	1	21
2007–08	LAK	9	2	4	1	28	247	219	.887	3.43	0	489	0	0	0	2
NYR Totals	-	34	10	13	4	72	818	746	.912	2.62	0	1648	0	0	0	21
Career	-	351	139	142	37	874	8625	7751	.899	2.76	15	18,927	0	5	5	147

Playoffs

Season	Team	GP	W	L	T	GA	SA	SV	SV%	GAA	SO	MIN	G	A	PTS	PIM
2000–01	VAN	2	0	2	-	9	57	48	.842	4.63	0	117	0	0	0	0
2001–02	VAN	6	2	3	-	16	123	107	.870	3.51	0	273	0	0	0	0
2002–03	VAN	14	7	7	-	45	341	296	.868	3.24	0	833	0	0	0	8
2003–04	VAN	3	1	1	-	5	64	59	.922	2.18	0	138	0	0	0	2
Career	VAN	25	10	13	-	75	585	510	.872	3.31	0	1361	0	0	0	10

Fast Fact: Dan Cloutier was the first of three goaltenders to be selected by the Rangers in the first round of the NHL entry draft. The other two were Dan Blackburn (2001) and Al Montoya (2004).

Kirk McLean
Born: June 26, 1966 in Willowdale, Ontario
6-0, 180lb
Caught: Left
Rangers Debut: October 5, 1999 vs. Ottawa Senators
Uniform #30
Seasons with Rangers: 2, 1999–2000 to 2000–01
All-Star selections: 1991–92 (Second Team)
All-Star Games: 2, 1990, 1992

Courtesy of the New York Rangers

Kirk McLean played junior hockey with the Oshawa Generals of the OHA and was selected in the sixth round (107th overall) of the 1984 entry draft by the New Jersey Devils. Due to an overabundance of goaltenders in the Devils organization, McLean saw action in only six NHL games over two seasons and was traded to Vancouver in September of 1987 along with Greg Adams and a draft pick for Patrik Sundstrom and a pair of draft picks.

McLean came into his own in his 11 seasons with the Canucks, leading the NHL in wins and shutouts in 1991–92. In 1994, his goaltending took Vancouver to the Stanley Cup Finals against the Rangers, losing a dramatic seven-game series.

The well-traveled netminder was traded twice during the 1997–98 season, first to Carolina with Martin Gelinas for Sean Burke, Geoff Sanderson, and Enrico Ciccone and then to Florida at the March trading deadline for Ray Sheppard.

McLean signed as a free agent with the Rangers in 1999–2000. At thirty-three, he was utilized primarily as a backup for Mike Richter. He is one of only four goaltenders to play for both the Rangers and Devils, the others being John Vanbiesbrouck, Mike Dunham, and Kevin Weekes. McLean retired at the end of the 2000–01 season.

Regular Season

Season	Team	GP	W	L	T/O	GA	SA	SV	SV%	GAA	SO	MIN	G	A	PTS	PIM
1985–86	NJD	2	1	1	0	11	59	48	.814	5.98	0	110	0	0	0	0
1986–87	NJD	4	1	1	0	10	72	62	.861	3.75	0	160	0	0	0	0
1987–88	VAN	41	11	27	3	147	1178	1031	.875	3.78	1	2334	0	2	2	8
1988–89	VAN	42	20	17	3	127	1166	1039	.891	3.08	4	2477	0	1	1	6
1989–90	VAN	63	21	30	10	216	1797	1581	.880	3.47	0	3739	0	3	3	6
1990–91	VAN	41	10	22	3	131	983	852	.867	3.99	0	1969	0	0	0	4
1991–92	VAN	65	38	17	9	176	1780	1604	.901	2.74	5	3852	0	5	5	0
1992–93	VAN	54	28	21	5	184	1615	1431	.886	3.39	3	3261	0	1	1	16
1993–94	VAN	52	23	26	3	156	1430	1274	.891	2.99	3	3128	0	4	4	2
1994–95	VAN	40	18	12	10	109	1140	1031	.904	2.75	1	2374	0	1	1	4
1995–96	VAN	45	15	21	9	156	1292	1136	.879	3.54	2	2645	0	2	2	6
1996–97	VAN	44	21	18	3	138	1247	1109	.889	3.21	0	2581	0	2	2	2
1997–98	VAN	29	6	17	4	97	800	703	.879	3.68	1	1583	0	0	0	0
1997–98	CAR	8	4	2	0	22	181	159	.878	3.29	0	401	0	1	1	0
1997–98	FLA	7	4	2	1	22	207	185	.894	3.25	0	406	0	0	0	0
1998–99	FLA	30	9	10	4	73	727	654	.900	2.75	2	1597	0	0	0	2
1999–00	NYR	22	7	8	4	58	558	500	.896	2.94	0	1206	0	1	1	2
2000–01	NYR	23	8	10	1	71	639	568	.889	3.49	0	1220	0	0	0	0
NYR Totals	-	45	15	18	5	129	1197	1068	.892	3.22	0	2426	0	1	1	2
Career	-	612	245	262	72	1904	16,871	14,967	.887	3.26	22	35,043	0	23	23	58

Playoffs

Season	Team	GP	W	L	T/O	GA	SA	SV	SV%	GAA	SO	MIN	G	A	PTS	PIM
1988–89	VAN	5	2	3	-	18	167	149	.892	3.57	0	302	0	0	0	0
1990–91	VAN	2	1	1	-	7	66	59	.894	3.41	0	123	0	0	0	0
1991–92	VAN	13	6	7	-	33	364	331	.909	2.52	2	785	0	1	1	0
1992–93	VAN	12	6	6	-	42	369	327	.886	3.34	0	754	0	3	3	0
1993–94	VAN	24	15	9	-	59	820	761	.928	2.29	4	1544	0	1	1	0
1994–95	VAN	11	4	7	-	36	336	300	.893	3.27	0	660	0	1	1	0
1995–96	VAN	1	0	1	-	3	12	9	.750	8.62	0	21	0	0	0	0
Career	VAN	68	34	34	-	198	2134	1936	.907	2.84	6	4189	0	6	6	0

Milan Hnilicka
Born: June 25, 1973 in Pardubice, Czechoslovakia
6-1, 190lb
Caught: Left
Rangers Debut: October 14, 1999 vs. Pittsburgh Penguins
Uniform #33
Seasons with Rangers: 1, 1999–2000

Milan Hnilicka was originally selected by the Islanders in the fourth round (70th overall) of the 1991 entry draft. He spent a season with the Swift Current Broncos of the WHL and then turned pro, playing for Salt Lake and Denver (IHL) as well as Richmond (ECHL). He then returned to his native Czechoslovakia where he eventually caught the attention of pro scouts as the starting netminder for Sparta Praha and was signed as a free agent by the Rangers in July 1999.

The twenty-six-year-old rookie made his Rangers debut in October 1999, relieving starter Kirk McLean and surrendering two goals during a seven-minute span in a 5–2 loss to the Penguins. Hnilicka's final appearance came in the last game of that season when he stopped 36 shots but lost, 4–1, to the Flyers.

He signed with Atlanta that summer and spent three seasons with the Thrashers, playing a total of 117 games. He was dealt to the Kings after the 2002–03 season but played in only two games for them due to a hand injury and returned to Czechoslovakia at the end of the year.

Regular Season

Season	Team	GP	W	L	T/O	GA	SA	SV	SV%	GAA	SO	MIN	G	A	PTS	PIM
1999–00	NYR	2	0	1	0	5	44	39	.886	3.48	0	86	0	0	0	0
2000–01	ATL	36	12	19	2	105	951	846	.890	3.41	2	1879	0	0	0	4
2001–02	ATL	60	13	33	10	179	1956	1777	.908	3.17	3	3367	0	2	2	8
2002–03	ATL	21	4	13	1	65	605	540	.893	3.56	0	1097	0	0	0	2
2003–04	LAK	2	0	1	0	5	42	37	.881	3.76	0	80	0	0	0	0
NYR Totals	-	2	0	1	0	5	44	39	.886	3.48	0	86	0	0	0	0
Career	-	121	29	67	13	359	3598	3239	.900	3.31	5	6509	0	2	2	14

Jean-Francois Labbe
Born: June 15, 1972 in Sherbrooke, Quebec
5-10, 175lb
Caught: Left
Rangers Debut: April 5, 2000 vs. Montreal Canadiens
Uniform #31
Seasons with Rangers: 1, 1999–2000

Jean-Francois Labbe played junior hockey with Trois-Rivieres, Sherbrooke, and Hull of the QMJHL and was awarded the Jacques Plante Trophy as the league's best goaltender in 1992. He turned pro the following season with the Thunder Bay Senators of the Colonial Hockey League, where he gained Rookie of the Year, Goaltender of the Year and Playoff MVP honors.

He signed as a free agent with Ottawa in 1994 but was never given a shot by the Senators and was traded to the Colorado Avalanche in 1995.

He played for the Cornwall Aces in 1995–96 and then the Hersey Bears when the Avalanche changed their minor-league affiliation. Labbe won 34 games with the Bears in 1996–97, posted a 2.52 GAA and played a league-record 23 playoff games that spring, leading the Bears to the Calder Cup championship. Labbe earned a First Team All-Star berth as well as the Les Cunningham (Most Valuable Player), Baz Bastien Memorial (Most Valuable Goaltender) and Harry "Hap" Holmes Memorial (best goals-against average) Awards for his efforts. But with Patrick Roy blocking his path, he had little chance of making a name for himself with the Avalanche.

The next season Labbe signed as a free agent with the Edmonton Oilers where NHL veterans Bob Essensa and Curtis Joseph were in front of him on the depth chart so he spent the season with the AHL's Hamilton Bulldogs. That summer he was on the move again, this time signing a free-agent contract with the Rangers.

Labbe spent two seasons with the Hartford Wolfpack and scored a goal into an empty net against the Quebec Citadelles during a game on February 5, 2000. He was recalled three times during the season and finally made his NHL debut on April 5, stopping 19 of 22 shots in a 3–0 loss to Montreal.

Labbe then returned to Hartford where he led the Wolfpack to the Calder Cup championship.

The Rangers traded Labbe to Columbus in exchange for Bert Robertsson on November 9, 2000. He played 14 games over two seasons with Columbus and eventually moved to Europe where he played for teams in Russia, Germany, and Austria before finishing his career with Sherbrooke of the NAHL in 2010–11.

Regular Season

Season	Team	GP	W	L	T/O	GA	SA	SV	SV%	GAA	SO	MIN	G	A	PTS	PIM
1999–00	NYR	1	0	1	0	3	22	19	.864	3.00	0	60	0	0	0	0
2001–02	CBJ	3	1	1	0	6	68	62	.912	3.07	0	117	0	0	0	0
2002–03	CBJ	11	2	4	0	27	233	206	.884	3.59	0	451	0	0	0	2
NYR Totals	-	1	0	1	0	3	22	19	.864	3.00	0	60	0	0	0	0
Career	-	15	3	6	0	36	323	287	.889	3.44	0	628	0	0	0	2

CHAPTER TWELVE

Sather Swings and Misses

When Glen Sather took over as the Rangers' tenth general manager on June 1, 2000, it's doubtful that he realized the length of time it would take to turn the team around. While running the perpetually financially troubled Edmonton Oilers, Sather often said that if he had the Rangers' payroll, he'd never lose a game. But when "Slats" finally got a chance to run the deep-pocketed Blueshirts in 2000, he found that without pillars like Wayne Gretzky and Mark Messier to build a team around, it wasn't quite that easy.

Sather had enjoyed a 10-year NHL career as an agitating presence for Boston, Pittsburgh, the Rangers, St. Louis, Montreal, and Minnesota. He wrapped up his playing career with Edmonton of the WHA, being named player-coach late in the 1976–77 season. He retired after that season but remained as coach and soon took on the additional responsibilities of president and general manager as the Oilers were admitted into the NHL in 1979. Sather went on to build a team that won five Stanley Cups between 1984 and 1990 and was elected to the Hockey Hall of Fame in the builders category in 1997. He is also known to be a shrewd businessman, having made a fortune buying up property in Banf, Alberta.

Despite the fact that Sather's Oilers had not come close to winning another Cup, he was still considered to be one of the most accomplished and influential executives in hockey at that time, qualities that met Garden owner James Dolan's need to hire and rub elbows with the biggest names in sports. It also seemed inevitable that Sather would wind up back with the Rangers since he had supplied Neil Smith with several key players that contributed to the Rangers' 1994 Stanley Cup victory.

While most of his players loved him, Sather's been-there, done-that attitude coupled with an innate arrogance did not sit well with fans.

And when the Blueshirts failed to make the playoffs for the first four years of Sather's tenure, chants of "Fire Sather" were often heard at the Garden. Even after he had turned the team around, the chants and anti-Sather demonstrations continued. But Sather was never in danger of losing his job because Dolan admired him. For better or worse, Sather and Dolan formed an unshakable bond, based on a quality that both men appreciated in the other—loyalty. Sather preached it and Dolan demanded it. Dolan is also a meddler. His hands-on ownership approach to running the Garden's NBA franchise, the Knicks, has been a well-documented disaster. And even though he has often said that he doesn't understand hockey, it's conceivable that if it wasn't for the faith and trust he had in Sather, the Rangers could have been in an even worse situation than their basketball counterparts.

The team Sather inherited had missed the playoffs in 1999–2000, finishing in fourth place in the Atlantic Division, 15 points behind the third-place Penguins. They surrendered 28 more goals than they scored and their two leading scorers were Petr Nedved and Theo Fleury, a tandem that never reminded anyone of Gretzky and Messier.

Sather's first four years on the job were anything but successful. He used poor judgement in throwing big money at over-the-hill free agents. He brought back Mark Messier from Vancouver but eventually traded Brian Leetch, on his birthday no less, to the Maple Leafs for prospects and draft choices, a move that did not sit well with the paying customers nor with Leetch himself.

Ron Low, who had previously coached the Oilers for four-plus seasons, was Sather's first selection to run the bench. After two losing seasons, Low was let go and replaced by John Tortorella on an interim basis. Sather then faxed a nine-page questionnaire to candidates for the coaching position including former Islanders legend Bryan Trottier. "Trots," who had been an assistant coach with the Colorado Avalanche, replied with what was rumored to be a ninety-page, meticulously handwritten reply, explaining why he was the right man for the job. Sather either liked what he read or at least admired Trottier's handwriting. Trottier got the job but lasted only 54 games and was replaced by Sather himself as the Blueshirts once again missed the playoffs.

Sather started the 2003–04 season behind the bench but brought in Tom Renney with 20 games remaining in another losing season. Renney had been the team's vice president of player development and had previously coached the Vancouver Canucks.

Following the 2004–05 lockout in which the entire season was cancelled, the Rangers came back with a new look led by Jaromir Jagr and fellow Czechs Martin Rucinsky, Martin Straka, Petr Prucha, Petr Sykora, Marek Malik, and Michal Rozsival. The Rangers made the playoffs for the first of seven times under Sather, but lost in the opening round. Renney also got them into the postseason the next two seasons, losing in the second round each time. He was subsequently fired with 21 games remaining in the 2008–09 season when the Rangers slipped to sixth place and were in danger of missing the postseason. He was replaced by fiery John Tortorella who had won a Stanley Cup with the Tampa Bay Lightning in 2004. "Torts" could not replicate that success in New York and after four seasons his tough love act wore thin on the players and he was replaced by Alain Vigneault in 2013. Ironically, Vigneault, who had lost his job with the Canucks, was replaced by Tortorella. Vigneault took the Blueshirts to the Stanley Cup Finals in 2014, losing in five games to the LA Kings.

Overall, Sather didn't do too badly at the draft table. He got lucky in his first draft in 2000, selecting future Hall of Famer Henrik Lundqvist in the seventh round at number 205. But in 2003 he used a rare first-round pick to select 6-foot-6, 230-pound right winger Hugh Jessiman while players such as Zach Parise and Dustin Brown were still available. Jessiman never played a game for the Rangers and spent his entire career in the minor leagues. Sather once again went for size in 2010 when he drafted 6-foot-5, 230-pound defenseman Dylan McIlrath while many other more serviceable prospects were still on the board. McIlrath saw limited duty with the Rangers, appearing in only 38 games over three seasons and recording two goals with 22 assists and 84 penalty minutes. Sather did make several fine draft selections, however, including Chris Kreider, Brady Skjei, Marc Staal, Brandon Dubinsky, Pavel Buchnevich, J. T. Miller, Ryan Callahan, Jesper Fast, and Carl Hagelin among others.

The salary cap that was set in place in 2005 following the lockout may have kept Sather from throwing more money at aging mercenaries, but it did little to stop him from dealing away draft picks and young players in an all-in effort to go out in a blaze of glory.

In July 2012, he sent Artem Anisimov, Brandon Dubinsky, Tim Erixon, and a 2013 first-round draft pick to Columbus for high-scoring Rick Nash, who was a disappointment in New York, especially in the playoffs. At the trading deadline in March 2014 he overpaid for Martin St. Louis. The thirty-eight-year-old winger had demanded a trade to the Rangers yet Sather felt compelled to send a 2014 second-round pick plus a 2015 first-round pick along with captain Ryan Callahan, who was an impending free agent, to Tampa. St. Louis was, however, a key contributor to the Stanley Cup drive that year that ended in a five-game loss to the Kings in the Final.

Then, at the 2015 trading deadline, he sent top prospect Anthony Duclair, defenseman John Moore, a 2015 second-round pick and a conditional 2016 first-round pick to Arizona for defenseman Keith Yandle. Yandle played well but never became the power-play quarterback the Rangers hoped he would be. He was dealt to Florida for fourth- and sixth-round picks in 2016.

Finally, with the cupboard bare of prospects and draft picks, Sather, seventy-one, stepped down as general manager but retained the title of team president in July 2015. He was succeeded by assistant GM Jeff Gorton.

Rule Changes:

Following the lockout year of 2004–05 in which the entire season was cancelled, the NHL returned with many new rules meant to increase offense and cut down on the clutching and grabbing tactics that had become prevalent throughout the league.

- The width of goaltenders leg pads was limited to 11 inches. In addition, the blocking glove, upper-body protector, pants, and jersey were also reduced in size.
- Goaltenders were allowed to play the puck behind the goal line only within a trapezoid-shaped area defined by lines that began six feet from either goal post and extended diagonally to points 28 feet apart at the end boards. Goaltenders who played the puck behind the goal line but outside of the trapezoid were assessed a two-minute delay of game penalty. Goaltenders were also penalized for delaying the game if they froze the puck unnecessarily.

- The goal lines were moved back two feet, to 11 feet from the end boards.
- Each of the offensive zones were increased by four feet while the neutral zone was reduced to 50 feet.
- Passes from behind the defensive blue line to the attacking blue line were now considered to be legal. The center red line was ignored for purposes of the "two-line pass."
- For tied games, following a scoreless 4-on-4 five-minute overtime (amended to 3-on-3 in 2015), three players from each team participated in a shootout. Each team took three shots. The team with the most goals after those six shots was designated as the winner. If the score remained tied, the shootout proceeded to a sudden death format. Regardless of the number of goals scored during the shootout portion of overtime, the final score recorded for the game will give the winning team one more goal than its opponent, based on the score at the end of overtime. Shootout goals and saves were not included in a players' statistics.

Jason LaBarbera
Born: January 18, 1980 in Burnaby, British Columbia
6-3, 232lb
Caught: Left
Rangers Debut: October 14, 2000 at Pittsburgh Penguins
Uniform #34
Seasons with Rangers: 2, 2000–01, 2003–04

Courtesy of the New York Rangers

Neil Smith selected Jason LaBarbera in the third round (66th overall) of the 1998 entry draft. Jason's junior career took him to Tri-City, Portland, and Spokane of the WHL before being assigned to the ECHL's Charlotte Checkers during the 2000–01 season.

LaBarbera spent most of his Rangers career in Hartford with the Wolfpack. In 2003–04, he set an AHL record for shutouts with 13 while being named the league's top goaltender.

Although recalled numerous times as a backup he only managed to appear in five games with the Rangers, posting a 1–2–0 record with a 4.61 GAA.

He became an unrestricted free agent in 2005 and signed with the LA Kings, where he saw more NHL action. In December 2008, he was traded to Vancouver for a draft pick. That summer he moved to Phoenix and later played for Edmonton and Anaheim.

Regular Season

Season	Team	GP	W	L	T/O	GA	SA	SV	SV%	GAA	SO	MIN	G	A	PTS	PIM
2000–01	NYR	1	0	0	0	0	2	2	1.000	0.00	0	10	0	0	0	0
2003–04	NYR	4	1	2	0	16	91	75	.824	4.84	0	198	0	1	1	2
2005–06	LAK	29	11	9	2	69	688	619	.900	2.89	1	1433	0	1	1	0
2007–08	LAK	45	17	23	2	121	1341	1220	.910	3.00	1	2421	0	0	0	2
2008–09	LAK	19	5	8	4	47	439	392	.893	2.83	2	995	0	0	0	2
2008–09	VAN	9	3	2	2	20	235	215	.915	2.66	0	451	0	0	0	0
2009–10	PHX	17	8	5	1	33	459	426	.928	2.13	0	928	0	0	0	0
2010–11	PHX	17	7	6	3	48	529	481	.909	3.26	2	883	0	0	0	2
2011–12	PHX	19	3	9	3	43	486	443	.912	2.54	0	1015	0	0	0	2
2012–13	PHX	15	4	6	2	32	418	386	.923	2.64	0	726	0	0	0	0
2013–14	EDM	7	1	3	0	19	146	127	.870	3.27	0	348	0	0	0	0
2014–15	ANA	5	2	0	1	9	99	90	.909	2.60	0	207	0	0	0	0
NYR Totals	-	5	1	2	0	16	93	77	.828	4.61	0	208	0	1	1	2
Career	-	187	62	73	20	457	4933	4476	.907	2.85	6	9615	0	2	2	10

Johan Holmqvist
Born: May 24, 1978, in Tolfta, Sweden
6-3, 198lb
Caught: Left
Rangers Debut: October 27, 2000 vs. Pittsburgh Penguins
Uniform #32
Seasons with Rangers: 3, 2000–01 to 2002–03

Johan Holmqvist was selected by Neil Smith in the seventh round (175th overall) of the 1997 entry draft. He played four seasons in the Swedish Elite League and was a member of his country's world junior and national teams.

He made his NHL debut with the Rangers in October 2000 and appeared in four games over the next three seasons. He was traded to Minnesota in March 2003 for Lawrence Nycholat.

Holmqvist moved back to Sweden in 2004 but returned to the NHL in 2006, signing as a free agent with Tampa Bay. In 2008, he was dealt to the Dallas Stars along with Brad Richards for Jussi Jokinen, Jeff Halpern, Mike Smith, and a fourth-round pick in 2009. He returned to Sweden following that season and played there until 2013.

Regular Season

Season	Team	GP	W	L	T/O	GA	SA	SV	SV%	GAA	SO	MIN	G	A	PTS	PIM
2000–01	NYR	2	0	2	0	10	71	61	.859	5.05	0	119	0	0	0	2
2001–02	NYR	1	0	0	0	0	2	2	1.000	0.00	0	9	0	0	0	0
2002–03	NYR	1	0	1	0	2	18	16	.889	3.08	0	39	0	0	0	0
2006–07	TBL	48	27	15	3	121	1134	1013	.893	2.85	1	2548	0	3	3	4
2007–08	TBL	45	20	16	6	124	1129	1005	.890	3.01	2	2469	0	1	1	0
2007–08	DAL	2	1	0	0	5	35	30	.857	3.75	0	80	0	0	0	0
NYR Totals	-	4	0	3	0	12	91	79	.868	4.32	0	167	0	0	0	2
Career	-	99	48	34	9	262	2389	2127	.890	2.99	3	5264	0	4	4	6

Playoffs

Season	Team	GP	W	L	T	GA	SA	SV	SV%	GAA	SO	MIN	G	A	PTS	PIM
2006–07	TBL	6	2	4	-	18	168	150	.893	2.92	0	370	0	0	0	0
Career	TBL	6	2	4	-	18	168	150	.893	2.92	0	370	0	0	0	0

Vitali Yeremeyev
Born: September 23, 1975 in Ust-Kamenogorsk, USSR
5-10, 190lb
Caught: Left
Rangers Debut: December 27, 2000 at Carolina Hurricanes
Uniform #31
Seasons with Rangers: 1, 2000–01

Courtesy of the New York Rangers

Vitali Yeremeyev was the Rangers' ninth-round selection (209th overall) in the 1994 entry draft. He came to North America in 2000 and spent time with the Charlotte Checkers and Hartford Wolfpack before appearing in four games with the Rangers. He then spent part of the next season in Charlotte before returning to Europe.

Regular Season

Season	Team	GP	W	L	T/O	GA	SA	SV	SV%	GAA	SO	MIN	G	A	PTS	PIM
2000–01	NYR	4	0	4	0	16	104	88	.846	4.52	0	212	0	0	0	0
Career	NYR	4	0	4	0	16	104	88	.846	4.52	0	212	0	0	0	0

Guy Hebert
Born: January 7, 1967 in Troy, New York
5-11, 186lb
Caught: Left
Rangers Debut: March 9, 2001 at Washington Capitals
Uniform #31
Seasons with Rangers: 1, 2000–01
All-Star Game: 1, 1997

Guy Hebert was one of six goaltenders used by the Rangers during the 2000–01 season during which they gave up 290 goals, the most in the NHL. It was also the most goaltenders the Rangers had ever used since their inception in 1926.

Hebert was drafted by the St. Louis Blues (eighth round, 159th overall) in 1987 while playing for Hamilton College. He made his NHL debut with the Blues in December 1991 against Buffalo and played in 12 more games for St. Louis that year. By the next season he was the full-time backup for Curtis Joseph in St. Louis before being left exposed in the 1993 expansion draft and selected by Anaheim.

The native of Troy, New York, became Anaheim's starting goaltender for most of the next seven seasons, playing in the 1997 All-Star Game and representing the United States in the 1993 World Championships and the 1996 World Cup. But in 2000 he lost his job to Jean-Sebastien Giguere, who was ten years younger. Hebert was placed on waivers where he was picked up by the Rangers, who had just lost Mike Richter to reconstructive knee surgery.

In 13 games for the Rangers that season, Guy posted a 5–7–1 record with a 3.43 GAA. He became a free agent at the end of the season and retired.

Regular Season

Season	Team	GP	W	L	T/O	GA	SA	SV	SV%	GAA	SO	MIN	G	A	PTS	PIM
1991–92	STL	13	5	5	1	36	393	357	.908	2.93	0	738	0	1	1	0
1992–93	STL	24	8	8	2	74	630	556	.883	3.67	1	1210	0	0	0	2
1993–94	MDA	52	20	27	3	141	1513	1372	.907	2.83	2	2991	0	0	0	2
1994–95	MDA	39	12	20	4	109	1132	1023	.904	3.13	2	2092	0	0	0	2
1995–96	MDA	59	28	23	5	157	1820	1663	.914	2.83	4	3326	0	0	0	6
1996–97	MDA	67	29	25	12	172	2133	1961	.919	2.67	4	3863	0	1	1	4
1997–98	MDA	46	13	24	6	130	1339	1209	.903	2.93	3	2660	0	1	1	4
1998–99	MDA	69	31	29	9	165	2114	1949	.922	2.46	6	4083	0	1	1	0
1999–00	MDA	68	28	31	9	166	1805	1639	.908	2.51	4	3976	0	2	2	2
2000–01	MDA	41	12	23	4	115	1112	997	.897	3.11	2	2215	0	0	0	0
2000–01	NYR	13	5	7	1	42	409	367	.897	3.43	0	735	0	0	0	0
NYR Totals	-	13	5	7	1	42	409	367	.897	3.42	0	735	0	0	0	0
Career	-	491	191	222	56	1307	14,400	13,093	.909	2.82	28	27,889	0	6	6	22

Playoffs

Season	Team	GP	W	L	T/O	GA	SA	SV	SV%	GAA	SO	MIN	G	A	PTS	PIM
1992–93	STL	1	0	0	-	0	1	1	1.000	0.00	0	2	0	0	0	0
1996–97	MDA	9	4	4	-	18	255	237	.929	2.02	1	534	0	0	0	0
1998–99	MDA	4	0	3	-	15	124	109	.879	4.33	0	208	0	0	0	0
Career	-	14	4	7	-	33	380	347	.913	2.66	1	744	0	0	0	0

Dan Blackburn
Born: May 20, 1983 in Montreal, Quebec
6-1, 180lb
Caught: Left
Rangers Debut: October 10, 2001 vs. Washington Capitals
Uniform #31
Seasons with Rangers: 2, 2001–02 to 2002–03

Courtesy of the New York Rangers

Dan Blackburn was selected by Glen Sather in the first round of the 2001 entry draft (10th overall). It was only the second time the Rangers had ever selected a netminder in the first round (Dan Cloutier, 1994) and many considered Blackburn to be their goaltender of the future.

The Montreal, Quebec, native spent two seasons with the Kootenay Ice, being named the WHL's Rookie of the Year in 2000 and finishing second in wins and save percentage. He was also named the MVP of the playoffs as he backstopped Kootenay to their first WHL championship. The next season Blackburn led the league in wins and placed second in save percentage and third in goals-against average.

In 2001, the eighteen-year-old netminder attended Blueshirts training camp and made quite an impression, earning the Lars-Erik Sjoberg Award as the best rookie. He began the season in Hartford of the AHL but was recalled after only four games and won his first NHL start, an impressive 2–1 victory over the Canadiens in Montreal. The rookie saw action in 31 games that season and was slated to be Mike Richter's backup again in 2002–03. But when Richter suffered a concussion in early November Blackburn shouldered the workload, starting 17 consecutive games until Mike Dunham was acquired from Nashville.

Blackburn injured his left shoulder lifting weights in training camp the following fall and missed the entire 2003–04 season. The Rangers were one of the few NHL teams that did not have a full-time goaltending coach at the time so the young netminder was left to train on his own which led to the injury. He underwent exploratory surgery on his shoulder in March 2004 which led to the discovery that the nerves in his shoulder did not regenerate properly. He had trouble reacting with his glove hand and could no longer rotate that hand with his palm facing out while raising his arm for a shot.

Blackburn joined the Victoria Salmon Kings of the ECHL in February 2005 wearing a modified glove on his catching hand. The glove consisted of a blocker with the webbing and pocket from a regular catching glove attached to the underside. The customized glove allowed Blackburn to redirect high shots without rotating his hand, while still being able to catch low shots and cover pucks at his feet. He appeared in 12 games with the Salmon Kings, posting a 3–9–0 record with a 3.54 GAA before retiring at the end of the season.

Blackburn's injury led to the Rangers finally hiring a full-time goalie coach, Benoit Allaire, who would eventually become an important influence in Henrik Lundqvist's career.

Regular Season

Season	Team	GP	W	L	T/O	GA	SA	SV	SV%	GAA	SO	MIN	G	A	PTS	PIM
2001–02	NYR	31	12	16	0	95	935	840	.898	3.32	0	1737	0	0	0	10
2002–03	NYR	32	8	16	4	93	842	749	.890	3.17	1	1762	0	0	0	2
Career	NYR	63	20	32	4	188	1777	1589	.894	3.24	1	3499	0	0	0	12

Mike Dunham
Born: June 1, 1972 in Johnson City, New York
6-3, 200lb
Caught: Left
Rangers Debut: December 16, 2002 vs. San Jose Sharks
Uniform #30
Seasons with Rangers: 2, 2002–03, 2003–04
William Jennings Trophy: 1996–97 (with New Jersey, shared with Martin Brodeur)

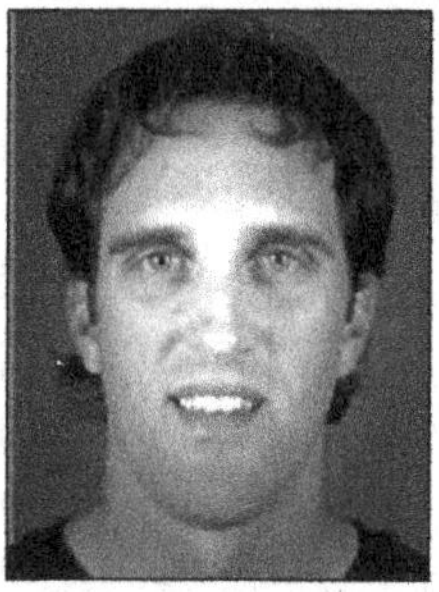
Courtesy of the New York Rangers

Following Mike Richter's second concussion in the span of eight months early in the 2002–03 season, the Rangers found themselves in need of a legitimate starting goaltender, so GM Glen Sather sent forward Rem Murray and defensemen Tomas Kloucek and Marek Zidlicky to the Nashville Predators for thirty-year-old Mike Dunham on December 12, 2002.

Dunham played high school hockey at Canterbury High in Connecticut and then moved to the University of Maine in 1990 where he was a teammate of Garth Snow. He was selected 53rd overall in the 1990 entry draft by the New Jersey Devils. He played for Team USA in the 1994 Olympics, where he once again shared the goaltending duties with Snow.

He made his NHL debut with the Devils in 1996–97 and shared the William Jennings Trophy for the lowest team goals-against average with Martin Brodeur. He was left unprotected in the 1998 expansion draft and selected by the Nashville Predators. Dunham was named to the 2002 United States Olympic team that won a silver medal in Salt Lake City and was dealt to the Rangers later that season.

Dunham was a decent goaltender who had the misfortune of playing for the Rangers while they were in the midst of a downward slide in which they did not make the playoffs for seven consecutive seasons. He also did not make a single playoff appearance in 10 seasons as an NHL goalkeeper.

Dunham became a free agent following the 2003–04 season and later played with the Atlanta Thrashers and New York Islanders, becoming the only netminder besides John Vanbiesbrouck to play for the Rangers, Devils, and Islanders.

Regular Season

Season	Team	GP	W	L	T/O	GA	SA	SV	SV%	GAA	SO	MIN	G	A	PTS	PIM
1996–97	NJD	26	8	7	1	43	456	413	.906	2.55	2	1013	0	0	0	2
1997–98	NJD	15	5	5	3	29	332	303	.913	2.25	1	773	0	1	1	0
1998–99	NSH	44	16	23	3	127	1387	1260	.908	3.08	1	2472	0	0	0	4
1999–00	NSH	52	19	27	6	146	1584	1438	.908	2.85	0	3077	0	0	0	6
2000–01	NSH	48	21	21	4	107	1381	1274	.923	2.33	4	2810	0	0	0	2
2001–02	NSH	58	23	24	9	144	1525	1381	.906	2.62	3	3316	0	2	2	2
2002–03	NSH	15	2	9	2	43	397	354	.892	3.15	0	819	0	0	0	0
2002–03	NYR	43	19	17	5	94	1229	1135	.924	2.29	5	2467	0	1	1	0
2003–04	NYR	57	16	30	6	159	1522	1363	.896	3.03	2	3148	0	0	0	0
2005–06	ATL	17	8	5	2	36	336	300	.893	2.77	1	779	0	0	0	0
2006–07	NYI	19	4	10	3	61	552	491	.889	3.74	0	979	0	1	1	0
NYR Totals	-	100	35	47	11	253	2751	2498	.908	2.70	7	5615	0	1	1	0
Career	-	394	141	178	44	989	10,701	9712	.908	2.75	19	21,653	0	5	5	16

Jussi Markkanen
Born: May 8, 1975 in Imatra, Finland
6-0, 182lb
Caught: Left
Rangers Debut: October 11, 2003 at Columbus Blue Jackets
Uniform #40
Seasons with Rangers: 1, 2003–04

Jussi Markkanen was one of five goaltenders the Rangers used during the 2003–04 season attempting to fill the void left by Mike Richter's retirement due to multiple concussions. Markkanen came up through the Finnish Junior and Elite leagues and was selected in the fifth round (133rd overall) by the Edmonton Oilers in the 2001 entry draft.

Markkanen posted a shutout over Anaheim in his NHL debut and appeared in 36 games over two seasons in Edmonton, going 13–12–5 with five shutouts and a 2.21 GAA. In June 2003, Jussi was traded to the Rangers along with a 2004 fourth-round draft pick for the rights to Brian Leetch, who was due to become an unrestricted free agent. Leetch eventually re-signed with the Rangers.

While in New York he played well and appeared in 26 games, going 8–12–1 with two shutouts and a 2.56 GAA.

But his stay in New York was brief. At the March 2004 trading deadline, he was sent back to Edmonton with Petr Nedved in exchange for Dwight Helminen, Steve Valiquette, and a 2004 second-round draft pick.

Markkanen spent the next two seasons with the Oilers before returning to Europe. In September 2008 Jussi and his wife Sanna suffered a tragic blow when one of their two sons, Olli-Matias, died after falling out of a fifth-story window while playing in the living room with his older brother, Juho. He was only four years of age.

Regular Season

Season	Team	GP	W	L	T/O	GA	SA	SV	SV%	GAA	SO	MIN	G	A	PTS	PIM
2001–02	EDM	14	6	4	2	24	336	312	.929	1.88	2	784	0	0	0	0
2002–03	EDM	22	7	8	3	51	533	482	.904	2.59	3	1180	0	1	1	2
2003–04	NYR	26	8	12	1	53	611	558	.913	2.56	2	1244	0	0	0	0
2003–04	EDM	7	2	2	2	12	182	170	.934	1.83	0	394	0	0	0	2
2005–06	EDM	37	15	12	6	105	873	768	.880	3.13	0	2016	0	1	1	0
2006–07	EDM	22	5	9	1	52	457	405	.886	3.14	0	992	0	0	0	0
NYR Totals	-	26	8	12	1	53	611	558	.913	2.56	2	1244	0	0	0	0
Career	-	128	43	47	15	297	2992	2695	.901	2.70	7	6610	0	2	2	4

Playoffs

Season	Team	GP	W	L	T	GA	SA	SV	SV%	GAA	SO	MIN	G	A	PTS	PIM
2002–03	EDM	1	0	0	-	1	12	11	.917	4.30	0	14	0	0	0	0
2005–06	EDM	6	3	3	-	13	137	124	.905	2.16	1	360	0	0	0	0
Career	EDM	7	3	3	-	14	149	135	.906	2.24	1	374	0	0	0	0

Jamie McLennan
Born: June 30, 1971 in Edmonton, Alberta
6-0, 199lb
Caught: Left
Rangers Debut: March 13, 2004 at Florida Panthers
Uniform #33
Seasons with Rangers: 1, 2003–04
Bill Masterton Trophy: 1997–98 (with St. Louis Blues)

Courtesy of the New York Rangers

Following three solid seasons in the WHL with the Spokane Chiefs and Lethbridge Hurricanes, Jamie McLennan was selected by the Islanders in the third round (48th overall) of the 1991 entry draft. After two seasons in the minors McLellan made his NHL debut with the Islanders in 1993–94 and appeared in 56 games over the next three seasons. He signed with the St. Louis Blues in 1996 and stayed for three seasons, appearing in 82 games. While with the Blues, Jamie came down with bacterial meningitis but recovered and was awarded the Bill Masterton Trophy for perseverance, sportsmanship, and dedication to hockey in 1997–98.

McLennan was later selected by the Minnesota Wild in the 2000 expansion draft, stayed there for a season, and was then dealt to Calgary in June 2002 for a draft choice.

He remained in Calgary until the March 2004 trading deadline when he was sent to the Rangers along with Blair Betts and Greg Moore for Chris Simon and a draft pick. He saw action in four games with the Rangers at the tail end of the 2003–04 season, going 1–3–0 with a 2.96 GAA.

Following his brief stint with the Blueshirts, McLennan signed with the Florida Panthers and later moved to England during the lockout year and returned to the NHL with Calgary in 2006. In 2007 he played in Japan and retired at the end of the season.

Regular Season

Season	Team	GP	W	L	T/O	GA	SA	SV	SV%	GAA	SO	MIN	G	A	PTS	PIM
1993–94	NYI	22	8	7	6	61	639	578	.905	2.84	0	1287	0	1	1	6
1994–95	NYI	21	6	11	2	67	539	472	.876	3.39	0	1185	0	0	0	2
1995–96	NYI	13	3	9	1	39	342	303	.886	3.68	0	636	0	0	0	2
1997–98	STL	30	16	8	2	60	618	558	.903	2.17	2	1658	0	0	0	4
1998–99	STL	33	13	14	4	70	640	570	.891	2.36	3	1763	0	0	0	0
1999–00	STL	19	9	5	2	33	341	308	.903	1.96	2	1009	0	0	0	2
2000–01	MIN	38	5	23	9	98	1032	934	.905	2.64	2	2230	0	1	1	4
2002–03	CGY	22	2	11	4	58	537	479	.892	2.99	0	1165	0	0	0	14
2003–04	CGY	26	12	9	3	53	587	534	.910	2.20	4	1446	0	1	1	4
2003–04	NYR	4	1	3	0	12	97	85	.876	2.96	0	244	0	0	0	0
2005–06	FLA	17	2	4	2	34	360	326	.906	2.85	0	678	0	0	0	0
2006–07	CGY	9	3	5	1	32	304	272	.895	3.60	0	533	0	0	0	16
NYR Totals	-	4	1	3	0	12	97	85	.876	2.96	0	244	0	0	0	0
Career	-	254	80	109	36	617	6036	5419	.898	2.67	13	13,834	0	3	3	54

Playoffs

Season	Team	GP	W	L	T	GA	SA	SV	SV%	GAA	SO	MIN	G	A	PTS	PIM
1993–94	NYI	2	0	1	-	6	47	41	.872	4.37	0	82	0	0	0	0
1997–98	STL	1	0	0	-	1	4	3	.750	4.25	0	14	0	0	0	0
1998–99	STL	1	0	1	-	0	7	7	1.000	0.00	0	37	0	0	0	6
2006–07	CGY	1	0	0	-	0	0	0	-	0.00	0	1	0	0	0	12
Career	-	5	0	2	-	7	58	51	.879	3.13	0	134	0	0	0	18

Steve Valiquette
Born: August 20, 1977 in Etobicoke, Ontario
6-6, 210lb
Caught: Left
Rangers Debut: March 27, 2004 at Philadelphia Flyers
Uniform #45, 40
Seasons with Rangers: 5, 2003–04, 2006–07 to 2009–10

Courtesy of the New York Rangers

Steve Valiquette played four seasons of junior hockey for the Sudbury Wolves and Erie Otters of the OHL and was selected by the LA Kings in the eighth round (190th overall) of the 1996 entry draft. Steve never got an opportunity with Los Angeles and signed as a free agent with the Islanders in 1996. He played six games for the Isles in 1999–2000 and at 6-foot-6, was the tallest goaltender to ever play in the NHL at that time.

In July 2003, Steve signed as a free agent with the Edmonton Oilers, who left him exposed in the waiver draft that October, where he was claimed by the Florida Panthers. Six days later he was once again an Oiler, having been re-claimed on waivers from Florida. Steve wound up playing in only one game with Edmonton before being traded to the Rangers along with Dwight Helminen and a draft pick for Petr Nedved and Jussi Markkanen on March 3, 2004.

Steve appeared in two games for the Rangers during the 2003–04 season and spent the next year with the Hartford Wolfpack of the AHL. He played in Russia during the lockout year and returned to the Rangers in 2006–07, sharing the backup role behind Henrik Lundqvist with Kevin Weekes. He spent the next two seasons as Lundqvist's sole backup, which meant that he didn't play too often. To his credit, he kept himself ready and was dependable, if not spectacular when needed.

Valiquette struggled at the beginning of the 2009–10 season and was demoted to Hartford, where he stayed the rest of the year. He then played in Russia and Italy for two years and retired following the 2011–12 season. He is now an analyst on Ranger broadcasts on MSG Network and is also President and CEO. of Clear Sight Analytics, a company that collects and analyzes team and player-based performance data.

Regular Season

Season	Team	GP	W	L	T/O	GA	SA	SV	SV%	GAA	SO	MIN	G	A	PTS	PIM
1999–00	NYI	6	2	0	0	6	117	111	.949	1.87	0	193	0	0	0	0
2003–04	EDM	1	0	0	0	2	7	5	.714	8.65	0	14	0	0	0	0
2003–04	NYR	2	1	1	0	6	71	65	.915	3.00	0	120	0	0	0	0
2006–07	NYR	3	1	2	0	6	45	39	.867	3.14	0	115	0	0	0	0
2007–08	NYR	13	5	3	3	25	296	271	.916	2.19	2	686	0	0	0	2
2008–09	NYR	15	5	5	2	39	421	382	.907	2.84	1	823	0	1	1	2
2009–10	NYR	6	2	3	0	19	128	109	.852	3.74	1	305	0	0	0	0
NYR Totals	-	39	14	14	5	95	961	866	.901	2.78	4	2049	0	1	1	4
Career	-	46	16	14	5	103	1085	982	.905	2.74	4	2256	0	1	1	4

Playoffs

Season	Team	GP	W	L	T	GA	SA	SV	SV%	GAA	SO	MIN	G	A	PTS	PIM
2008–09	NYR	2	0	0	-	0	9	9	1.000	0.00	0	40	0	0	0	0
Career	NYR	2	0	0	-	0	9	9	1.000	0.00	0	40	0	0	0	0

Kevin Weekes
Born: April 4, 1975 in Toronto, Ontario
6-2, 215lb
Caught: Left
Rangers Debut: October 5, 2005 at Philadelphia Flyers
Uniform #80
Seasons with Rangers: 2, 2005–06 through 2006–07

Courtesy of the New York Rangers

Kevin Weekes was selected by the Florida Panthers in the second round (41st overall) of the 1993 entry draft following a junior career that included time with the Owen Sound Platers and Ottawa 67's of the OHL. With John Vanbiesbrouck and Mark Fitzpatrick firmly ensconced in the top spots with the Panthers, Weekes spent his first two pro seasons with Carolina of the AHL. In 1997–98, Fitzpatrick was traded and Weekes saw action in 11 games with the Panthers, but failed to notch a win.

Weekes was back in the minors the next season as Florida went with veterans Sean Burke and Kirk McLean. He was assigned to the Detroit Vipers of the IHL, where he went 19–5–7 with a 2.07 GAA, and won the James Norris Memorial Trophy awarded to the goaltender with the fewest goals against.

In January 1999, he was sent to Vancouver along with Ed Jovanovski, Dave Gagner, Mike Brown, and a first-round draft pick in a blockbuster deal that brought Pavel Bure, Bret Hedican, Brad Ference, and a third-round pick to Florida.

However, after less than a year in Vancouver he was on the move again, this time to the Islanders in December 1999. The deal also included Dave Scatchard and Bill Muckalt and sent goaltender Felix Potvin to the Canucks along with two draft choices. On Long Island

Weekes teamed with young Roberto Luongo, but the Isles struggled at the end of the season and GM Mike Milbury traded both of his goaltenders to the state of Florida in separate deals. Luongo wound up with the Panthers and Weekes was sent to Tampa Bay in June 2000 along with Kristian Kudroc and a second-round pick for the Lightning's first-, fourth-, and seventh-round picks.

Weekes had a good first year in Tampa Bay. He was one of six goaltenders used by the Lightning that season but appeared in a career-high 61 games and recorded four shutouts and a 3.14 GAA. But late in the season, the Lightning acquired goaltender Nikolai Khabibulin from Phoenix and Weekes was forced back to the bench, seeing action in only 19 games in 2001–02.

In March 2002, Weekes was traded once again, this time to the Carolina Hurricanes for Shane Wells and Chris Dingman. He won his only two starts at the end of the regular season and then went 3–2 with a 1.62 GAA in the playoffs as the Hurricanes made it to the Stanley Cup Finals for the first time in franchise history. Although Carolina lost to the Detroit Red Wings, Weekes established himself as the team's starter, appearing in 117 games over the next two seasons.

Weekes became a free agent in the summer of 2004 and signed with the Rangers, who hoped to team him with young Henrik Lundqvist. The plan was for Lundqvist to be worked into the lineup slowly. However, the Swedish rookie took over the starter's role by early November after winning three of his first five starts while losing the other two in overtime. Weekes saw action in 32 games that season and only 14 the next after being sidelined by a strained quadricep muscle. He became a free agent at the end of the 2006–07 season and signed with the Devils, becoming only the third goaltender to play for the Rangers, Islanders, and Devils. He served as a backup for Martin Brodeur for two seasons before retiring in 2009 to become an analyst for *Hockey Night in Canada*.

Regular Season

Season	Team	GP	W	L	T/O	GA	SA	SV	SV%	GAA	SO	MIN	G	A	PTS	PIM
1997–98	FLA	11	0	5	1	32	247	215	.870	3.96	0	485	0	0	0	0
1998–99	VAN	11	0	8	1	34	257	223	.868	3.83	0	532	0	0	0	0
1999–00	VAN	20	6	7	4	47	461	414	.898	2.85	1	987	0	0	0	0
1999–00	NYI	36	10	20	4	115	1173	1058	.902	3.51	1	2026	0	1	1	0

Season	Team	GP	W	L	T/O	GA	SA	SV	SV%	GAA	SO	MIN	G	A	PTS	PIM
2000–01	TBL	61	20	33	3	177	1742	1565	.898	3.15	4	3378	0	1	1	4
2001–02	TBL	19	3	9	0	40	470	430	.915	2.89	2	830	0	0	0	0
2001–02	CAR	2	2	0	0	3	41	38	.927	1.50	0	120	0	0	0	0
2002–03	CAR	51	14	24	9	126	1438	1312	.912	2.50	5	2965	0	0	0	2
2003–04	CAR	66	23	30	11	146	1652	1506	.912	2.33	6	3765	0	0	0	6
2005–06	NYR	32	14	14	3	91	867	776	.895	2.86	0	1850	0	1	1	4
2006–07	NYR	14	4	6	2	43	355	312	.879	3.39	0	761	0	0	0	0
2007–08	NJD	9	2	2	1	17	160	143	.894	2.97	0	343	0	0	0	2
2008–09	NJD	16	7	5	0	32	399	367	.920	2.42	0	795	0	0	0	0
NYR Totals	-	46	18	20	5	134	1222	1088	.890	3.01	0	2611	0	1	1	4
Career	-	348	105	163	39	903	9262	8359	.903	2.87	19	18,837	0	3	3	18

Playoffs

Season	Team	GP	W	L	T	GA	SA	SV	SV%	GAA	SO	MIN	G	A	PTS	PIM
2001–02	CAR	8	3	2	-	11	180	169	.939	1.62	2	408	0	0	0	0
2005–06	NYR	1	0	1	-	4	25	21	.840	4.01	0	60	0	0	0	2
NYR Totals	-	1	0	1	-	4	25	21	840	4.01	0	60	0	0	0	2
Career	-	9	3	3	-	15	205	190	.927	1.93	2	468	0	0	0	2

Henrik Lundqvist—Franchise Goaltender
Born: March 2, 1982 in Are, Sweden
6-1, 180lb
Caught: Left
Rangers Debut: October 8, 2005 at New Jersey Devils
Uniform #30
Seasons with Rangers: 14, 2005–06 to present
Vezina Trophy: 2011–12
All-Star selections: 2005–06, 2011–12 (First Team); 2012–13 (Second Team)
All-Star Games: 2009, 2011–12, 2018–19

Courtesy of the New York Rangers

Henrik Lundqvist has excelled at every level of hockey. The native of Are, Sweden, began his career with Vastra Frolunda of the Swedish Elite League in 2001–02 and led them to the championship a year later.

In 2004–05, he led the league with 33 wins, a 1.79 GAA, a .936 save percentage and six shutouts while capturing another championship with Frolunda. That same season he set many national playoff records and was named Sweden's best player and the league's MVP. Lundqvist was also named the Swedish goaltender of the year in 2003, 2004, and 2005.

Lundqvist was scouted by Christer Rockstrom and selected in the seventh round (205th overall) in the 2000 entry draft. He was named the winner of the Lars-Erik Sjoberg Award as the best rookie in training camp in 2005 and made his NHL debut on October 8 of that year, a 3–2 overtime loss to the Devils. He bounced right back with a 4–1 victory over New Jersey in his next start five days later.

The original plan was for "Hank" to be worked into the lineup gradually during his rookie season. The Blueshirts had signed veteran Kevin Weekes to assume the starter's role while Lundqvist became acclimated to the league and the smaller North American rinks. But after winning three of his first five starts while losing the other two in overtime, Lundqvist took over the number one spot by early November. He then went on to appear in 53 of the Rangers' 82 games, was a finalist for the Vezina Trophy as the NHL's top netminder, and earned a spot on the NHL's All-Rookie Team.

Lundqvist's 30 victories that season broke the team record for wins by a rookie goaltender (29) which was previously shared by Sugar Jim Henry (1941–42) and Johnny Bower (1953–54). He went on to become the standard against which every future Ranger netminder will be judged, breaking almost every franchise goaltending mark, including regular season shutouts and games and minutes played in both the regular season and playoffs. His fine play also catapulted the Rangers into the playoffs for the first time since 1996–97 and helped revive interest in the franchise after nearly a decade of mediocre hockey.

Lundqvist was also a standout in international competition as well. His 12 career Olympic wins rank second to Vladislav Tretiak's 17 and he led Sweden to a gold medal in the 2006 Winter Olympics and a silver medal in 2014. Lundqvist also represented his country in the 2010 games, leading all netminders with a 1.34 GAA and a pair of shutouts. He also played for Sweden in the World Championships four times, winning a silver medal in 2004.

"King Henrik," who possessed a quick glove hand and lightning fast reflexes, proved to be a durable performer despite suffering two potential career-ending injuries.

In January 2015 he suffered a vascular injury when struck in the throat by a puck. The injury occurred when defenseman Ryan McDonagh's stick accidentally pushed up the throat protector that hung from the bottom of Lundqvist's mask just as a shot by Carolina center Brad Malone was headed towards the net. Lundqvist shook off the injury, stopping 31 shots, as the Rangers beat the Hurricanes, 4–1. He played in the team's next game as well, beating Florida, 6–3. But when he began experiencing a stiff neck, breathing difficulties, headaches, and lightheadedness, he was diagnosed and missed the next 24 games.

Lundqvist also suffered an eye injury in the first game of the 2016 quarterfinals against Pittsburgh when teammate Marc Staal's stick blade slipped between the bars of his mask and speared him in the eye. Other than a black eye, there was no serious damage and Henrik didn't miss a game.

Lundqvist won 30 games or more eleven times and was nominated for the Vezina Trophy in 2006, 2007, and 2008 before finally winning the award in 2012. He was also a solid playoff netminder for the Rangers leading them to the conference finals eight times and the Stanley Cup Final in 2013–14, when they lost a dramatic five-game series to the LA Kings.

Henrik was voted Rangers MVP twelve times and given the coveted Steven McDonald Extra Effort award twice. He won the John Halligan Good Guy Award voted on by the media in 2008 and the Ceil Seidel award for dedication to the organization both on and off the ice in 2006 and 2009. He was also a two-time winner of the now-defunct Rangers Fan Club's Frank Boucher Trophy.

The twin brother of Joel, who was a center for the Dallas Stars, Lundqvist enjoyed fine fashion and being in the spotlight. He was named to numerous best-dressed and best-looking lists and was deemed the "Most Stylish Athlete" at the 2012 Style Awards during Mercedes Benz Fashion Week. He was active in MSG's Garden of Dreams Foundation and donated a percentage of his Crown Collection clothing line to the charity. Lundqvist was featured in an MSG Network series *The Mask with Henrik Lundqvist* in 2015. The series featured Henrik in one-on-one interviews with celebrities such as Michael J. Fox, Jeff Gordon, and John McEnroe as they designed one-of-a-kind goalie masks that Henrik wore during the 2014–15 season. The masks were then auctioned off and raised over $220,000 for charity. Lundqvist also auctioned off the customized mask he created for the 2012 Winter Classic following the Rangers' 3–2 victory over the Flyers, raising over $37,000 for the Garden of Dreams.

In 2014, the goaltender established the Henrik Lundqvist Foundation which through its fundraising efforts and community outreach, strove to create positive change in the lives of children and adults throughout the world through education and health services.

The future Hall of Famer won only 26 games during the 2017–18 season as the entire team struggled. It was the first time he failed to reach the 30-win plateau in a full season. (He won 24 games during the lockout shortened 2012–13 season.) He also faced 40 or more shots 13 times during the season—his previous career high was six times in any campaign. In February 2018, Rangers GM Jeff Gorton announced that they would be undergoing a rebuilding process and would be trading away many of their high-priced veterans for draft picks and younger prospects. Gorton gave his franchise goaltender the opportunity to be dealt elsewhere, to a team where he would have another chance of winning a Stanley Cup. Lundqvist declined, saying that he was committed to the Rangers, their fans, and the club's rebuilding process.

Regular Season

Season	Team	GP	W	L	T/O	GA	SA	SV	SV%	GAA	SO	G	A	PTS	PIM
2005–06	NYR	53	30	12	9	116	1485	1369	.922	2.24	2	0	2	2	0
2006–07	NYR	70	37	22	8	160	1927	1767	.917	2.34	5	0	0	0	0
2007–08	NYR	72	37	24	10	160	1823	1663	.912	2.23	10	0	0	0	2
2008–09	NYR	70	38	25	7	168	2007	1839	.916	2.43	3	0	2	2	0
2009–10	NYR	73	35	27	10	167	2109	1942	.921	2.38	4	0	1	1	0
2010–11	NYR	68	36	27	5	152	1965	1813	.923	2.28	11	0	4	4	6
2011–12	NYR	62	39	18	5	123	1753	1630	.930	1.97	8	0	2	2	4
2012–13	NYR	43	24	16	3	88	1190	1102	.926	2.05	2	0	1	1	0
2013–14	NYR	63	33	24	5	144	1810	1666	.920	2.36	5	0	4	4	0
2014–15	NYR	46	30	13	3	103	1329	1226	.922	2.25	5	0	1	1	0
2015–16	NYR	65	35	21	7	156	1944	1788	.920	2.48	4	0	4	4	4
2016–17	NYR	57	31	20	4	148	1650	1502	.910	2.74	2	0	1	1	0
2017–18	NYR	63	26	26	7	174	2036	1862	.915	2.98	2	0	1	1	0
2018–19	NYR	52	18	23	10	158	1699	1541	.907	3.07	0	0	3	3	0
Career	NYR	857	499	298	93	2017	24,727	22,710	.918	2.41	63	0	26	26	16

Playoffs

Season	Team	GP	W	L	T	GA	SA	SV	SV%	GAA	SO	MIN	G	A	PTS	PIM
2005–06	NYR	3	0	3	-	13	79	66	.835	4.40	0	177	0	0	0	0
2006–07	NYR	10	6	4	-	22	291	269	.924	2.07	1	637	0	0	0	0
2007–08	NYR	10	5	5	-	26	287	261	.909	2.57	1	608	0	0	0	0
2008–09	NYR	7	3	4	-	19	207	188	.908	3.00	1	380	0	0	0	0
2010–11	NYR	5	1	4	-	13	156	143	.917	2.26	0	346	0	0	0	0
2011–12	NYR	20	10	10	-	38	554	516	.931	1.82	3	1251	0	0	0	0
2012–13	NYR	12	5	7	-	27	411	384	.934	2.14	2	756	0	0	0	0
2013–14	NYR	25	13	11	-	54	737	683	.927	2.14	1	1516	0	1	1	0
2014–15	NYR	19	11	8	-	41	570	529	.928	2.11	0	1166	0	0	0	0
2015–16	NYR	5	1	3	-	15	113	98	.867	4.39	0	205	0	0	0	0
2016–17	NYR	12	6	6	-	29	395	366	.927	2.25	1	775	0	0	0	0
Career	NYR	128	61	65	-	297	3800	3503	.922	2.28	10	7817	0	1	1	0

Chris Holt
Born: June 5, 1985 in Vancouver, British Columbia
6-3, 221lb
Caught: Left
Rangers Debut: December 3, 2006 at Washington Capitals
Uniform #40
Seasons with Rangers: 1, 2005–06

Courtesy of the New York Rangers

Chris Holt was the Rangers' sixth-round pick (180th overall) in the 2003 entry draft. After finishing his collegiate career with the University of Nebraska-Omaha Mavericks, Chris began the 2005–06 season with the Hartford Wolfpack of the AHL. He was recalled in December to back up Henrik Lundqvist when Kevin Weekes was injured. Holt was called upon to relieve Lundqvist for 10 minutes in a game against Washington on December 3, 2006. He did not give up a goal.

He was returned to Hartford and after two seasons of bouncing between the Wolfpack and the Charlotte Checkers of the ECHL signed a free agent contract with the St. Louis Blues. He saw 19 minutes of action with the Blues in 2008–09 and once again did not surrender a goal. He returned to the minor leagues and signed with Riga (KHL) in 2010.

Regular Season

Season	Team	GP	W	L	T/O	GA	SA	SV	SV%	GAA	SO	MIN	G	A	PTS	PIM
2005–06	NYR	1	0	0	0	0	2	2	1.000	0.00	0	10	0	0	0	0
2008–09	STL	1	0	0	0	0	3	3	1.000	0.00	0	19	0	0	0	0
NYR Totals	-	1	0	0	0	0	2	2	1.000	0.00	0	10	0	0	0	0
Career	-	2	0	0	0	0	5	5	1.000	0.00	0	29	0	0	0	0

Chad Johnson
Born: June 10, 1986 in Saskatoon, Saskatchewan
6-3, 196lb
Caught: Left
Rangers Debut: December 30, 2009 vs. Philadelphia
Uniform #29
Seasons with Rangers: 2, 2009–10 through 2010–11

Courtesy of the New York Rangers

After playing four seasons with the University of Alaska, Chad Johnson was named the Central Collegiate Hockey Association's Player of the Year, as well as a Hobey Baker Award finalist in 2009.

He was selected by the Pittsburgh Penguins in the fifth round (125th overall) in the 2006 entry draft and eventually sent to the Rangers in June 2009 for a fifth-round pick in that year's draft. Ironically, the Penguins used that pick to select Andy Bathgate, the grandson of the former Rangers great.

Johnson made five appearances for the Rangers in 2009–10 and saw action in one game the following season, going 1–2–0 with a 2.59 GAA.

In July 2012, he signed a free-agent contract with the Phoenix Coyotes but played only four games for them in 2012–13 following the lockout. The next season he signed with Boston and saw regular duty with the Bruins, appearing in 39 games.

In July 2014, Johnson was on the move again, signing with the Islanders as a backup to Jaroslav Halak. The Isles then sent him to Buffalo at the trading deadline for Michael Neuvirth. He was signed as a free agent by Calgary in 2016 and traded to Arizona at the end of the season. He then signed with Buffalo in 2017. Johnson and Martin Biron are the only two goaltenders to have played for all three teams located within the state of New York. Johnson signed with the St. Louis Blues as a free agent in July 2018 and was claimed on waivers by Anaheim in December 2018.

Regular Season

Season	Team	GP	W	L	T/O	GA	SA	SV	SV%	GAA	SO	MIN	G	A	PTS	PIM
2009–10	NYR	5	1	2	1	11	135	124	.919	2.35	0	281	0	1	1	0
2010–11	NYR	1	0	0	0	2	11	9	.818	6.00	0	20	0	0	0	0
2012–13	PHX	4	2	0	2	5	108	103	.954	1.22	1	247	0	0	0	0
2013–14	BOS	27	17	4	3	53	708	655	.925	2.10	2	1511	0	0	0	0
2014–15	NYI	19	8	8	1	54	488	434	.889	3.08	0	1053	0	0	0	0
2015–16	BUF	45	22	16	4	102	1270	1168	.920	2.36	1	2591	0	2	2	0
2016–17	CGY	36	18	15	1	87	969	882	.910	2.59	3	2013	0	0	0	0
2017–18	BUF	36	10	16	3	105	962	857	.891	3.55	0	1774	0	0	0	0
2018–19	STL	10	2	6	0	29	250	221	.884	3.55	1	491	0	0	0	0
2018–19	ANA	9	0	5	0	20	156	136	.872	3.75	0	320	0	0	0	0
NYR Totals	-	6	1	2	1	13	146	133	.911	2.59	0	301	0	1	1	0
Career	-	192	80	72	15	468	5057	4985	.907	2.73	8	10,301	0	3	3	0

Playoffs

Season	Team	GP	W	L	T	GA	SA	SV	SV%	GAA	SO	MIN	G	A	PTS	PIM
2016–17	CGY	1	0	1	-	1	21	20	.952	1.16	0	52	0	0	0	0
Career	CGY	1	0	1	-	1	21	20	.952	1.15	0	52	0	0	0	0

Alex Auld
Born: January 7, 1981 in Cold Lake, Alberta
6-4, 215lb
Caught: Left
Rangers Debut: March 6, 2010 at Washington Capitals
Uniform #31
Seasons with Rangers: 1, 2009–10

Courtesy of the New York Rangers

Alex Auld played his junior hockey with the Ontario Hockey League's North Bay Centennials and was selected by the Florida Panthers in the second round (40th overall) of the 1999 entry draft. He was traded to Vancouver in 2001 and saw limited action with the Canucks until 2005–06 when he became their starter and appeared in 67 games.

In June 2006, Auld was dealt to Florida with Todd Bertuzzi as part of a blockbuster trade that brought Bryan Allen, Roberto Luongo, Lukas Krajicek, and a draft pick in return. Auld spent that season in Florida and then signed a one-year deal with Phoenix in the offseason and was later traded to Boston in December 2007. Auld's tour of NHL clubs continued as he played for Ottawa and Dallas before being claimed off waivers by the Rangers in February 2009.

Auld appeared in three games for the Rangers that season as Henrik Lundqvist's backup, posting an 0–1–0 record with a 2.52 GAA and was released at the end of the year.

Auld then went on to play for the Canadiens and rejoined the Senators in 2011 before playing for Salzburg in Austria.

Regular Season

Season	Team	GP	W	L	T/O	GA	SA	SV	SV%	GAA	SO	MIN	G	A	PTS	PIM
2001–02	VAN	1	1	0	0	2	22	20	.909	2.00	0	60	0	1	1	0
2002–03	VAN	7	3	3	0	10	165	155	.939	1.57	1	382	0	0	0	0
2003–04	VAN	6	2	2	2	12	168	156	.929	2.06	0	349	0	0	0	0
2005–06	VAN	67	33	26	6	189	1938	1749	.902	2.94	0	3859	0	2	2	4
2006–07	FLA	27	7	13	5	82	729	647	.888	3.34	1	1471	0	1	1	2
2007–08	PHX	9	3	6	0	30	249	219	.880	3.54	1	509	0	0	0	0
2007–08	BOS	23	9	7	5	47	578	531	.919	2.32	2	1213	0	0	0	0
2008–09	OTT	43	16	18	7	101	1141	1040	.911	2.47	1	2449	0	0	0	2
2009–10	DAL	21	9	6	3	59	558	499	.894	3.00	0	1181	0	2	2	2
2009–10	NYR	3	0	1	0	5	52	47	.904	2.53	0	119	0	0	0	0
2010–11	MTL	16	6	2	2	33	383	350	.914	2.64	0	749	0	1	1	2
2011–12	OTT	14	2	4	2	36	310	274	.884	3.35	0	645	0	0	0	0
NYR Totals	-	3	0	1	0	5	52	47	.904	2.52	0	119	0	0	0	0
Career	-	237	91	88	32	606	6293	5687	.904	2.80	6	12,986	0	7	7	12

Playoffs

Season	Team	GP	W	L	T	GA	SA	SV	SV%	GAA	SO	MIN	G	A	PTS	PIM
2002–03	VAN	1	0	0	-	1	5	4	.800	3.00	0	20	0	0	0	0
2003–04	VAN	3	1	2	-	9	88	79	.898	2.44	0	222	0	0	0	0
Career	VAN	4	1	2	-	10	93	83	.892	2.48	0	242	0	0	0	0

Matt Zaba
Born: July 14, 1983 in Yorkton, Saskatchewan
6-1, 185lb
Caught: Left
Rangers Debut: January 23, 2010 at Montréal Canadiens
Uniform #31
Seasons with Rangers: 1, 2009–10

Matt Zaba played for four seasons at Colorado College of the WCHA and was selected by the LA Kings in the eighth round (231st overall) of the 2003 entry draft. He spent his first pro season playing for Charlotte of the ECHL before signing with the Rangers as a free agent in August 2007.

Zaba made his only appearance for the Rangers on January 23, 2010, when he relieved Henrik Lundqvist for 34 minutes in a 6–0 loss in Montreal. He gave up two goals and finished his Rangers career with a 3.54 GAA.

Zaba left the Rangers organization that summer and finished his career in Europe.

Regular Season

Season	Team	GP	W	L	T/O	GA	SA	SV	SV%	GAA	SO	MIN	G	A	PTS	PIM
2009–10	NYR	1	0	0	0	2	16	14	.875	3.56	0	34	0	0	0	0
Career	NYR	1	0	0	0	2	16	14	.875	3.56	0	34	0	0	0	0

Martin Biron
Born: August 15, 1977 in Lac St. Charles, Quebec
6-2, 186lb
Caught: Left
Rangers Debut: October 21, 2010 at Toronto Maple Leafs
Uniform #43
Seasons with Rangers: 4, 2010–11 through 2013–14

Courtesy of the New York Rangers

The Buffalo Sabres selected Martin Biron in the first round (16th overall) in the 1995 entry draft following an outstanding junior career in the QMJHL. Biron, a native of Lac St-Charles, Quebec, turned pro with Rochester of the AHL where he recorded five shutouts and a 2.93 GAA in 41 games during the 1997–98 season. The following year he led the league with a 2.07 GAA and six shutouts and took the Amerks to the Calder Cup finals. He was also named a First Team All-Star and won the Baz Bastien Memorial Trophy as the league's best goaltender as well as sharing the Harry "Hap" Holmes Memorial Trophy with teammate Tom Draper for allowing the fewest goals during the regular season. Biron also made six appearances with the Buffalo Sabres that season.

Biron earned a spot on the Sabres roster as Dominick Hasek's backup in 1999–2000 and took over as the starter in 2001–02 when Hasek was traded. He held onto the starter's role until 2005–06 when he was bumped by youngster Ryan Miller and was traded to the Philadelphia Flyers in February 2007 for a second-round draft pick.

He recorded 30 wins for the Flyers in 2007–08 and led them to the Eastern Conference finals where they were beaten by Pittsburgh in five games.

In July 2009, he signed with the Islanders as a free agent but lost the starting job to former Buffalo teammate Dwayne Roloson.

The following summer Biron signed with the Rangers, thus completing his tour of New York-based hockey teams.

Biron provided reliable backup for Henrik Lundqvist while seeing limited duty in three full seasons with the Rangers. He was a good teammate and a positive presence in the locker room. However, after two poor outings at the beginning of the 2013–14 season in which he surrendered nine goals in a total of 71 minutes, Biron was placed on waivers and decided to retire rather than be assigned to the Blueshirts'

AHL affiliate in Hartford. He then became a between periods analyst on Rangers broadcasts. He currently works as a studio analyst with the Sabres and is the director of goaltending at the Academy of Hockey at the Buffalo Harbor Center.

Regular Season

Season	Team	GP	W	L	T/O	GA	SA	SV	SV%	GAA	SO	MIN	G	A	PTS	PIM
1995–96	BUF	3	0	2	0	10	64	54	.844	5.05	0	119	0	0	0	0
1998–99	BUF	6	1	2	1	10	120	110	.917	2.14	0	281	0	0	0	0
1999–00	BUF	41	19	18	2	90	988	898	.909	2.42	5	2229	0	0	0	6
2000–01	BUF	18	7	7	1	39	427	388	.909	2.55	2	918	0	0	0	0
2001–02	BUF	72	31	28	10	151	1781	1630	.915	2.22	4	4085	0	1	1	8
2002–03	BUF	54	17	28	6	135	1468	1333	.908	2.56	4	3170	0	1	1	12
2003–04	BUF	52	26	18	5	125	1442	1317	.913	2.52	2	2972	0	2	2	10
2005–06	BUF	35	21	8	3	93	980	887	.905	2.88	1	1934	0	1	1	10
2006–07	BUF	19	12	4	1	54	533	479	.899	3.04	0	1066	0	0	0	25
2006–07	PHI	16	6	8	2	47	509	462	.908	3.01	0	935	0	0	0	0
2007–08	PHI	62	30	20	9	153	1865	1712	.918	2.59	5	3539	0	1	1	8
2008–09	PHI	55	29	19	5	146	1718	1572	.915	2.76	2	3177	0	4	4	0
2009–10	NYI	29	9	14	4	89	859	770	.896	3.27	1	1634	0	1	1	2
2010–11	NYR	17	8	6	0	33	426	393	.923	2.13	0	928	0	0	0	0
2011–12	NYR	21	12	6	2	50	519	469	.904	2.46	2	1220	0	3	3	0
2012–13	NYR	6	2	2	1	13	156	143	.917	2.32	0	336	0	0	0	0
2013–14	NYR	2	0	1	0	9	38	29	.763	7.65	0	71	0	0	0	0
NYR Totals	-	46	22	15	3	105	1139	1034	.908	2.47	2	2555	0	3	3	0
Career	-	508	230	191	52	1247	13,893	12,646	.910	2.61	28	28,614	0	14	14	81

Playoffs

Season	Team	GP	W	L	T	GA	SA	SV	SV%	GAA	SO	MIN	G	A	PTS	PIM
2007–08	PHI	17	9	8	-	52	540	488	.904	2.98	1	1049	0	1	1	2
2008–09	PHI	6	2	4	-	16	198	182	.919	2.56	1	375	0	0	0	0
Career	PHI	23	11	12	-	68	738	670	.908	2.87	2	1424	0	1	1	2

Fast Fact: Martin Biron and Chad Johnson are the only two goaltenders to have played for all three NHL teams located within New York State: the Rangers, Islanders and Buffalo Sabres.

Cam Talbot
Born: June 5, 1987 in Caledonia, Ontario
6-4, 200lb
Catches: Left
Rangers Debut: October 24, 2013 at Philadelphia Flyers
Uniform #33
Seasons with Rangers: 2, 2013–14 to 2014–15

Cam Talbot spent the first two seasons of his NHL career as Henrik Lundqvist's backup while showing the rest of the NHL that he was good enough to be a starter for any team in the league.

Talbot was signed by the Rangers as an undrafted free agent in March of 2010 after three strong seasons with the University of Alabama. He spent his first four seasons in the Rangers organization playing for the Greenville Road Warriors (ECHL) and Hartford Wolf Pack (AHL) and was called up to the Rangers in 2013–14 to replace Marty Biron as Lundqvist's backup.

The twenty-six year-old rookie lost his first start, 2–1, in Philadelphia, but bounced back two nights later with a 3–2 overtime victory in Detroit and registered his first shutout in a 1–0 win at Montreal. Talbot had an outstanding rookie season going 12–6–1 with three shutouts and a 1.64 GAA.

But it was during the 2014–15 season when Talbot was called upon to provide more than an occasional rest for Lundqvist. On February 3, 2015, Lundqvist was struck in the throat with a puck, injuring his neck and forcing him out of the lineup for six weeks. Talbot stepped up and went 17–4–3 over the next 24 games, helping the Blueshirts win the Presidents' Trophy as the team with the NHL's best record. Due to salary cap restrictions, Talbot's time with the Rangers came to an end in June 2015 when he was traded to the Edmonton Oilers with a seventh-round draft pick in exchange for three draft picks. Talbot played very well in Edmonton but was traded to the Philadelphia Flyers on February 15, 2019, for goaltender Anthony Stolarz.

Regular Season

Season	Team	GP	W	L	T/O	GA	SA	SV	SV%	GAA	SO	MIN	G	A	PTS	PIM
2013–14	NYR	21	12	6	1	33	560	527	.941	1.64	3	1211	0	0	0	0
2014–15	NYR	36	21	9	4	77	1038	961	.926	2.21	5	2095	0	0	0	0
2015–16	EDM	56	21	27	5	137	1648	1511	.917	2.55	3	3223	0	1	1	0
2016–17	EDM	73	42	22	8	171	2117	1946	.919	2.39	7	4294	0	0	0	4
2017–18	EDM	67	31	31	3	188	2036	1848	.908	3.02	1	3730	0	1	1	8
2018–19	EDM	31	10	15	3	95	888	793	.893	3.36	1	1696	0	1	1	0
2018–19	PHI	4	1	2	0	13	109	96	.881	3.70	0	211	0	0	0	0
NYR Totals	-	57	33	15	5	110	1598	1488	.931	2.00	8	3306	0	0	0	0
Career	-	288	138	112	24	714	8396	7682	.915	2.60	20	16,459	0	3	3	12

Playoffs

Season	Team	GP	GS	W	L	T	GA	SA	SV	SV%	GAA	SO	MIN	G	A	PTS	PIM
2013–14	NYR	2	0	0	1	-	2	13	11	.846	2.59	0	46	0	0	0	0
2016–17	EDM	13	13	7	6	-	33	437	404	.924	2.48	2	799	0	1	1	0
NYR Totals	-	2	0	0	1	-	2	13	11	.846	2.59	0	46	0	0	0	0
Career	-	15	13	7	7	-	35	450	415	.922	2.48	2	845	0	1	1	0

Mackenzie Skapski
Born: June 15, 1994 in Abbotsford, British Columbia
6-3, 192lb
Caught: Left
Rangers Debut: February 20, 2015 at Buffalo Sabres
Uniform #70
Seasons with Rangers: 1, 2014–15

Courtesy of the New York Rangers

Mackenzie Skapski played junior hockey with the Kootenay Ice of the WHL and was selected by the Rangers in the seventh round (170th overall) of the 2013 entry draft.

Skapski turned pro in 2014–15 and started the season with the Greenville Road Warriors of the ECHL, but after just one game was called up to the Hartford Wolf Pack of the American Hockey League.

That same season Skapski was brought up to the Rangers to fill in for the injured Henrik Lundqvist. The twenty-one-year-old rookie made his NHL debut on February 20, 2015, against the Buffalo Sabres, making 24 saves in a 3–1 victory. He faced the Sabres again on March 14, stopping all 20 shots and earning his first NHL shutout.

Skapski required hip surgery at the end of the 2014–15 season and is currently playing in Europe following two seasons in the ECHL.

Regular Season

Season	Team	GP	W	L	T/O	GA	SA	SV	SV%	GAA	SO	MIN	G	A	PTS	PIM
2014–15	NYR	2	2	0	0	1	45	44	.978	0.50	1	119	0	0	0	0
Career	NYR	2	2	0	0	1	45	44	.978	0.50	1	119	0	0	0	0

CHAPTER THIRTEEN

A New Beginning

Jeff Gorton took over as Rangers general manager on July 1, 2015, after serving for eight seasons in a variety of front office positions including assistant GM, assistant director of player personnel, and scout.

Gorton graduated from Bridgewater State College with a degree in physical education in 1991. He then went on to earn a master's degree from Springfield College in sports management in 1993. Before joining the Rangers in 2007, Gorton spent 15 seasons with the Boston Bruins organization, working his way up through the public relations and scouting departments before being named assistant general manager. He replaced GM Mike O'Connell on an interim basis in 2006, and was instrumental in the selections of Phil Kessel, Brad Marchand, and Milan Lucic in that season's entry draft.

Gorton's biggest challenge as Rangers general manager was the lack of first-round draft choices and prospects, assets that Glen Sather had traded away in deals for big-name players. The league was getting younger and faster while the Rangers were standing still.

During Gorton's first two seasons as GM the Rangers compiled 100-plus point seasons but lost in the first and second round of the playoffs respectively. In his third season the Blueshirts struggled out of the gate and in February 2018, Gorton and Sather announced that the team would undergo a major rebuilding process and that most of the veteran players were on the trading block for draft picks and young prospects.

At the trading deadline that season, Rick Nash, Ryan McDonagh, J. T. Miller, Michael Grabner, and Nick Holden were sent away for high draft picks and prospects. Coach Alain Vigneault was dismissed at the end of the season and replaced by former Boston University coach David Quinn as the rebuilding of the Rangers began to take shape.

Antti Raanta
Born: May 12, 1989 in Rauma, Finland
6-0, 195lb
Catches: Left
Rangers Debut: October 19, 2015 vs. San Jose Sharks
Uniform #32
Seasons with Rangers: 2, 2015–16 to 2016–17

Antti Raanta had five seasons of amateur and professional experience under his belt in his native Finland when he signed a free-agent contract with the Chicago Blackhawks in 2013.

The undrafted twenty-four year old then spent the next two seasons bouncing between the Blackhawks and the Rockford IceHogs of the AHL. He appeared in 39 games for Chicago over two seasons, posting a 20–9–5 record with three shutouts and a 2.41 GAA.

Raanta was acquired from the Blackhawks for forward Ryan Haggerty in June 2015 to take over as Henrik Lundqvist's backup after Cam Talbot was dealt to Edmonton. Raanta made his Rangers debut on October 19, 2015, beating the San Jose Sharks 6–0. Raanta joined Hal Winkler, John Ross Roach, and Marcel Paille as the only netminders to post a shutout in their first game with the Blueshirts. He played extremely well in the backup role for two seasons but with teams only allowed to protect one netminder in the 2017 expansion draft Raanta was traded to Arizona along with Derek Stepan for Anthony DeAngelo and a first-round pick in the 2017 draft.

Regular Season

Season	Team	GP	W	L	T/O	GA	SA	SV	SV%	GAA	SO	MIN	G	A	PTS	PIM
2013–14	CHI	25	13	5	4	63	610	547	.897	2.71	1	1397	0	1	1	0
2014–15	CHI	14	7	4	1	25	389	364	.936	1.89	2	792	0	0	0	0
2015–16	NYR	25	11	6	2	43	530	487	.919	2.24	1	1145	0	0	0	0
2016–17	NYR	30	16	8	2	61	782	721	.922	2.26	4	1617	0	1	1	0
2017–18	ARI	47	21	17	6	97	1388	1291	.930	2.24	3	2599	0	0	0	0
2018–19	ARI	12	5	6	0	33	351	318	.906	2.88	0	687	0	1	1	0
NYR Totals	-	55	27	14	4	104	1312	1208	.921	2.25	5	2762	0	1	1	0
Career	-	153	73	46	15	322	4050	3728	.920.	2.34	11	8237	0	3	3	0

Playoffs

Season	Team	GP	W	L	T	GA	SA	SV	SV%	GAA	SO	MIN	G	A	PTS	PIM
2015–16	NYR	3	0	1	-	4	38	34	.895	2.56	0	94	0	0	0	0
Career	NYR	3	0	1	-	4	38	34	.895	2.55	0	94	0	0	0	0

Magnus Hellberg
Born: April 4, 1991 in Uppsala, Sweden
6-6, 209lb
Caught: Left
Rangers Debut: December 20, 2015 vs. Washington Capitals
Uniform #45
Seasons with Rangers: 2, 2015–16 through 2016–17

Magnus Hellberg came up through the Swedish Elite League and was selected by the Nashville Predators in the second round (38th overall) of the 2011 entry draft.

Hellberg made his NHL debut with the Predators on October 26, 2013, relieving starter Carter Hutton. He was acquired by the Rangers in July 2015 for a 2017 sixth-round draft pick and spent most of his time with the Hartford Wolfpack of the AHL. He made three appearances over two seasons with the Rangers and moved to Russia in 2017, signing with Kunlun Redstar as a free agent.

Regular Season

Season	Team	GP	W	L	T/O	GA	SA	SV	SV%	GAA	SO	MIN	G	A	PTS	PIM
2013–14	NSH	1	-	-	-	1	4	3	.750	4.92	0	12	0	0	0	0
2015–16	NYR	1	0	0	0	2	6	4	.667	6.00	0	20	0	0	0	0
2016–17	NYR	2	1	0	0	2	28	26	.929	1.53	0	79	0	0	0	0
NYR Totals	-	3	1	0	0	4	34	30	.882	2.44	0	99	0	0	0	0
Career	-	4	1	0	0	5	38	33	.868	2.71	0	111	0	0	0	0(

Ondrej Pavelec
Born: August 31, 1987 in Kladno, Czech Republic
6-3, 212lb
Caught: Left
Rangers Debut: October 7, 2017 at Toronto Maple Leafs
Uniform #31
Seasons with Rangers: 1, 2017–18

Ondrej Pavelec was selected by the Atlanta Thrashers in the second round (41st overall) of the 2005 entry draft. After honing his skills in his native Czechoslovakia, he joined Cape Breton of the QMJHL in 2005–06 and posted a 55–29 record with a 2.51 GAA over two seasons. He was the league's top netminder in 2005–06 and the next season was awarded the Jacques Plante Trophy, given annually to the goalie with the lowest GAA in the league.

Pavelec turned pro with the AHL's Chicago Wolves in 2007–08 and made his NHL debut with the Thrashers in an early regular-season game against the Tampa Bay Lightning.

Pavelec saw steady action with the Thrashers over the next three seasons and moved to Winnipeg with the franchise in 2011. During the 2014–15 season, Pavelec set a Winnipeg Jets franchise record with three consecutive shutouts, going 187:05 without allowing a goal. His strong play in 50 games that season helped the Jets qualify for the Stanley Cup playoffs for the first time since the franchise relocated from Atlanta.

Pavelec struggled out of training camp in October 2016 and was sent to the Manitoba Moose of the AHL. He returned to Winnipeg for eight games and signed a one-year contract as a free agent with the Rangers in July 2017.

Pavelec showed quickness and agility and proved to be a reliable backup for Henrik Lundqvist in 2017–18, appearing in 19 games and posting a 4–9–1 record. However, he injured his knee in February and was replaced by Alexandar Georgiev. Pavelec announced his retirement in September 2018.

Regular Season

Season	Team	GP	W	L	T/O	GA	SA	SV	SV%	GAA	SO	MIN	G	A	PTS	PIM
2007–08	ATL	7	3	3	0	18	190	172	.905	3.11	0	347	0	0	0	2
2008–09	ATL	12	3	7	0	36	301	265	.880	3.60	0	599	0	0	0	0
2009–10	ATL	42	14	18	7	127	1353	1226	.906	3.29	2	2317	0	1	1	0
2010–11	ATL	58	21	23	9	147	1705	1558	.914	2.73	4	3225	0	0	0	4
2011–12	WPG	68	29	28	9	191	2036	1845	.906	2.91	4	3932	0	2	2	0
2012–13	WPG	44	21	20	3	119	1251	1132	.905	2.80	0	2553	0	0	0	2
2013–14	WPG	57	22	26	7	163	1644	1481	.901	3.01	1	3248	0	3	3	0
2014–15	WPG	50	22	16	8	108	1353	1245	.920	2.28	5	2838	0	0	0	2
2015–16	WPG	33	13	13	4	88	918	830	.904	2.78	1	1899	0	0	0	0
2016–17	WPG	8	4	4	0	26	233	207	.888	3.55	0	440	0	0	0	0
2017–18	NYR	19	4	9	1	46	510	464	.910	3.05	1	904	0	0	0	2
NYR Totals	-	19	4	9	1	46	510	464	.910	3.05	1	904	0	0	0	2
Career	-	398	156	167	48	1069	11,494	10,425	.907	2.88	18	22,302	0	6	6	12

Playoffs

Season	Team	GP	W	L	T	GA	SA	SV	SV%	GAA	SO	MIN	G	A	PTS	PIM
2014–15	WPG	4	0	4	-	15	137	122	.891	3.74	0	241	0	0	0	0
Career	WPG	4	0	4	-	15	137	122	.891	3.74	0	241	0	0	0	0

Brandon Halverson
Born: March 29, 1996 in Traverse City, Michigan
6-4, 208lb
Catches: Left
Rangers Debut: February 17, 2018 at Ottawa Senators
Uniform #75
Seasons with Rangers: 1, 2017–18

Brandon Halverson was the Rangers' second-round selection (59th overall) in the 2014 entry draft. He had three outstanding seasons (2012–13 to 2015–16) with the Sault Ste. Marie Greyhounds of the OHL, becoming the first draft pick in franchise history to earn at least 40 wins in one season of junior hockey.

He then split most of the next two seasons between the Hartford

Wolfpack of the AHL and the Greenville Swamp Rabbits, their ECHL affiliate.

Halverson also played on two US National Junior Teams. He posted a 1–0 record with a 0.65 GAA and a .973 SV% in two appearances while helping the United States earn a bronze medal at the 2016 IIHF World Junior Championship. Previously he went 1–0, posting a shutout in his only appearance in the 2015 IIHF World Junior Championship.

Halverson made his Rangers debut on February 17, 2018, allowing one goal in 13 minutes of play in a 6–3 loss in Ottawa.

Regular Season

Season	Team	GP	W	L	T/O	GA	SA	SV	SV%	GAA	SO	MIN	G	A	PTS	PIM
2017–18	NYR	1	0	0	0	1	6	5	.833	4.78	0	13	0	0	0	0
Career	NYR	1	0	0	0	1	6	5	.833	4.78	0	13	0	0	0	0

Alexandar Georgiev
Born: February 10, 1996 in Rue, Bulgaria
6-1, 180lb
Catches: Left
Rangers Debut: February 22, 2018 at Montreal Canadiens
Uniform #40
Seasons with Rangers: 2, 2017–18 to present

Courtesy of the New York Rangers

Alexandar Georgiev is the Rangers' first Bulgarian-born netminder. He began playing for the Moscow-based Penguins, then moved to Khimik Voskresensk. In 2014, he saw action with TPS Turku of the Finnish Elite League. He also helped Russia earn a silver medal at the 2016 IIHF World Junior Championships, posting a 3–1 record with a 2.52 GAA in five appearances.

Georgiev was not selected in the 2017 NHL entry draft but was invited to participate in the Rangers developmental camp in July 2017. He signed a three-year, entry-level contract with the Rangers and made his NHL debut on February 22, 2018, making 38 saves in a 3–1 loss to the Canadiens in Montreal. He earned his first NHL victory on March 3, a 3–2 win over Edmonton. Georgiev compiled a 4-4-1 record in his rookie year and continued his fine play in his sophomore season despite playing behind the Rangers' young defense and figures to have a bright future in the NHL.

Regular Season

Season	Team	GP	W	L	T/O	GA	SA	SV	SV%	GAA	SO	MIN	G	A	PTS	PIM
2017–18	NYR	10	4	4	1	27	331	304	.918	3.15	0	515	0	0	0	0
2018–19	NYR	33	14	13	4	91	1057	966	.914	2.91	2	1874	0	2	2	2
Career	NYR	43	18	17	5	118	1388	1270	.915	2.96	2	2389	0	2	2	2

CHAPTER FOURTEEN

The Next Generation

Moving forward, the Blueshirts are blessed with a number of fine goaltending prospects throughout their system. But it remains to be seen if any of these young netminders will become the Rangers' next starter and eventually develop into their next Franchise Goaltender.

In the opinion of Jess Rubenstein, longtime editor of *The Prospect Park*, the four goalies to watch are Alexandar Georgiev, Igor Shestyorkin, Adam Huska, and Olof Lindbom.

Alexandar Georgiev (6-1, 180 lbs. Born: February 10, 1996 in Bulgaria) "I like him," says Rubenstein, "and if any anything happened to Henrik I would be confident in him. I was so impressed by his poise and self-confidence in his game. This was not your average twenty-three-year-old goalie, as he plays as if he was doing this forever. His ability to read the ice and square up to the shooters is first-rate. If anything, he does remind me of a young Henrik Lundqvist as nothing about the game scares him. The best part about Georgiev is that he is still learning how to play the position. The more he gets to play the better I can see him getting. The Rangers must agree as they did not resign Ondrej Pavelec and went into the 2018–19 season with Georgiev as their backup goalie. That is saying a lot about a kid with just 10 NHL games under his belt."

Igor Shestyorkin (6-1, 190 lbs. Born: December 30, 1995 in Moskva, Russia) was the Rangers' fourth-round pick (118th overall) in the 2014 entry draft. Described as acrobatic with a good glove hand, scouts have also noted that he sometimes loses focus after giving up a goal and was once suspended for getting into a fight with a fan.

Although Shestyorkin has been called one of the best young goaltenders outside of the NHL, Rubenstein has his doubts. "I might be the only one who wonders if he is really the heir apparent. It has been a headscratcher watching Shestyorkin play 'lights out' during the regular season as SKA's starter only to be replaced by his backup during the 2018 KHL playoffs. It has not been because of his play or due to his health. It would be one thing if the replacement was a "stud" goalie but it has been a guy who couldn't make it in the NHL. I hope I'm wrong about Shestyorkin but to me it is the playoffs where a goalie earns his reputation.

Adam Huska (6-3, 190 lbs. Born: May 12, 1997 in Zvolen, Slovakia) was selected in the seventh round (184th overall) in the 2015 entry draft. In 69 games over three seasons with the University of Connecticut, Adam posted a 20-38-8 record with two shutouts and a 2.90 GAA. He also has played for the Green Bay Gamblers of the USHL and represented Slovakia in the IIHF World Championships. "[Rangers goaltending coach] Benoit Allaire loves him," says Rubenstein. "I think the Rangers arranged for his UConn scholarship. He has a shot. He has been a surprise to many, but his development has not. Huska has been playing at a higher level since he was just 14 in his native Slovakia and playing at the Under-18 level. Huska has represented Slovakia at the international level playing on Slovakia's Under-17, Under-18, and Under-20 junior teams. Only twenty-one, Huska is a huge 6-4, 210 lbs, but he moves like a smaller player. He is the type of goalie who the more shots he faces in a game the better he plays. He does need some work on his positioning but everything else is rock solid. The best thing for Huska would be to remain at UConn for two more years working on his development."

The Rangers scouting staff thought very highly of **Olof Lindbom** (6-2, 180 lbs. Born July 23, 2000 in Stockholm, Sweden) selecting him in the second round (39th overall) in the 2018 entry draft. Lindbom is described as having average reflexes but makes up for it with very sound positioning and excellent anticipation. Drafted as a seventeen-year-old, Lindbom is several years away from making the jump to North American hockey.

New York Rangers Goaltending Records

Individual Career Records through the 2018–19 season

MOST APPEARANCES: 857, Henrik Lundqvist
MOST WINS: 449, Henrik Lundqvist
MOST LOSSES: 298, Henrik Lundqvist
MOST SHUTOUTS: 63, Henrik Lundqvist
MOST MINUTES PLAYED: 50,221, Henrik Lundqvist
LOWEST GOALS AGAINST AVERAGE: (Min. 100 appearances) 2.07, Dave Kerr
MOST ASSISTS: 26, Henrik Lundqist
MOST PENALTY MINUTES: 212, John Vanbiesbrouck

Individual Single Season Records through the 2018–19 season

MOST APPEARANCES: 73 - Henrik Lundqvist, 2009–10
MOST WINS: 42 - Mike Richter, 1993–94
MOST WINS (Including Playoffs): 58 - Mike Richter, 1993–94
MOST LOSSES: 39 - Ken McAuley, 1943–44
MOST SHUTOUTS: 13 - John Ross Roach, 1928–29
MOST MINUTES: 4,305 - Henrik Lundqvist, 2007–08
LOWEST GOALS AGAINST AVERAGE: 1.41 - John Ross Roach, 1928–29
MOST ASSISTS: 5 - John Vanbiesbrouck, 1984-85 and 1987-88; Mike Richter, 1992–93
HIGHEST SAVE PERCENTAGE: .930 - Henrik Lundqvist, 2011–12

Single Game Records through the 2018–19 Season

MOST SAVES: 59 - Mike Richter, at Vancouver on 1/31/91 (3–3 tie)
MOST ASSISTS: 2 - Ed Giacomin, vs. Toronto, at Madison Square Garden on 3/19/72; John Vanbiesbrouck, at Winnipeg on 1/9/85; Mike Richter, at Washington on 2/23/90; vs. Quebec, at Madison Square Garden on 10/29/92

Playoff Records

Career

MOST APPEARANCES BY A GOALTENDER: 128 - Henrik Lundqvist
MOST WINS: 61 - Henrik Lundqvist
MOST SHUTOUTS: 10 - Henrik Lundqvist

Playoff Year

MOST CONSECUTIVE SHUTOUTS: 3 - John Ross Roach, 1928–29: 3/19 vs. NY Americans (0–0); 3/21 vs. NY Americans (1–0); 3/24 vs. Toronto (1–0)
MOST MINUTES PLAYED BY A GOALTENDER: 1,515:35 - Henrik Lundqvist, 2013–14 (25 games)
MOST WINS BY A GOALTENDER: 16 - Mike Richter, 1993–94
MOST SHUTOUTS: 4 - Mike Richter, 1993–94; Dave Kerr, 1936–37
Single Playoff Series
MOST SHUTOUTS: 3 - Dave Kerr, 1940, semifinals vs. Boston in Game One (4–0), Game Four (1–0), and Game Five (1–0)

New York Rangers Top 10 Goaltender Rankings

Career Regular Season

Games Played		Goals Against Average*		Shutouts	
H. Lundqvist	857	L. Chabot	1.63	H. Lundqvist	63
M. Richter	666	C. Talbot	2.00	E. Giacomin	49
L. Worsley	581	D. Kerr	2.07	D. Kerr	40
E. Giacomin	539	J. R. Roach	2.16	J. R. Roach	30
J. Vanbiesbrouck	449	H. Lundqvist	2.41	L. Worsley	24
C. Rayner	377	J. Bower	2.56	M. Richter	24
D. Kerr	324	G. Villemure	2.62	C. Rayner	24
J. Davidson	222	E. Giacomin	2.74	L. Chabot	21
G. Villemure	184	M. Richter	2.89	J. Vanbiesbrouck	16
J. R. Roach	180	C. Rayner	2.98	G. Villemure	13

*** Minimum of 50 games**

Wins		Losses		Ties & OT Losses	
H. Lundqvist	449	H. Lundqvist	298	L. Worsley	101
M. Richter	301	L. Worsley	270	H. Lundqvist	93
E. Giacomin	267	M. Richter	258	E. Giacomin	89
L. Worsley	204	C. Rayner	179	M. Richter	73
J. Vanbiesbrouck	200	J. Vanbiesbrouck	177	C. Rayner	73
D. Kerr	157	E. Giacomin	172	D. Kerr	57
C. Rayner	123	D. Kerr	170	J. Vanbiesbrouck	47
G. Villemure	98	J. Davidson	90	J. R. Roach	37
J. Davidson	93	K. McAuley	64	J. Davidson	25
J. R. Roach	80	J. R. Roach	63	G. Villemure	23

Assists		Penalty Minutes	
H. Lundqvist.	26	J. Vanbiesbrouck	212
J. Vanbiesbrouck	25	L. Worsley	85
M. Richter	11	E. Giacomin	64
Ed Giacomin	8	J. Davidson	42
G. Healy	5	G. Hanlon	38
J. Davidson	5	M. Richter	34
S. Weeks	5	C. Rayner	26
M. Biron	3	D. Cloutier	21
E. Mio	3	D. Soetaert	20
W. Thomas	3	G. Healy	16
G. Hanlon	3	H. Lundqvist	16

Career Playoffs

Games Played		Goals Against Average*		Shutouts	
H. Lundqvist	128	L. Chabot	1.36	H. Lundqvist	10
M. Richter	76	A. Aitkenhead	1.48	M. Richter	9
E. Giacomin	65	D. Kerr	1.57	D. Kerr	7
J. Vanbiesbrouck	38	B. Gardiner	1.66	J. R. Roach	5
D. Kerr	32	J. R. Roach	1.82	A. Aitkenhead	3
J. Davidson	30	J. Henry	1.90	J. Vanbiesbrouck	2
J. R. Roach	21	H. Lundqvist	2.28	L. Chabot	2
L. Worsley	20	C. Rayner	2.43	Six tied with	1
C. Rayner	18	J. Davidson	2.44		
E. Mio	16	M. Richter	2.68		

*** appeared in a minimum of 5 games**

Wins		Losses		Penalty Minutes	
H. Lundqvist	61	H. Lundqvist	65	E. Giacomin	23
M. Richter	41	E. Giacomin	35	G. Hanlon	18
E. Giacomin	29	M. Richter	33	J. Vanbiesbrouck	10
D. Kerr	17	J. Vanbiesbrouck	20	B. Froese	7
J. Davidson	16	L. Worsley	15	J. Davidson	6
J. Vanbiesbrouck	13	D. Kerr	13	S. Weeks	5
J. R. Roach	9	J. Davidson	13	S. Baker	4
C. Rayner	9	J. R. Roach	10	M. Richter	2
E. Mio	9	C. Rayner	9	L. Worsley	2
S. Baker	7	S. Baker & G. Hanlon	7	K. Weekes	2

Assists	
J. Vanbiesbrouck	2
H. Lundqvist	1
M. Richter	1
B. Froese	1

ACKNOWLEDGMENTS

Writing may be a solitary endeavor, but that doesn't mean that there isn't a load of people I need to thank for their assistance, support and cooperation in the completion of this book.

I'd like to start by thanking my late parents, Grace and George Grimm, for instilling in me the joy of reading and the value of books. I'm also very grateful to Dr. Alexander Palacios who has helped me battle glaucoma and saved my vision several times over the last forty-odd years.

My wife, Theresa, also deserves a lot of credit for her patience and support. I could not have even thought about attempting to write another book without her cooperation.

I'd also like to thank my two oldest friends, Dianne Wolfsohn and Steve Carroll, for their longtime support and encouragement. They've both been putting up with me and my stories for a very long time.

I'm very grateful to Michael Rappaport and the New York Rangers PR Department for allowing me to use some of the photos that appear in this book. I also want to thank Jay Moran (author of *The Rangers, The Bruins and the End of an Era*), Tony Accordino, Ken Tash, Steve Baker, and Michael Cosby for their encouragement and photo contributions.

A big tap on the pads to Stan Fischler, Frank Brown, Hal Bock, Jess Rubenstein, and Patrick Hoffman for their generous contributions to this project.

I also want to thank fellow authors Matthew DiBiase, Brad Kurtzberg, and Kevin Shea for their support and advice. I'm also grateful to Kevin Greenstein of *Insidehockey.com* for posting my *Retro Rangers* columns on his site, and to Rangers beat writer and columnist Rick Carpiniello of *The Athletic* for his continued encouragement and support.

I also want to thank the people at Sports Publishing, and my editors, Jason Katzman and Ken Samelson, as well as their staff for their fine work, extreme patience, and assistance.

Of course, I never would have ever dreamed of writing any books at all if it hadn't been for the encouragement of former Rangers publicist, the late John Halligan, who always took the time to give me feedback about my newsletter *SportStat...The Ranger Report* in the 1980s. I would also like to thank former Rangers PR Director Barry Watkins, who gave me a press pass when I was writing *SportStat*, introduced me to the working relationship between the Rangers and the media, and gave me one of the best pieces of advice I've ever received: "It never hurts to ask."

In closing I'd also like to take this opportunity to thank everyone who read my previous book, *We Did Everything but Win*, about the Emile Francis-era Rangers, and who helped make it a success and in a way made this one possible. Thank you also for your many kind emails and Facebook and Twitter comments. I appreciate every one of them. And I sincerely hope that you enjoy this offering as much as the last one.

BIBLIOGRAPHY

Allen, Kevin and Duff, Bob. *Without Fear* (Triumph Books, 2012)

Andrahtas, Tom: *The 60s: Goaltending's Greatest Generation* (CreateSpace, 2018)

Boucher, Frank. *When the Rangers Were Young* (Dodd Mead, 1973)

Bower, Johnny. Duff, Bob. *The China Wall, The Legendary Life of Johnny Bower* (Fenn Publishing, 2008)

Chadwick, Bill. *The Big Whistle* (Hawthorn Books, 1974)

Diamond, Dan. *The Official National Hockey League Stanley Cup Centennial Book* (Tormont, 1993)

____________. *The Official National Hockey League 75th Anniversary Commemorative Book* (Firefly Books, 1994)

____________. *Hockey: Twenty Years* (Doubleday Canada, 1987)

Delano, Hugh. *Eddie: A Goaltender's Story* (Atheneum, 1976)

Denault, Todd. *Jacques Plante: The Man Who Changed the Face of Hockey* (McClelland & Stewart, 2009)

Eskenazi, Gerald. *A Year on Ice* (Coward-McCann, 1970)

Eskenazi, Gerald. *A Sportswriter's Life* (University of Missouri, 2004)

____________. *Hockey* (Follett Publishing Co., 1969)

____________. *The Fastest Sport: A Blood and Guts History of the National and World Hockey Leagues* (Follett Publishing Co., 1974)

Ferguson, John and Stan and Shirley Fischler. *Thunder and Lightning* (Prentice Hall Canada, 1989)

Fischler, Stan. *Slap Shot* (Grosset & Dunlap, 1973)

Fischler, Stan. *Fischler's Hockey Encyclopedia* (Crowell, 1975)

Fischler, Stan and Tom Sarro. *Metro Ice* (H & M Productions, 1999)

Gratton, Gilles, and Greg Oliver. *Gratoony the Loony* (ECW Press, 2017)

Grimm, George. *We Did Everything but Win* (Sports Publishing, 2017)

Halligan, John. *New York Rangers: Seventy Five Years* (Barnes & Noble, 2000)

Halligan John and John Kreiser. *The Game of My Life: New York Rangers* (Sports Publishing, 2006)

Halligan, John, Russ Cohen, and Adam Raider. *100 Ranger Greats* (Wiley, 2009)

Hunt, Jim. *The Men in the Nets* (Follett Publishing Company, 1967)
Hunter, Douglas. *A Breed Apart* (Viking Press, 1995)
Irvin, Dick. *In the Crease: Goaltenders Look at Life in the NHL* (McClelland & Stewart, 1996)
Irvin, Dick. *Behind the Bench* (McClelland & Stewart, 1993)
Kendall, Brian. *Shutout: The Terry Sawchuk Story* (Penguin Books Canada, Limited, 1996)
Kiczek, Gene. *Forgotten Glory: The Story of Cleveland Barons Hockey* (Blue Line Publications, 1994)
Kreiser, John and Lou Friedman. *The New York Rangers: Broadway's Longest Running Hit* (Sagamore Publishing, 1997)
McFarland, Brian. *New York Rangers Original Six* (Stoddart, 1997)
Martin, Gil. *Ice Wars* (AuthorHouse, 2016)
Moran, Jay. *The Rangers, The Bruins and the End of an Era* (Author House, 2009)
Sears, Thom. *Straight Shooter: The Brad Park Story* (Wiley, 2012)
Shea, Kevin. *The Toronto Maple Leaf Hockey Club: Official Centennial Publication* (McClelland & Stewart 2016)
Villemure, Gilles and Mike Shalin. *Tales from the Rangers Locker Room* (Sports Publishing, 2002)
Whitehead, Eric. *The Patricks: Hockey's Royal Family* (Doubleday, 1980)
Worsley, Lorne "Gump" and Tim Moriarty. *They Call Me Gump* (Dodd, Mead, 1975)

Publications

New York Rangers Blue Books/Media Guides (1965–present)
New York Times
SportStat... The Ranger Report (1988–1993)
The Hockey News Top 100 Goalies (2018)